otl aicher
architecture and landscape

edited by
gillermo zuaznabar

otl aicher architecture and landscape

braun
rotis
metro bilbao

BILBOKO ARTE EDERREN MUSEOA
MUSEO DE BELLAS ARTES DE BILBAO

metro bilbao

LA FABRICA

On 11 November 1995, an event occurred that would change the physiognomy of Bizkaia and the lives of its inhabitants forever: the inauguration of the long-awaited Bilbao Metro, which finally gave citizens fast, clean, efficient access to a large number of municipalities on both sides of the estuary. Today, twenty-five years later, I have the honour of presenting an exhibition at our beloved Bilbao Fine Arts Museum that celebrates this happy moment in our recent history while also paying tribute to one of the people who made it possible. That person is none other than Otl Aicher, one of the most influential graphic designers of the twentieth century, who created the corporate identity of the Bilbao Metro.

In the 1950s, Aicher co-founded the Hochschule für Gestaltung or Ulm School of Design in Germany, which pioneered a method of teaching design based on reflection, science, technology and close ties to industry. Using the same principles, he devised a communication system for the Bilbao Metro by exhaustively researching the architecture and landscape of the Basque Country, which undoubtedly explains why Basque society was so quick to embrace the underground rail system's identifying image. Aicher's extensive research for the Bilbao Metro project, documented in more than eighty unpublished drawings, is the centrepiece of this exhibition, although it also includes some of the German designer's widely recognised and recognisable creations for other clients such as Braun, Lufthansa, ERCO and the 1972 Olympic Games in Munich.

Moreover, with this show the museum opens its doors to graphic design, a discipline that is often overlooked in traditional art circles and yet shares an unbreakable bond with art, for both are creative processes, though art asks questions and design offers answer.

We therefore have many reasons to be enthusiastic about welcoming the exhibition *Otl Aicher: Metro Bilbao: Architecture and Landscape*, and just as many reasons to be grateful to all the individuals and institutions that helped to make it a reality: the curator Gillermo Zuaznabar, who selected the materials now on display and edited this catalogue, creating a vital resource for scholars of European graphic design and Otl Aicher; Florian Aicher, Otl's son, and the Hochschule für Gestaltung Ulm archive, which carefully preserves the designer's legacy, for their unconditional support throughout the entire process; and, of course, Metro Bilbao, whose directors eagerly welcomed the idea of an exhibition to mark its twenty-fifth anniversary and made it possible with their sponsorship. To all of them, and to all the museum staff who participated, congratulations and thank you.

Bingen Zupiria Gorostidi
Basque Minister of Culture and Linguistic Policy
and chair of the Bilbao Fine Arts Museum Foundation

The opening of Metro Bilbao's first underground line in November 1995, which connected the Old Quarter of the city with the coastal town of Plentzia, was a major milestone in the profound overhaul that the city and its metropolitan area had been experiencing since the 1980s. At that time, the exhaustion of the industrial model had to lead to the quest for new economic mainstays and an in-depth reconfiguration of the city. Bilbao and Bizkaia managed to rise to this challenge, which required the creation of effective transports to connect the neighbourhoods in the big city, which at that time were highly fragmented, and to connect with the surrounding towns in the region. Two decades later, the role of Metro Bilbao in shaping the new urban habitat is undeniable, as is its role in improving the environmental quality and overcoming the imbalances in its social fabric caused by industrialisation. In short, it generated a new city and a better environment.

However, the economic and social reconstruction of a region cannot be understood without the impetus of cultural activity as a driving force. In recent years, the construction of new facilities and promotion of the existing ones have turned Bizkaia into an international cultural touchstone. In this sense, the modernisation project that the Bilbao Fine Arts Museum undertook one year after the opening of the Metro can be regarded as yet another milestone that for the first time linked up both institutions' trajectories until they ultimately merged in 2001, when Metro Bilbao joined the board of the Foundation that manages the museum.

This shared history is now revealed in an extraordinary fashion in the exhibition in the museum celebrating the 25 years of history of Metro Bilbao through the work of the person who managed to create a brand that is now part of the collective imagination of the citizens of Bizkaia. The German designer Otl Aicher developed an image that aligned with the philosophy of the architecture designed by Norman Foster, with whom he partnered on countless projects. The symbol that identifies the urban area is an abstract figure comprised of three hoops which can be associated with tunnels, or with wheels in motion, as well as with the red-hot rings that came out of the ironworks of Bizkaia. The typography created by the designer sought to improve legibility and reading speed, and colours also play a prominent role: the basic colour, red—once again, fire—allows the signal system to stand out in stations where grey tones predominate.

It is important to recall the intense research that Aicher conducted on the Basque culture and landscape when designing this project. All of it—his sketches, drawings, notes, tests, etc.—is now available to visitors to this original exhibition. I cannot close without thanking the Bilbao Fine Arts Museum for this wonderful initiative which reminds us of design's invaluable role in changing the image of a region and a city not only outward, but also inward among their own inhabitants. My most sincere congratulations to Metro Bilbao for these 25 years of success, and to the museum and its team for helping us extend the celebration to all citizens.

Unai Rementeria Maiz
General deputy of the Provincial Council of Bizkaia
and CEO of Metro Bilbao

Otl Aicher in Rotis during the work
for the Metro Bilbao project.
Photograph: Hansjörg Brucklacher

The Bilbao Fine Arts Museum is celebrating the 25th anniversary of the city's metro system with the largest international exhibition that any institution has ever dedicated to Otl Aicher (1922–1991). This is also the first time our museum has hosted a major show devoted entirely to a designer. These two novelties are warranted for a number of reasons.

Otl Aicher was the most influential European designer of the mid to late twentieth century. With his wife and fellow activist Inge Scholl and Max Bill, in 1951 he founded the Hochschule für Gestaltung Ulm (Ulm School of Design), and from February 1954 he co-directed the school alongside Tomás Maldonado and Hans Gugelot. In the West Germany of the 1950s and 60s, the Ulm School defined the profession we now know as that of 'designer'. Aicher and his colleagues at Ulm believed that design was the economic and aesthetic tool that would enable their society to recover from the violence and destruction of the 1930s and 40s.

The Bilbao Metro has probably had a greater impact on the life of the city and its inhabitants than any other architectural and engineering project. Thanks to their collaboration, Norman Foster brought us Aicher's talent to give the city a new aesthetic and a new image, not only in the eyes of the world but also in the minds of its own citizens. Its implementation changed the relationship between neighbourhoods for the better, and at the same time it created a different environment with fresh aesthetic values to lift the spirits of users besieged by an economic and social crisis. We firmly believe that the investment in the Bilbao Metro and its radical design was vital, in both form and substance, to helping our society overcome those troubled times. We trust that both the exhibition and this catalogue will allow visitors to appreciate the importance of this contribution.

Our museum's collection and exhibitions are at once the reflection and catalyst of twentieth and twenty-first-century aesthetics in the Basque Country. Honouring Aicher's work gives us a chance to feel the pulse of the city, to chart its current life and its past history, and to gauge the impact of design on European industry and culture.

This landmark exhibition coincides with the preparation of Foster's definitive plans for the imminent expansion of the museum, closing the circle that began with the Metro three decades ago. At the same time, adding design to our sphere of interests opens up a new horizon which I am certain will continue to yield fresh fruit and opportunities to serve the community, while also increasing our presence in the European museum network of which we are a part.

In conclusion, I want to express my sincere gratitude to Gillermo Zuaznabar for his excellent curatorial work, his judicious and enthusiastic selection and his meticulous spatial arrangement of this first major Otl Aicher retrospective. We were aided in our endeavours by the generous cooperation of the Ulm School, which holds the designer's archive, and of course the involvement of Otl's son, Florian Aicher. This catalogue features outstanding contributions from various experts on the German designer's work, to whom we are also indebted for their diligent efforts, and Norman Foster's heartfelt personal recollections of his friendship and collaboration with Aicher, bridging the distance between Rotis and Bilbao.

Neither the exhibition nor the book would have been possible without the generous sponsorship of Metro Bilbao, a trustee of our museum since 2001 and closer to us now than ever before, thanks to the experience of studying its visual identity with the common goal of sharing culture to improve the wellbeing of society.

Miguel Zugaza
Director of the Bilbao Fine Arts Museum

index

otl aicher in bilbao

norman foster

Otl Aicher and Norman Foster at the ERCO Technical Centre, Ludenscheid, May 1989. Photograph: Rudi Meisel

I had wanted to collaborate with Otl Aicher on the graphics and signage for the Hongkong and Shanghai Bank. Frustratingly, the politics of commissioning on that project ruled it out, but I remember someone asking me why we needed him and responding, 'Because he is the best living designer in the world.' I could have added that he was a co-founder and subsequently the principal of the Ulm School of Design, and how he virtually invented the pictogram in his work for the 1972 Munich Olympic Games. In other words, he was a legendary figure in the design world.

A close friendship grew from our first meetings, so naturally when the publisher Watermark suggested a series of monographs on our work, I turned to Otl. This led to many intensive working sessions, reviewing material and discussing layouts. Otl's graphic concept communicated at several levels. He established a hierarchy of information in which the reader could scan a visual story or delve deeper through the medium of the written word. He was also interested in informal sketches, as ideas made visible, and the relationship of drawings, models and prototypes to the final thing. Joint working sessions might last a week or merely a single intensive day. Spaces would be 'wallpapered' with mock-ups of page layouts so the book could be viewed as a continuous sequence or examined a page at a time. The discipline he set as a designer initially seemed quite rigid. But, as work progressed, I saw that it provided an overall order within which there was almost infinite scope for choice and variation.

Sometimes Otl would come to my studio at Compton Bassett, in Wiltshire, and at other times we would happily escape to his studio at Rotis, in southern Germany. Otl, who had a passion for history, provided insights into the culture of Swabia and its strong Celtic traditions, which also happen to permeate the West Country of England. The end of each day was an opportunity for sightseeing and the rituals of food and drink, which for Otl merited the same attention to detail as the books. To paraphrase Charles Eames, both Otl and his wife Inge liked to take their pleasures seriously. Seriousness, though, was leavened by a dry sense of humour and a healthy dollop of self-deprecation.

Having known them both so well, I find it impossible to think of one without the other. They seemed intellectually, socially and politically united, but they were each strong and individual spirits. There is relatively little awareness outside Germany of the anti-Nazi resistance movement there, but Inge's younger siblings Hans and Sophie Scholl were founders of the White Rose movement in Munich and were executed for their beliefs. Inge chronicled this period in her book *Die Weiße Rose* (1952), which is still in print. Otl also resisted—he was arrested in 1937 for refusing to join the Hitler Youth and subsequently failed on his *abitur*, or college entrance examination, by the authorities.

When we first met, Otl told me that every August he escaped to Greenland. Only much later did he confide that Greenland was in fact the lush green paradise of Rotis, where he guarded his privacy fiercely. The studio complex he created there was a classic modern ensemble. The top-lit wooden structures were beautifully detailed and related perfectly to the old farmhouse, which Otl had restored and where he and Inge lived. Rotis was green in another sense, too. By harnessing a turbine generator to an old mill race, Otl ensured that his autonomous kingdom would always be energy self-sufficient.

I always told colleagues that they would learn something from the experience of working with and listening to Otl. I would explain that, brilliant designer though he was—and better architect than most—he was primarily a philosopher. Sometimes their scepticism was apparent, but afterwards it was always clear that they had shared the benefit of his insights.

Otl was a natural communicator and no doubt an inspirational teacher. I remember his extraordinary rigour and his very personal way of looking at the world. He had a way of working and living in which the creation of a new typeface, the design of a book or a graphic mark, attitudes to politics or the environment, how you peeled an onion or cut a rose, were all related and integral parts of a personal world view. But while no detail was ever considered too small, conceptual clarity was paramount. Which brings me to the design of the Bilbao Metro, where Otl's influence was felt so fundamentally.

I was once in Bilbao, where I had given a presentation about our work on the Prado, and noticed an elderly woman approaching. She stopped me and said, 'You're Norman Foster, aren't you?' I wondered what to expect next, but she continued, 'You did the Metro in Bilbao—it's fantastic! Thank you so much.' It was very touching. She really cared that someone had done something positive for her city. It also made me realise just how much some communities care about their environment. And in Bilbao they certainly care about the Metro. Its stations today are as fresh and as immaculately maintained as ever; and the graffiti that everyone told us to expect, and for which we prepared, has never materialised. For the reality is that there is such a sense of civic pride in the Metro that nobody would think of defacing it. That is until, at the last anniversary celebration, I was handed a thick black marker pen and asked to leave my signature on a station wall—a very moving compliment.

Thinking about the project, twenty-five years after the first stations opened, is an opportunity to reflect on its genesis. The Basque Government's brief for the Metro specified that 'beyond its obvious functionality [the system] must have its own aesthetic personality'. They determined that architects, in collaboration with engineers, should design the stations, their furnishings and the Metro's corporate identity. Eight teams of internationally recognised architects were invited to submit

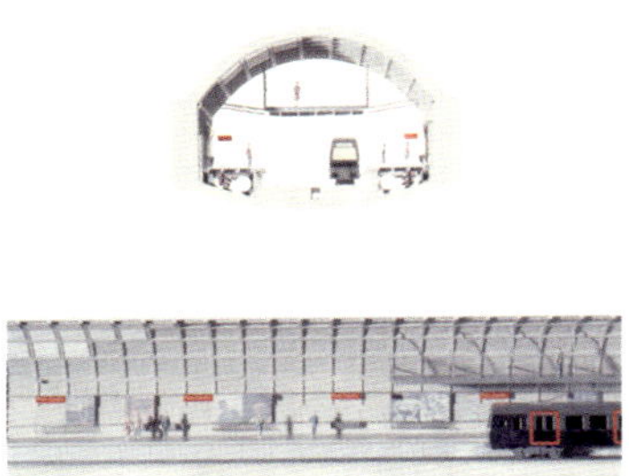

Foster + Partners, Metro Bilbao project, station design

Norman Foster, Otl Aicher and Inge Scholl at Rotis

proposals. The first thing to note is that none of us—architects, engineers and graphic designers—had worked on the design of a metro system before. What we didn't know was that our inexperience would be regarded by our client, IMEBISA, as a positive, not a negative. It meant we had no preconceptions about how a metro system should look or work.

From the beginning, our design philosophy ran counter to what is usually expected from architects. I think people assumed that we would add something to the engineering shell, which if you look at most underground systems is exactly what happens. The idea that you could eliminate everything except the shell and that you could direct all the creative energy into making the most efficient, expressive, poetic space was quite new.

I have in front of me one of the sequence of boards that formed our submission to the competition, dated 30 March 1988. It is drawn by me, with handwritten annotations and typewritten translations into Spanish. It is entirely a product of the analogue age—clear, intuitive and readable at a glance—just like the stations themselves. It concludes with the statement: 'We try to achieve simplicity ... a struggle ... much more difficult than accepting complexity ... but far more poetic and worthwhile.' Otl's Metro logo, with its overlapping rings—'the symbol'—forms the final punctuation point on the page.

Reading the competition assessors' report, what they liked about our scheme was that the engineering was the architecture; and whereas most of the other schemes proposed cladding the tunnel walls, or building boxes for the stations, we left the concrete structure bare. The same clarity applied to wayfinding. Otl's view was that the architecture should provide the signage—if you had to stick up a notice that said THIS WAY then you'd failed at some point along the line. Our signage begins at street level, with the crystalline canopies that announce the station entrances—the *Fosteritos*. From there, the routes down to the station caverns are completely intuitive. Only at platform level does Otl's elegantly minimal graphic system truly come into play.

The graphic identity was a key component of our competition submission. Even at this early stage, it encompassed everything from network maps to wristwatches—nothing was overlooked. The Metro logo and the station nameplates are rendered in a signature colour that Otl named 'Bilbao red'. What most people will not know is that the red was suggested by the colour of the river in the past, so it encapsulates both the city's industrial heritage and its wonderful rebirth.

One of the things that distinguishes the Bilbao Metro stations from those of most other systems is an absence of clutter—both physical and visual. Here the graphics and the architecture are completely of a piece. There is no redundancy, no overstatement. There are no flourishes. Every element is working hard. The aesthetic personality of the space emerges through the discipline of the ensemble. Tragically, this was

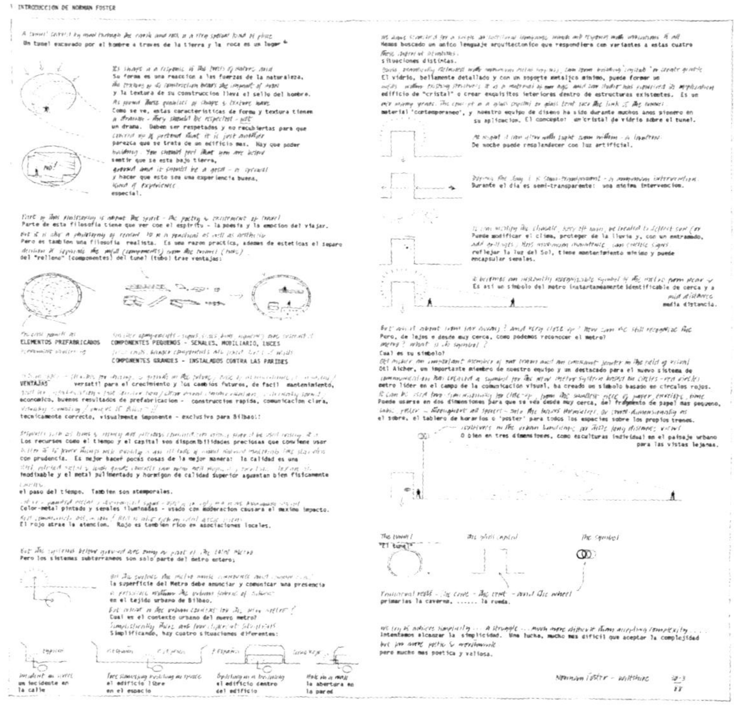

Foster + Partners, project brief for the Metro Bilbao competition

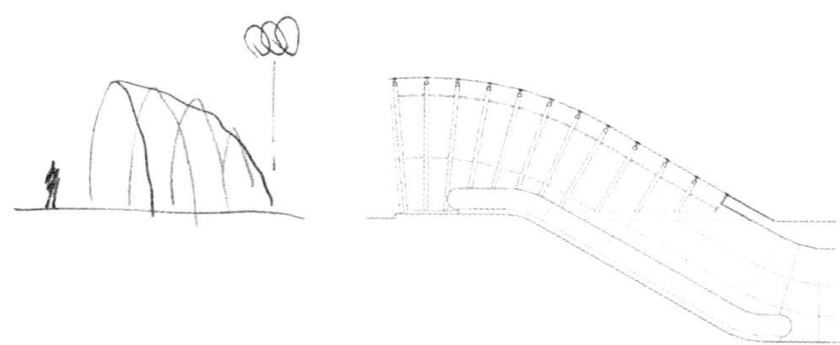

Foster + Partners, Metro Bilbao project, entrance canopy design

to be Otl's last major commission and he never saw the completed stations.

In August 1991, the month before he died, I was in the studio one afternoon and was struck by an impulse to call him, so I did. 'Norman,' he replied, 'I've been calling you at Compton Bassett. You never answer and I just wanted to hear your voice.' I explained that I was mostly in London and suggested that we met for dinner. Why not straight away—that evening? 'Wonderful,' he said, 'Where are you—in Germany?' I said no, but that London wasn't so far away and I could fly and be at Leutkirch—a tiny airstrip close to Rotis—just after seven o'clock, his time. I could stay overnight, so we would be able to have breakfast together, too.

We had one of those wonderfully spontaneous evenings, shared with Inge and Eberhart, an architect friend who had come from Munich to spend a couple of days cycling with him. Early the next morning, the two of us cycled to the village to buy bread and pretzels. On the way, Otl stopped and pointed to a church in the distance. 'That spire … tell me about it,' he said. 'It's leaning,' I replied. 'Exactly, but no one else can see that.'

Our time together was all too brief and by mid-morning I was on my way home. Within weeks I was back, this time dazed and tearful. I was there for Otl's funeral. I saw Eberhart after the service, as we stood in line to throw flowers on the coffin, the silence broken only by the sound of cowbells. Eberhart said that he and Otl had talked long into the night after that dinner about why I had come, out of the blue. 'You must have had a feeling,' he said.

Having such a rare person as a true friend makes it hard to pay adequate tribute. We shared a chemistry and a rapport, which even now I find difficult to explain.

Metro Bilbao entrance canopy in Gran Vía.
Photograph: Richard Davies

otl aicher: a personal experience[1]

yves zimmermann

In the early 1960s I was invited to become a lecturer in graphic design at the Elisava School in Barcelona, the first school to teach a discipline that was then quite novel, if not unknown. Elisava was a school for women. Under Franco, it was unthinkable that boys and girls might share the same classroom. Even so, there was always a priest present to keep an eye on teachers and students. After four years, the majority of the faculty, myself included, decided to leave due to disagreements with Elisava's director. In 1967, a group of those professors founded the Eina School of Design, also in Barcelona.

These years of teaching experience opened my eyes to the paucity of literature in Spanish on topics related to design, typography, photography, semiotics, etc. In the mid-1970s, I went to visit the publisher Gustavo Gili and proposed that he publish books on these themes to fill that gap. He was interested, but he warned me that he did not know the market for such books, and therefore proposed to start out with a broader thematic scope. That was how we ended up creating the Visual Communication collection. We invited relevant names in the field of communication to join the reading team: Román Gubern, Tomàs Llorens, Albert Ràfols Casamada, Ignasi Solà-Morales, Gustavo and myself formed the group that proposed books we had read in French, Italian, English or German to be translated and published in Spanish. Five years later, in 1979, we had published between forty and fifty titles, including several on graphic design, industrial design, typography, photography, semiotics, etc.

At this point, Gustavo told me he finally had a good handle on the market: the books that sold best were about mass media and design, and he invited me to oversee a collection on this topic. One of the first books I proposed for the collection was by none other than Otl Aicher, *Zeichensysteme der visuellen Kommunikation* [Sign Systems of Visual Communication].[2] This illustrated book describes different sign systems such as Morse code, where every letter is represented by dots and lines, or the Braille system for the blind. It also shows pottery symbols, Zodiac signs, etc.—and, of course, Otl Aicher's pictogram system.

In the 1980s, I attended a conference on typography and design held in Paris. One of the speakers was the great Otl Aicher. After his lecture, I approached him and we had a friendly chat. He mentioned that he had to travel to Barcelona to collect some data for a project he was working on.[3] When he came, I invited him over for dinner. He was a man who spoke slowly and thoughtfully. We immediately 'hit it off', and in addition to discussing topics related to the profession and the Ulm School he and his wife had founded, we also talked about personal things, including our memories of World War II. I was born in Basel, a city in northern Switzerland on the border with Germany and France. When the war began in 1939, I was two and half years old. Images of the air battles

[1] Lecture given by Yves Zimmermann on 12 January 2012 as part of the public programme accompanying the exhibition *Systems Design: The Ulm School* at Museu del Disseny, Barcelona, 21 September 2011–20 May 2012. In this written version, every effort has been made to indicate the source of the quotations.

[2] Spanish edition: Otl Aicher and Martin Krampen, *Sistemas de signos en la comunicación visual* (Barcelona: Gustavo Gili, 1979). Original edition: *Zeichensysteme der visuellen Kommunikation: Handbuch für Designer, Architekten, Planer, Organisatoren* (Stuttgart: Alexander Koch, 1977).

that could be seen overhead in 1943 or 1944 were seared into my memory: images of aircraft fighting in the heavens, and a few that shot down and plummeted to earth.

He also shared his experiences from that time. He had been close friends with the siblings Hans and Inge Scholl, founders of the anti-Nazi group Die Weiße Rose (The White Rose). He told me that one day he went to visit them at their house, carrying a satchel, and when he went inside he found two Gestapo officers interrogating the brother and sister. Aicher said, 'It was a miracle that those Gestapo men didn't ask me to open my satchel; if I'd had to do that, I wouldn't be here today.' Without saying it outright, he was implying that the satchel contained incriminating evidence of his association with the resistance group. Two of the Scholl siblings were condemned to death for their activities.

Aicher refused to join the Hitler Youth and was imprisoned for it in 1937. Later, in 1941, the Nazi regime prohibited him from sitting the baccalaureate exams. He was forced to join the army and sent to the Russian front. There he was offered the chance to enrol in an officer training programme, but he turned it down. True to his principles, he rejected a military career. When he saw the atrocities committed by the Nazi army against the Russian population, he deserted. After a long journey home, he surrendered to American troops. Years later, he published a book about his experiences during the war, *Innenseiten des Kriegs* [Inside the War].[4]

When the war ended, Aicher married Inge Scholl, sister of Hans and Sophie Scholl, who had been executed by the Nazis. Together they created the Geschwister Scholl Stiftung [Scholl Siblings Foundation]. The government funding they received was used to co-finance the creation of the Hochschule für Gestaltung Ulm, where prominent personalities like Max Bill, Tomás Maldonado and Aicher himself taught in the 1950s and 60s. The purpose of the Ulm School was not to design beautiful objects, a primary aim of Swiss arts and crafts schools at the time, but rather to incorporate design in the world of industry and shape our material culture. This process was driven, not by economic prosperity, but by a profound crisis of values and resources. They seized the opportunity to rethink what it means to create forms in the modern world, and to democratise access to design.

According to Gui Bonsiepe, 'The school accepted industry as a bedrock of contemporary society and saw industry and technology as cultural phenomena.' As a consequence of this position, the designer's profession was redefined from an entirely new perspective. Up until that point, the aim of design schools had been to teach students how to make ordinary objects beautiful. William Morris's workshop, the Werkbund and the Bauhaus were all made up of artists.

The school's influence was felt internationally, especially at the arts and crafts schools of Basel and Zurich, which taught what came to be known as 'Swiss Design' in the 1980s and 90s. At the Ulm School, even in those early years, they were already debating the 'eternal' problem of the relationship between art and design. The Swiss painter Max Bill believed that the two should not be separated, and his differences with Aicher on this subject eventually led to his resignation.

In the 1980s and 90s, the debate about whether design should be considered art also surfaced in Spain. For most *grafistas*, as Spanish graphic designers were then called, making design and making art were one and the same. This question gave me and Anna Calvera—with whom I had long been in the habit of meeting weekly or fortnightly to discuss design-related themes—the idea of putting together a book, in which we invited twelve Spanish and Latin American designers to share their thoughts on the connection, or lack thereof, between art and design. They all agreed that making art was one thing, and making design was quite another. In 2004, Gustavo Gili published the book under the title *Arte ¿? Diseño* [Art ? Design].

Aicher owed much of his fame to the corporate identities he had designed. Everyone was familiar with his work for the 1972 Munich Olympic Games, including his acclaimed pictogram system. He designed the corporate identity of Lufthansa Airlines and other major companies. One of them was ERCO, which manufactured lighting elements. The logo with the company's name in capital letters, designed by Aicher in 1975, features a sans-serif typeface, where the bold black lines of the first letter grow thinner on each subsequent character. Aicher's design illustrates different light intensities, especially in the negative version of the logo, with white letters on a black ground. By simply varying the weights of different characters from the same alphabet, he visually expressed several levels of luminous intensity. Today, forty years after it was designed, the logo is still in use. Master Aicher never signed his designs; he said that he was not like an artist who signed pictures. He refused to draw attention to himself and never wanted to appear in the media. He was a man who rarely agreed to give interviews and even turned down the highest distinction granted by the German government to honour its most illustrious citizens. In his opinion, politicians had no business using the work of others for their own glory.

In a report about Aicher that included interviews with him and several of his clients, who talked about their professional and personal relationship with the designer, his personality and his way of approaching problems, someone said, 'He had a talent for singling out the substance, the essence of a company's philosophy or attitude. He managed to make the company think about itself and express what it wanted to be; an idea of what it could be.' Some of his former clients described the designer as 'the corporate philosopher'. For Aicher, creating a 'corporate identity' was not merely a question of designing a graphic image with the company's

[3] [Editor's Note / EN] Based on the dates, it is quite likely that Aicher visited Barcelona in 1988, and that the project in question was a signage system (never materialised) for the Collserola telecommunications tower designed by Norman Foster.

[4] Otl Aicher, *Innenseiten des Kriegs* (Frankfurt am Main: S. Fischer, 1985).

logo or symbol; it went much deeper than that. According to him, the client first had to think long and hard about his or her company and then develop a corporate image policy that would be manifested on every level of the company's operations. A few companies even published books in which they described the experience of working with Aicher on this type of project.[5]

'Essentialist' is probably the best word for what characterises Aicher's graphic work. Allow me to explain. Years ago, someone recommended that I read a book on physics called *The Dancing Wu Li Masters: An Overview of the New Physics*.[6] In it, the author described Einstein's famous E = mc2 formula as something beautiful, a work of art. The idea that an equation could be considered beautiful was surprising, since for me, and presumably for many other people, beauty is associated with sight and sound: a beautiful landscape, a beautiful figure, a beautiful work of art or musical composition. One day I ran into the physicist Jorge Wagensberg and asked him why Einstein's equation was beautiful, and he replied, 'Because it's the synthesis of the synthesis of the synthesis. It can't be boiled down any further.' His response was like a revelation, and I suddenly understood that there was such a thing as 'intellectual beauty'. He made me see that, actually, something similar happens when designers get to work: they have to take a complex design problem and boil it down to the bare minimum, to its essence, and visualise it as a sign. That is precisely what characterises Otl Aicher's creations, which undoubtedly explains why his work is still relevant today. It is not a product of passing fads; the Deutsche Bank logo is a case in point.

When Aicher was a renowned and respected designer, he often turned down juicy contracts on principle, because he felt that the company requesting his services made products that were harmful to society or unsuitable for use, or for other ethical reasons. The case of the Bulthaup kitchen company reveals another salient trait of his personality as a designer. When he was hired to design the company's corporate identity, Aicher decided that he first had to write a book about kitchens,[7] in order to truly understand what a kitchen is and what it means to cook. Only afterwards did he begin to work on the corporate image.

In the foreword to the Spanish translation of his book *The World as Design*, I wrote:

> What characterises Aicher's work is not merely the excellence of his graphic solutions, but also the fact that, through his proposals, he convinced the companies he worked for to revise all of their actions, because they realised that every action, not just those on the visual plane, creates identity. Aicher made his clients see that the visual identity of their companies could not be a simple cosmetic fix, for ultimately, in an age so firmly anchored in 'the visual', communication and audiences,

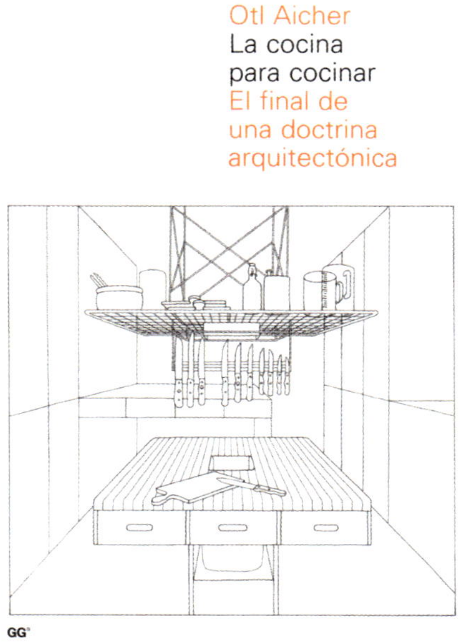

[7] Spanish edition: Otl Aicher, *La cocina para cocinar: el final de una doctrina arquitectónica* (Barcelona: Gustavo Gili, 2004). Original edition: *Die Küche zum Kochen: das Ende einer Architekturdoktrin* (Munich: Callwey Verlag, 1982).

[5] Otl Aicher, *Die Küche zum Kochen: das Ende einer Architekturdoktrin* (Munich: Callwey Verlag, 1982); *Kritik am Auto: schwierige Verteidigung des Autos gegen seine Anbeter: eine Analyse* (Munich: Callwey Verlag, 1984); *Johannes Potente, Brakel: Design der 50er Jahre* (Cologne: Verlag der Buchhandlung König, 1989); *ERCO Lichtfabrik: ein Unternehmen für Lichttechnologie* (Berlin: Ernst & Sohn, 1990).

[6] Gary Zukav, *The Dancing Wu Li Masters: An Overview of the New Physics* (New York: William Morrow & Co., 1979).

a company becomes what its image and public conduct in the broadest sense say about it. Aicher's efforts always aimed to achieve that unity between a company's visual appearance and its way of being and acting. For him, design was not just the means of devising a visual image; it was a tool for addressing larger issues that extend beyond the bounds of what we normally understand as graphic design. His philosophy posited that all corporate actions, visual or not, must share and be based on the same *Weltanschauung*,[8] because only then will the company attain a truly distinctive identity.[9]

Aicher's approach highlighted a very important aspect of corporate identity design, one that is often overlooked. It often happens that, when ordinary citizens interact with a company or an institution, either in person or over the phone, they end up feeling irritated and even offended by how an employee or civil servant treats them. This unfortunately all too common scenario also occurs at companies or institutions with a good or excellent corporate graphic image. The incensed citizens may therefore wonder, and with just cause, 'What good is having such a great visual identity if my personal experience with the company creates such a bad "image"?' In this case, they are perfectly justified in thinking that the 'pretty' and 'attractive' corporate graphics are mere window dressing, if their experience proves that the company's way of being and way of appearing—in other words, its true identity and its visual image—are not only inconsistent but directly at odds with each other.

The human targets of these corporate images are not passive subjects. How citizens are treated by an employee or civil servant elicits an emotional response that will determine whether they have a positive or negative image of the company or institution in question. The impressions gleaned from personal, first-hand experience are more real than everything the symbolic representation of the graphic image tries to convey. Consequently, the treatment received from a single employee can shape the customer's entire image of the company, because that employee represents the entire organisation.

Certain behaviour or attitudes are conveyed through signs that carry meaning. A smiling face or a surly frown are perceived as signs, and the same is true of an inviting or aloof gaze, a kind or rude gesture, a warm or cool tone of voice, and clear or unintelligible speech. The sum of these signs elicits a spontaneous emotional response from citizens, which may be positive or negative, and for them that response is the 'true' measure of the company's identity. And if the citizen's personal experience contradicts the message conveyed by a corporate visual image, both that image and the company it represents lose all credibility. When this happens, the design of this image becomes a mere cosmetic operation.

Given the universal meaning that the word 'design' has acquired today, this aspect of the corporate image is barely taken into account. This raises the following question: Is it possible to 'design' the conduct of employees of the companies for which corporate visual identities are designed? On this subject, Wilhelm Vossenkuhl, author of the foreword to Otl Aicher's book *Analogous and Digital*, wrote:

> Aicher's philosophical reflections are an introduction to design, creativity and developing. For him there is nothing that should not be designed, created and developed. This is true of one's own self, of life with others and with nature, the objects of everyday life, living and thinking. We acquire the ability to design and create by doing it. What we do and in what profession is secondary. We should simply not allow ourselves to be guided by pre-formed designs and previously devised plans.[10]

The assertion that everything can be designed, even oneself or, say, one's romantic partnership, was quite stunning back in 1991, when most people still thought of design as an activity limited to the fields of graphic, industrial, architectural or textile design. So, intrigued by the notion that it was possible to design oneself and find an answer, and drawing on my own experience as a graphic designer, I asked myself this question: What is the most fundamental, basic characteristic of any design project, whether graphic or industrial? I concluded that it was the fact that every project begins with a person, a business owner, who presents the designer with a certain PROBLEM (for example, designing a corporate identity, a book, a poster, a website, etc.) and simultaneously outlines the type of SOLUTION s/he wants the designer to offer. In order to meet this requirement, the designer must then come up with a DESIGN that leads to the SOLUTION of said PROBLEM. That is the design process in a nutshell, making the journey from PROBLEM to SOLUTION. Having arrived at this basic, elementary understanding of design, it follows that whenever someone encounters a PROBLEM and embarks on a project/journey to find a SOLUTION, that person is DESIGNING.

Otl Aicher was a prolific author. He published thirteen books, several of which have been translated into English and Spanish. In addition to the aforementioned titles, he also published the breathtakingly lovely *Gehen in der Wüste* [Walking in the Desert],[11] which narrates his travels on foot through the deserts of North Africa. The large number of photographs illustrating his texts reveal landscapes so beautiful that we can only assume the time he spent in that setting must have constituted a 'total' experience for Aicher: in the desert, man is not *before* but *in* and *surrounded* by absolute beauty. The sensuality of the dunes combined with his marvellous writings offer the reader a kind of visually erotic experience. During the countless hours he spent walking by

[8] [EN] In English, 'worldview'.

[9] Spanish edition: Otl Aicher, *El mundo como proyecto*. (Barcelona: Gustavo Gili, 1994), 7–8. Original edition: *Die Welt als Entwurf: Schriften Zum Design* (Berlin: Ernst & Sohn, 1991). English edition: *The World as Design*, trans. Michael Robinson (Berlin: Ernst & Sohn, 2015). [EN] The excerpt quoted here differs significantly from the text of the published foreword.

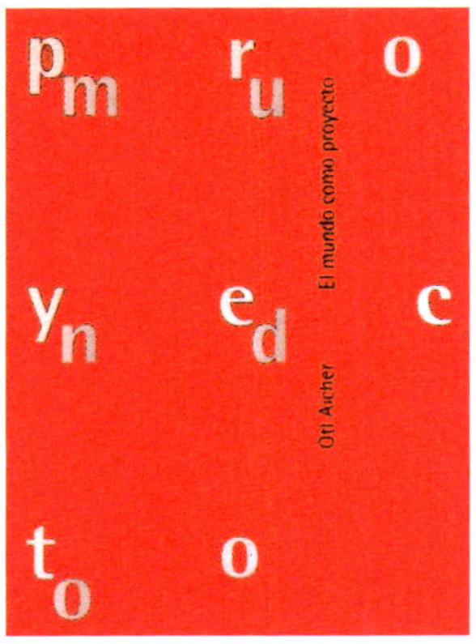

[10] English edition: Otl Aicher, *Analogous and Digital*, trans. Michael Robinson (Berlin: Ernst & Sohn, 2015), 16. Original edition: *Analog und Digital: Schriften zur Philosophie des Machens* (Berlin: Ernst & Sohn, 1991).

day and resting by night in those barren lands, deprived of all customary visual points of reference, and in such extreme conditions, Aicher must have experienced the concrete and the real in a very compelling way. His words reveal that he developed such an intense relationship with his surroundings that he could not stop thinking about what was genuinely necessary in any given situation. He reflected on the concrete reality of his own circumstances: shoes, clothes, gear, shelter, food, drink. He painstakingly examined everything he wore or carried in his pack, because his very life might depend on the quality and efficacy of each object, tool or garment.

The aforementioned book *Analogous and Digital* contains sixteen essays written between 1979 and 1991, the year it was published in German, which address a variety of themes. In the chapter titled 'Design and Philosophy', Aicher asked:

> What is design today? What does designing mean? The discussion about design extends even further. It all comes down to the question of whether we can still allow ourselves the luxury of simply recognizing the world, rather than designing it. Is our rationalistic culture of knowledge and our scientific morality of neutral objectivity not at an end, a point where annihilation of life is within the realms of the possible and can only be averted by a creative design intervention, a design in the dimension of what is feasible, of manufactured reality, not just of the insight in principle? Design is no longer a shaping concept, it moves into the realms of philosophy, of explanations of the world and understanding of the times.[12]

In this respect, Vossenkuhl wrote in the introduction, 'Aicher's imperative is that we should redesign the world. In his thinking the world as design is the theme that connects design and philosophy directly. Design requires concrete developments, not abstract planning. We should not just be designing material objects such as houses and cities for living and working in, but developing and changing ourselves.'[13] In other words, human beings must also design themselves.

The wide range of topics discussed by the author in *Analogous and Digital*, often straying far from anything related to our conventional notion of design, reveals the breadth and depth of his learning and his thought processes. In the afterword Aicher explained, 'The texts address the philosophical bases of design and architecture, the interconnection of sensory perception and thought, the role of physical experience and manual intelligence and philosophies that made important contributions to these subject areas.'[14] Essentially, his discourse is a defence of practical knowledge as opposed to theoretical knowledge. As Vossenkuhl noted, 'A characteristic feature of Modernism is the fact that theoretical knowledge is considered superior to practical knowledge. The practical knowledge that is learned in historical making attracts little attention.'[15]

In the world of design and typography, Aicher is also known as the inventor of the Rotis typeface. As graphic designers know, typefaces are characterised or classified by family: sans-serif, serif, blackletter, Hybrida and others, each with a regular, bold and italic version. Some typefaces also include condensed or extended variations. Aicher's particular alphabetical family consists of four members: Rotis sans-serif, Rotis semi-sans, Rotis semi-serif and Rotis serif. This typeface programme was quite novel and, in a way, reminiscent of how Adrian Frutiger designed the Univers family, approaching it as a typographical programme.

Aicher named his new alphabet after Rotis, the place where he lived and work with his wife Inge Aicher-Scholl and their daughter Eva. On a large property, the availability of water, energy and kitchen gardens gave the family independence, a defining trait in the life and work of this man who prided himself on his Celtic heritage. The three residents considered their territory an 'independent republic', nestled between two *länder* in southern Germany. And like other countries, this 'republic' had its own political agenda. The points were as follows:

- Promote freedom of speech, thought and assembly
- Eliminate aircraft noise
- Develop counter-models of centralised economics and politics

Like the political position, the cultural aims at Rotis were clear and emphatic:

- Eliminate the distinction between culture and civilisation
- Reinstate the concrete, whose value is derived from its use, not from higher, universal or ideal general concepts[16]

This statement of independence was nothing less than a proclamation, for the inhabitants of Rotis saw it as a universally valid proposition: 'territorial' independence equalled independence of thought—and above all, insofar as it were possible, independence from the state.

One of the most gratifying experiences I had with Gustavo Gili while managing the GD Diseño book collection came when I suggested that we should publish Aicher's *World as Design* in Spanish. When I showed Gustavo the German edition, he leafed through it and then shook his head. Finding that it contained not a single illustration, he told me, 'You know books without pictures don't sell.' I retorted that, while that might well be true, this book had to be published in Spanish because Aicher was one of the very few thinker-designers in our profession and we needed people like him. He remained unconvinced, but I was so determined that I eventually made him a bold proposition: I would pay for the translation if he would cover the publishing costs. Gustavo took me up on

[11] Otl Aicher, *Gehen in der Wüste* (Frankfurt am Main: S. Fischer, 1982).

[12] Otl Aicher, *Analogous and Digital*, 78.

[13] In Aicher, *Analogous and Digital*, 18.

[14] Aicher, *Analogous and Digital*, 188.

[15] In Aicher, *Analogous and Digital*, 14.

[16] *In Rotis* (Rotis, 1987), 8.

the offer, and then the translation odyssey began. Aicher happened to be a man who refused to accept any form of authority or hierarchy, and because he believed that upper-case letters had established a hierarchy of dominance over lower-case characters, he eliminated capitals from all of his writings. This was particularly significant in his native language, German, where the first letter of every noun is always capitalised.

Aicher always wrote every word in lower-case letters, even after a full stop at the end of sentence. In his book *Typographie*, he made the following comment about the use of capitals:

> Language is transformed not only by new words in speech or in pronunciation, but also through its entire structure. The last substantial change in the structure of German happened some three hundred years ago, when it was decided that nouns should be capitalised. Nouns were promoted to a higher class, and after that point different classes of words emerged: nouns at the top of the hierarchy, followed by verbs, adjectives, etc. It was undoubtedly the result of the political and social changes of that era.[17]

And, of course, *the world as design* was written without a single upper-case letter. Suspecting that this might pose a problem in translation, I advised Gustavo to have his translator do just the first chapter and send it to me for review. My suspicions were confirmed: the absence of capitalised nouns confused the translator, as some of these words, written in lower-case, could be mistaken for verbs. In total, I had to reject three different translators who could not understand the text owing to the lack of capital letters—and this despite the fact that they all claimed to be highly proficient in German! As the Italian saying goes, 'traduttore = traditore' (translator = traitor).

At last I found a translator who produced an excellent translation, and his text in Spanish used capital letters where they would normally appear in that language, for instance after a full stop. However, when the book came out, I was amazed to find that the entire text had been printed in lower case. I expressed my surprise to Gustavo, but he told me that if Aicher had written his text in lower-case letters, he felt he should respect that choice. That volume was published in 1994, and a year and half later Gustavo Gili informed me that the book had sold so well that he had to print a second run. By 2007, it was already in its sixth reprinting! In the end, I did not have to pay for the translation. The bill was footed by a German institution that offered financial aid to publishers who commissioned translations of texts in German.

Otl Aicher died as the result of an accident in 1991, at the age of 69. When the sad tidings reached me, I sent a letter to his widow expressing my condolences. In her reply, she told me that his untimely death was a sad loss, because our relationship was the beginning of a beautiful friendship.

[17] Spanish edition: Otl Aicher, *Tipografía* (Valencia: Campgràfic, 2004), 60. Original edition: *Typographie* (Berlin: Ernst & Sohn, 1988).

virtues and limitations of otl aicher's design approach

rené spitz

The city of Ulm in ruins after the air raids of World War II, 1945

The basic problem is a question. It is a question with two facets, one verbal and one visual: What should we show, what can we say?

The question is not: What do we want to hear, what do we want to say? When we ask this, it's about our impression. But the problem is expression. What should we show, what can we say?

Nor is the question: What do you want to hear, what do you want to tell me? These are the questions that sellers, social media and propaganda deal with.

Think! Convince me! Prove it to me! This is the categorical imperative of enlightenment. Think because you can! The reasonable use of the mind leads to a humane life. *Ratio* should dominate, that is a moral commandment. Then we are mature. The use of the mind is a mandate of responsibility.

For if feeling, the irrational dominates, then we let ourselves be carried away. Overpowered. Manipulated. We submit to the momentary mood. We are minors. Will-less. Then there are felt truths. Facts felt. Then there is murder and manslaughter, screaming and ecstasy from calculation. Because not everyone is stupid enough to rely on their feelings: they like to use emotions and manipulate others for their own purposes.

Otl Aicher was born in 1922 in Ulm and died 1991 in Günzburg. He was one of the most important designers of the twentieth-century industrial West. His relevance stems from four factors:

1. His achievements as a designer
2. His commitment to the foundation and operation of the Ulm School of Design and thus to the formation of the still-current professional profile in design
3. His contributions to design theory
4. His influence on designers today

Otl Aicher was born during the Weimar Republic (1918–1933), the first democracy in Germany. The cruel experiences of World War I (1914–1918) had profoundly shaken German society. The slogans of radical parties stirred the mood; their supporters battled each other on the street. Thus, during Otl Aicher's childhood, most people's everyday lives were marked by violence, economic uncertainty and political extremes.

Otl Aicher was ten years old when the National Socialists came to power. Throughout his youth, their physical brutality, inhuman recklessness and intellectual incapacity were omnipresent.

The children of the Scholl family in Ulm were among Otl Aicher's childhood friends. He later described Sophie Scholl as his childhood sweetheart. Sophie and her older brother Hans Scholl joined the resistance group Die Weiße Rose (The White Rose). They distributed flyers at the University of Munich. In February 1943, they were arrested. A few days later, the Nazis murdered them. By sheer luck, Otl Aicher narrowly escaped his own arrest and probable murder.

After the end of World War II (1939–1945), German society lay in ruins. Houses were destroyed and the streets and city squares full of rubble and ashes. The country was occupied and divided among the four principal victorious powers. The destruction was almost total. It was not limited to the physical environment. Families and friends mourned their dead and missing. In addition, the spiritual foundations of society were fundamentally damaged. All societal values that had hitherto been taken for granted now seemed questionable, because they had not helped people to resist the Nazis.

Without this prehistory, the history of the Ulm School of Design and the work of Otl Aicher cannot be not fully understood. The Ulm School was not founded to remedy an aesthetic deficit. Otl Aicher, Inge Scholl and Max Bill, the founders of the Ulm School, were not primarily interested in designing beautiful posters and lamps. They wanted to contribute to the development of a peaceful, democratic, free society. Because the world had changed so fundamentally due to the Nazi regime, Otl Aicher was deeply convinced that Germans could not simply pick up where they had left off in 1933.

Otl Aicher believed that the traditional dominance of art for any given form of design was a mistake. He wanted to emancipate the valuation of everyday objects from the standards that were applied to art. Aicher's goal was to formulate independent criteria for the design of equipment and information aimed at a broad population.

That is why he was not interested in the embellishment of fine holiday porcelain. He believed that modern people need dishes for every day of the year which are not only practical and affordable but also have their own particular form. Aicher rejected all references to historical authorities and sentimentality as backward and politically irresponsible. Therefore, it was out of the question for him to imitate the appearance of elegant luxury goods. Modern commodities should not be identifiable by a designer's personal style, by an artistic hand in the sense of a signature; nor should they pretend fine materials or precious workmanship through ornament. Modern mass media should inform clearly and precisely: from Aicher's point of view, a legible train timetable and a factual educational poster about the importance of healthy eating were more socially relevant than artistic painting.

Aicher aimed for a design based on reason, because feeling had no claim to legitimacy as a framework for evaluation: because the Nazis had constantly appealed to people's emotions, this dimension was discredited in Aicher's eyes.

Aicher demanded that design should not manipulate people with tricks but rather persuade them by conclusive

Otl Aicher and Inge Scholl at the Ulmer Volkshochschule, 1949. Photographs: Ike and Hannes Rosenberg

argumentation. Better results should be obtained from better reasonable foundations, not from the loud and shrill, short-lived surprise or fashionable effect. He vehemently rejected any tendency to disguise, deceive and lie by means of design. He rejected the concept of style: he did not want to develop a new style for a new era, as had been regularly propagated since the Arts and Crafts Movement, creating absurd labels like Bauhaus-style or machine-style for the purpose of short-term sales pitches.

Aicher insisted that societal responsibility was the basis for answering questions regarding the shaping the world. What contribution must design make to resist the temptations of a tyrannical, inhuman regime? So that something like the Nazi era would never happen again? Aicher's creative answer to these questions can therefore be described as an aesthetic of rational objectivity and of the morally appropriate.

In lieu of symbols and slogans, Aicher proposed sober, convincing arguments. Design should be an activity based on reason. It was not about inspiring and bubbling ideas, but about freedom from prejudice and a thorough exploration of the context of a task; objective weighing and balancing of the analysis results; systematic and interdisciplinary production of systems instead of unique pieces. However, he did not see science and technology as ends in themselves; within them lay the potential of an efficient instrument for a democratic, liberal society. To lift this society up, technicians, scientists and engineers must not be one-track specialists who, uninterested in social contexts, accumulate their specialised knowledge in isolation.

These considerations were based, firstly, on the diagnosis that the (Western) world had become technical since the mid-nineteenth century through the historic process of industrialisation, and secondly, on the assumption that this world could be shaped. In contrast to the avant-garde movement of modern art, from Arts and Crafts to the Bauhaus, Aicher concluded that technical civilisation must be managed on the basis of a new understanding of culture: culture is not an exceptional 'Sunday-best' creation that concerns only a few areas of life (in particular poetry, theatre, opera, classical music, painting, sculpture and philosophy), for it has long encompassed all machine-made objects and everyday actions. The design of these things and their connections within industrial society must therefore be treated as a cultural task. He coined the programmatic formula: the cultural mastering of technical civilisation.

So far, so good. These are the general indications.

If we now take a closer look at Aicher's reception, a homogeneous, conclusive overall picture of Aicher's design emerges. The cliché, so to speak, of Aicher's design.

It could be articulated as the thesis of the 'geometric man': because rationally justified and systematically executed design seemed morally necessary to him, Aicher always based his work on a general construction grid, from which his concrete solutions then logically and inevitably emerged by themselves. They were almost objective results based on scientific knowledge. Aicher was a designer for whom even the dachshund was the result of a rational programme.

We have to examine this picture from two perspectives: to what extent does the thesis of the 'geometric man' tally with the reality of Aicher's design practice? And to what extent are there statements in his own theoretical contributions that support this thesis?

I grew up in a household with technical drawing equipment. My father had an engineering office, we had drawing boards, rulers, Rapidographs, transparent paper and razor blades. As a design enthusiast and mission-conscious student, I wanted to place Otl Aicher's pictograms at school. But the school did not want to buy the originals from ERCO. It didn't matter; nothing is easier than drawing yourself.

The operating instructions are unsurpassed in simplicity and logical stringency. Democratic design at its best. Simply construct a grid of 10 squares, which are halved lengthwise and vertically and crossed by diagonals at 45-degree angle. Why else did I have drawing boards, rulers, Rapidographs and transparent paper?

Let's start with the football player. First one leg, hanging on the two diagonals that intersect in the centre. Then the second leg. Widths, lengths, radii and distances inevitably result from the grid. The angled arm with the shoulder. The upper body and the second arm. Head and ball. Done. All elements are nicely neat and strict in the grid. I could be content. Perfect. A real Aicher. The copy template was ready.

My girlfriend at the time, now my wife, saw the result. Her devastating verdict: 'Terrible. It doesn't look good.' She said, 'It's an offence to the eye.' That was true, because although she didn't know it, I knew that Aicher had said exactly the same thing (albeit in another context). But I was prepared to argue. My answer was obvious: 'Look here. It must be beautiful because it is right. Because it can't be ugly, which is logical.' My girlfriend replied, 'You confuse background and foreground. You only pay attention to the grid. But the grid is only the background, that's not the point. It's about the figure. You have to pay attention to the figure, and it looks horrible. The original by Aicher is much more elegant, by the way.'

Excuse me? What was that supposed to mean? There could be no difference between Aicher and me! But when I compared my pictogram to his, I realised that he did not stick to his own rules at all. Gross. Look at where the short leg is placed. And the upper body. And the outstretched arm. The head. The ball. As a teenager who had just discovered and devoured Aicher's writings, I found it unbelievable ... I don't want to say that my world collapsed, but a few cracks had definitely appeared in the pillars of the earth.

Otl Aicher. 'Gruppe 5' at the HfG: Study '1400/0'. Lufthansa image, October 1962

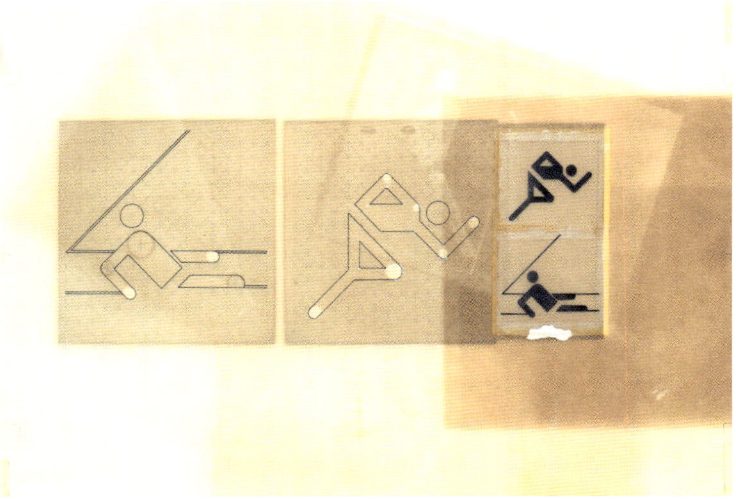

Otl Aicher and Gerhard Jo<sch.
Sports pictograms for the 1972
Munich Olympics

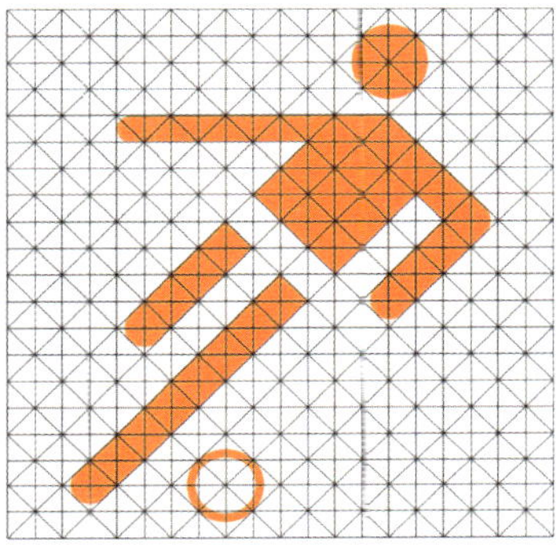

Football pictogram.
Illustration: René Spitz

Otl Aicher and Gerhard Joksch. Football pictogram for the 1972 Munich Olympics

Otl Aicher's design team / Dept. XI.
Guidelines and standards for the 1972
Munich Olympics

I've been peddling this little observation ever since. I often use the image in discussions about the applicability of mathematical rules or scientific laws to design.

I usually get two reactions. First, silence. Staggered silence. And second, suspicion: Mr Spitz, that's not true, you manipulated this image.

Then I show the picture of the original Aicher pictogram, which fans immediately identify as authentic. The figure stands on the grid. Not in the grid. The grid of the construction lines is the frame, the figure is framed. We see both the grid and the figure, but we only perceive the grid. We could say that we perceive only the theory and not the practice. We perceive the verbally expressed intention according to which the design should be logically founded. But we do not perceive the actual implementation. The grid acts as a smokescreen to distract us from the actual blurriness or arbitrariness of the work. For there is no construction formula that prescribes the shifts of the individual elements in this picture. The outcome of this design process does not result from a calculation or, as we might say today, from an algorithm.

This observation is repeated: the appearance of Lufthansa. The crane and the lettering are on the grid. They are not in the grid. The grid does not provide any information on how the crane is to be constructed, how the circle is arranged and how the two elements relate to each other.

The same applies to the coloured grounding of the Olympic rings. The five rings are not the same thickness. The yellow ring has the thickest line, the black the thinnest, and the other three are in between. Yet the exact dimensions do not result from a calculation but from Aicher's subjective perception of colour. Here, for example, it is not 0.9 but 0.92. We see the practical application of Josef Albers's *Interaction of Color*.

Just like with the mascot Waldi. Just like with advertising for the Herman Miller Collection.

Undoubtedly, Aicher's subjective interventions in the objective raster are precisely what create the decisive aesthetic quality. This intervention cannot be objectified. It is both the virtue and the limitation of Aicher's design practice. It is what is specific for Aicher.

Let's take a brief look at Aicher's theoretical statements. In 1962, Otl Aicher wrote a text at the HfG Ulm which summarises his theoretical design considerations better than any other. This text has not yet been published. Aicher himself reproduced it as a typescript under the title 'zur situation der hochschule für gestaltung 1962'. This text is so remarkable because in it Aicher makes central statements about design using few words and with extreme sharpness. The conciseness and fundamental nature of the arguments as well as the lack of evidence for the statements lend them the character of axioms. Otl Aicher literally describes his statements as doctrine. These are normative statements; in other words, here Aicher formulates what should be.

Aicher postulates that the designer is an equal partner of engineers and scientists, and that only rational methods make conceptual thinking legitimate: 'Design [is] no longer possible without working through scientific and technological foundations ... The designer [cannot] not sit on the artist's throne. He needs training that makes him an equal partner of the engineer and scientist. Rational methods make conceptual thinking legitimate in the first place.'

Aicher is not content to situate design in relation to science and technology. Rather, the nature of this relationship must be defined: 'A concept that generally postulates a classification of design, science and technology is too general. Science and design stand in a relationship that can only become fruitful if their differences are made clear and clearly distinguished from one another.'

Aicher maintains that the essential difference between design and science lies in the degree of abstraction: 'Science, including applied science, seeks generalisable insights, laws of a general nature, while design seeks objects of a concrete nature .... Design proves itself in the individual decision, in the individual object, not in the finding of truth. Its goal and its yardstick is the individual product result. In this respect, science and design are diverging activities as those that flow into abstraction, this into the concrete case.'

Aicher argues that the thought process in design and science is different: 'Science progresses from derivation to derivation, it draws conclusions. Design is a design activity that does not end with a conclusion, but with a concept that has been built up from ideas. Design and law are also intrinsically different.'

Aicher explains that the criteria for success differ from those of science and design: 'An insight can be true or false. Design, on the other hand, is based on the criteria of probity and correctness, how everything can be proven by the success of the application.' For Aicher Design, therefore, this is a 'process that has more to do with invention than investigation'. As Aicher puts it, 'The world doesn't just want to be recognised, it also wants to be made.'

Aicher notes that design consists in interpreting rather than merely collecting and processing facts. Design is based on qualitative judgements beyond quantitative methods: 'Design, however, is based precisely on reasons of meaning and purpose that cannot be given with the help of statistical-mathematical methods. Today, very few designers can do without data collection and data processing. But collecting facts does not explain the demands and necessities. Facts have to be included in the design, but facts do not yet result in a concept. Design consists precisely in interpreting them, in inserting them into a concept which is not satisfied with the fact that something exists, but also attempts to determine how and why. In this respect, value should be placed on a qualitative presentation of facts.'

Aicher claims that design is a moral, evaluative activity based on a cultural and social value system. For Aicher, this confirms 'the necessity of a precise design doctrine': 'Design is to a large extent a statement and thus a moral activity. It is based on both cultural and social values. It includes objectives, evaluations and commitment. Otherwise, it must degenerate into opportunistic styling. The design is in an educational position from the outset. It does not design what is wanted, but what should be. Freedom of value is the self-abandonment of design, regardless of whether it is sacrificed to market demands, public taste or corporate strategy. ... Value-free design becomes worthless.'

The result of my review is as follows: Aicher's design is based on the foundation of meaning and purpose. It is ultimately a moral, judgemental activity predicated on cultural and social values. Aicher's doctrine does not contain a formal aesthetic definition, which is why it would be wrong to assume that he was subservient to a particular style.

There is nothing in Aicher's practice or theory that would justify labelling him as a purely scientific or rational designer. Rather, Aicher is presented as an artist who did not want to be one, as Max Bill said. We can regard this as tragic, because his social goals cannot be seamlessly translated into a theory of design. The aesthetic qualities that Aicher preferred cannot be produced algorithmically. Design is not a simple input-output calculation.

However, more than tragedy, I see a circle that Aicher himself closed. That circle began with art and philosophy as a source of resistance against the Nazis. He came up with answers for socially responsible design. And at the end of his life, he worked as a sculptor, creating a bust of Sophie Scholl from memory. On the day he completed this work, Otl Aicher was struck by a motorcycle.

otl aicher and the definition of visual communication studies at the ulm school of design

neus moyano

Meeting of the governing body of the HfG Ulm, 1955. Max Bill at the front; Otl Aicher and Inge Aicher-Scholl on the right. Photograph: Hans Conrad

Otl Aicher was a radically modern thinker with strong religious and philosophical convictions who, after World War II, felt called to transform the field of visual communication studies, and the very concept of design, to adapt them to the needs and reality of the industrialised world.

And so Aicher, an artist with no training in graphic design, after undergoing a traumatic experience, decided to found a school, the Hochschule für Gestaltung Ulm—also known in English as the Ulm School of Design—in order to redirect the conception of design. His determination to modernise the discipline, working from yet simultaneously challenging the postulates of the Bauhaus, made him one of the most important designers of the second half of the twentieth century.

The Hochschule für Gestaltung Ulm opened in 1955 and went on to become the most important design school of the mid-to-late twentieth century. In 1946 its founders, Otl Aicher and Inge Scholl, started out with the Volkshochschule Ulm project, an adult education centre opened with the idea of providing democratic re-education for young Germans after the war.

In 1950, their focus shifted to establishing a design school, and artist and architect Max Bill was recruited to lead a kind of revival of the teachings of the legendary Bauhaus. Bill was also charged with the task of designing the building. The decision to make Max Bill director of the new design school was partly based on the fact that he had studied at the Bauhaus from 1927 to 1929. During that short period, Bill was deeply impressed by the school's teaching method, which he subsequently attempted to apply and renew, particularly the methodology of Josef Albers's preliminary course. The lessons of Wassily Kandinsky, to whom he dedicated various publications and exhibitions in the course of his life, and Paul Klee were also indelibly etched in his memory. But Josef Albers was the most immediate point of reference, and it was he who would inaugurate the new HfG Ulm with his famous preliminary course, which he taught in 1953 and 1954, when classes were still being held at the Volkshochschule Ulm.

View of the city of Ulm. In the foreground, the Hochschule für Gestaltung building. Photograph: Otl Aicher

In 1950s Europe, creating a brand-new type of design school was a difficult and risky venture. The memory of the Bauhaus and the myriad ways in which former students and teachers, and even people unconnected to the school, had chosen to interpret its teachings was directly opposed to the conservative training that continued to dominate the applied arts across Europe. The Ulm School initiative did not always meet with the approval of the academic establishment, and in Germany it clashed with other decorative arts projects and schools of art and architecture.

Shortly after its official inauguration in 1955, Max Bill began to have differences of opinion with the younger teachers and founders: Otl Aicher, Tomás Maldonado, Hans Gugelot and Walter Zeischegg. Hans Gugelot was the only one

Volkshochschule Ulm team: Inge Scholl, Herbert Wiegandt, Sven Anker Lindström, Hans Werner Richter, Otl Aicher, Irm Lindström, Hans Rupp and Peter Wackernagel, c. November 1949. Photograph: Hannes Rosenberg

of them who had received technical training; the rest all had visual arts backgrounds. In 1956, the recently inaugurated HfG decided to create a council of rectors comprising Otl Aicher, Tomás Maldonado, Hans Gugelot, Friedrich Vordemberge-Gildewart and Max Bill. As a result, Bill no longer had absolute control over the educational policy of the Ulm School, and he eventually left in 1957.

The programme drafted by the new rectors finally made it clear that the HfG was moving in a different direction. The introduction explained that the new directorial team was no longer convinced by Max Bill's theory that all the school's activities should be aimed at building a new culture which would help to create a lifestyle suited to the new technological era. Bill's vision reflected a desire to create a model of universal 'good' design, but the new rectors advocated a humbler attitude: instead of trying to create a universal culture, they believed they should focus on design problems. In this new approach, the designer was a scientific partner and 'critical coordinator' in the production system, well-versed in the areas of research, technology, communication and aesthetics. In contrast, according to Max Bill's old pedagogical theory, the engineer was subordinate to the designer in the production hierarchy, and art was upheld as the ultimate model for the configuration of all surrounding objects.

Otl Aicher served as rector of the HfG Ulm on two occasions: in 1956 as a member of the council of rectors, and in 1962 as sole rector. As a teacher, director of the Visual Communication Department for several terms since the school first opened, and director of the development team known as Gruppe 5, Aicher participated in every important industry-related project at the school. One such project was developing a corporate identity for Braun—which included designing free-standing pavilions for fairs—with Hans G. Conrad and Hans Gugelot. He also worked with Gugelot to design the diagrams for Braun's hi-fi devices and display structures for the brand. In addition, Aicher was involved in the 1961 Hamburg Metro project, one of the Ulm School's crowning achievements, and in the development of Lufthansa's corporate identity, a commission the school received in 1962 and one of the most important projects he ever supervised.

This last job, a pioneering communication system, entailed reviewing, reorganising and restructuring all of the company's identifying visual elements to create a new principle: the systematic coordination of all such elements. The most important identifying factor was colour as a recognisable sign. The company was already using a yellow-and-blue colour scheme, but the design team reworked it to emphasise yellow, a colour associated with speed, safety, activity and technology. They also switched to a Helvetica-Grotesk font, standardised the typography of all graphic elements, and incorporated photography as an illustrative medium. They revamped the image of the airline's ground support vehicles, offices and

Timetable of flights operated by Lufthansa, April–June 1967

ticket desks, on-board tableware and other brand-related items, treating everything as parts of a single communication system. Timetables, tickets, boarding passes and baggage labels were optically, functionally and economically organised by coordinating formats.

Outside the Ulm School, Aicher created the image of the 1972 Olympic Games in Munich, developing an innovative system of pictograms as well as all other visual identity elements. The Olympics are a mass sporting event that requires effective non-verbal signage. Aicher efficiently met this need by creating a system of pictograms whose geometric simplicity made them highly legible. This system proved so effective that it is still used today for visual communication in airports, where clear, efficient signage is paramount.

Philosophy and design

Aicher has been called a thinking designer,[1] and this description underscores an aspect that characterised his entire existence: his facet as a theoretician concerned with the fundamentals of design and architecture. He was a theoretician in the philosophical sense of the word, for Aicher never developed a specific learning method, and his teaching activity was focused on praxis rather than theory; his classes, always for small groups, often involved completing corporate commissions or competition proposals with his students, working alongside them as collaborators. Aicher, who took it upon himself to create an administrative structure that would allow hands-on experience, also formed the research groups and personally led Gruppe 5 to take on visual communication commissions at the school.

Through his own professional and teaching experience at the Hochschule für Gestaltung Ulm, Otl Aicher was able to formulate and pass on his design philosophy. As a principal co-founder, he played a very important role in setting up the school, although in the early days he focused on continuing his own education with people like Max Bill, Josef Albers, Walter Peterhans and Helene Nonné-Schmidt, whose teachings came from the defunct Bauhaus. At the same time, his sources of information were many and varied, given that Otl Aicher's design philosophy and ideas did not descend directly from art, design or architecture.

It is important to remember that Aicher fought as a soldier in World War II and as an anti-fascist activist in the ranks of the White Rose group. Two of his closest friends were executed for participating in a student uprising, a loss that clearly marked the fate of the future designer. When the war ended, he decided to study sculpture in Munich but only completed one year of the programme; after becoming aware of the pressing need to redefine the foundations of a morally and economically devastated society, he immediately shouldered the responsibility of doing his part to rebuild the country from his place of residence, Ulm, a city that had sustained serious damage. Aicher was keenly aware of the material necessities involved in the moral and political reconstruction of his homeland, which in turn called for design decisions about how that reconstruction should be effected from a fresh, modern, anti-Nazi perspective.

As René Spitz and Eva Moser have noted in two important monographs,[2] Aicher's sources of information were not those of formal design. Philosophy and religion were the themes that interested him most, although he approached philosophy as someone with no philosophical training but whose observations were pertinent to the problem he had to solve: namely, the justification of design beyond the formal world, design as a way of planning the world, of making it more human. The telling title of one of his books, *The World as Design*, reflects the fact that, for Aicher, everything could and should be designed. In the exercise of designing, the individual finds self-determination.

Modernism has had few great adherents of practical knowledge. Karl Marx became one of its principal advocates when he based man's capacity for emancipation on his own work,[3] even though selling that work for monetary value is the cause of his alienation. For Aicher, doing was not enough; one had to do thinking and think doing. In this way, Aicher connected disciplines as dissimilar as philosophy and architecture or design, abstract and concrete thought, the analogous and the digital, as expressed in another of his book titles. We should not necessarily be surprised by this connection. In fact, what is surprising is that a philosopher like Karl Marx, who devoted part of his work to describing the characteristics of the produced object, has not attracted more attention from designers, who after all talk about the same things: the products of human labour, their useful value and their exchange value.

Argentine artist and designer Tomás Maldonado, who sided with Aicher when the Ulm School broke away from concrete art, wrote in 1949, shortly before embarking on the new adventure of teaching design at the HfG Ulm: 'Industrial design today holds out the only possibility of effectively solving one of the most dramatic and pressing problems of our time, the divorce of art from life.'[4]

However, Aicher found the clearest conciliation of philosophy with design, not in Marx, but in the pragmatic ideas of Ludwig Wittgenstein, for whom both had to do with things, the experience of objective knowledge in the process of creating or, more accurately, redesigning objects. After all, designing is simply rethinking, redrawing objects and needs of everyday life or the world around us, and in the process redrawing our environment, which leads to a genuine philosophical debate on the idea of *Dasein* or being-in-the-world.

[1] Yves Zimmermann, *Del diseño* (Barcelona: Gustavo Gili, 2002).

[2] Eva Moser, *Otl Aicher: Gestalter* (Ostfildern: Hatje Cantz, 2012); René Spitz, *HfG Ulm: The View behind the Foreground: The Political History of the Ulm School of Design, 1953–1968* (Stuttgart/London: Axel Menges, 2002).

[3] Introduction by Wilhelm Vossenkuhl in Otl Aicher, *Analogous and Digital*, trans. Michael Robinson (Berlin: Ernst & Sohn, 2015), 10–21.

[4] Tomás Maldonado, 'Diseño industrial y sociedad' [1949] in Tomás Maldonado, *Escritos preulmianos* (Buenos Aires: Infinito, 1997), 63–65; Neus Moyano, 'Industria y diseño: ideología en la Hochschule für Gestaltung Ulm 1953–1968', PhD thesis, Universitat Rovira i Virgili, Tarragona, 2016.

Christian humanism and design

Christian humanism was the second source of Aicher's philosophy and pedagogy. In their early days at the Volkshochschule, Aicher and Scholl were quite close to the humanist philosopher Romano Guardini, a family friend and best man at the couple's wedding. In the final years of the war, Aicher also established ties with the Christian humanist philosopher Jacques Maritain and Theodor Haecker, a Catholic thinker and writer concerned with reconciling reason and faith and closely connected to the White Rose, the anti-Hitler resistance group to which Aicher and the Scholl siblings belonged.[5]

Towards the end of his life, Aicher embarked on a singular project that would encapsulate his theory of the connection between design, logic and Christianity: the exhibition on William of Ockham which he organised with Professor Wilhelm Vossenkuhl in 1986. According to Aicher, Ockham was one of the first thinkers and designers of modern science; thanks to him, thought abandoned abstraction and turned towards concretion.[6]

The exhibition panels that illustrated the life and philosophy of William of Ockham were based on a systematic order with a few simple rules. To create these panels, Aicher sought inspiration in medieval illuminations and Gothic architecture, whose forms strictly adhered to the structural principles that made it possible to construct buildings like the great Gothic cathedrals. Consequently, the structural and semantic order that Aicher found in medieval imagery was repeated in the exhibition: four bands organising the narrative, and the use of colour and isometric geometry to represent all the architectural and some of the figurative elements. Axonometric and isometric projections are used to represent cities and landscapes from above, the same aerial perspective Aicher used when preparing the Bilbao Metro project. That handful of elements were elevated to the category of signs, in the same way and following the same premise applied to the identity of the 1972 Olympic Games in Munich.

Ockham's inspiring influence on the Aicher's work is clearly expressed in the designer's ruminations on the Franciscan thinker: 'What is mind? What we see and understand.'[7]

Opposition to National Socialism

The creation of the Ulm School was motivated by a profound conviction of the need to rebuild the humanist roots of the German people, roots which were ultimately blamed for having led them into National Socialism. And as National Socialism had found its ultimate propagandistic expression in the manifest symbolism of design and architecture, it seemed likely that the sources of evil had contaminated the very core of design. Consequently, Aicher devoted his entire life to the primordial task of finding the antidotes to that worldview, and this dedication also decisively shaped his ideas about design. The idealistic vision that associated design with the world of art and forms was firmly rejected from the outset by the HfG Ulm, deeming it a one-sided point of view with no bearing on the actual task of the designer, which is to design a more human world. In fact, the school believed that any one-sided perspective, whether idealistic, artistic or based directly on ideological propaganda, was an obstacle to good design.

In 1972, the Munich Olympics gave the Ulm School a chance to oppose what the Berlin Games had represented in 1936 with their own design perspective. They wanted to reverse the ideological signs and language used in National Socialist iconography, which in practice meant resorting to a particular colour scheme, repetition and pathos—all of which the public found quite captivating. When setting out the design guidelines for the 1972 Olympic Games, Aicher carefully itemised the reasons for that opposition and the methods for achieving it based on his idea of communication through design.

Thus, repetition was replaced by the idea of a system as an organic whole that would have to fulfil the most basic requirement of an international mass sporting event: wayfinding. Repetition and monumentality do not facilitate wayfinding and in fact have the opposite effect: they paralyse, overwhelm, confound the senses. Clarity is the opposite of pathos, and diversity in organic connection is the antithesis of uniformity. The colour scheme of Munich '72, based on blue, orange, yellow and green, was a deliberate contrast to the black and red palette of the Berlin Games. Aicher established a handful of elements that, in his words, constituted the rules of the game, a game involving a large number of designers and items to which those few yet decisive design principles would have to be applied.[8]

In response to this need to invert the relationship between graphic design and ideological propaganda, the Ulm School created an Information Department whose mission was to analyse language, propaganda, persuasion and journalism, including those employed by television and other new media. This section complemented the Visual Communication Department.

Choice of design tools

These ideas were constants in every aspect of the Ulm School's development. The origins of that philosophy have to do with cybernetics, systems theory and information aesthetics, which permeated the school's educational procedures from its founding as planning and design tools.

[5] Otto Karl Werckmeister, 'Otl Aichers Bildtafeln zu Wilhelm von Ockham' in *form+zweck*, HfG Ulm, no. 20 (2003), 22–30.

[6] Otl Aicher, 'Universals and Capitals' in Otl Aicher, *Analogous and Digital*, trans. Michael Robinson (Berlin: Ernst & Sohn, 2015), 55–59.

[7] Aicher, 'Universals and Capitals', 59.

[8] Mark Holt, *Munich '72: The Visual Output of Otl Aicher's Dept. XI* (London: Mark Holt, 2019).

Norbert Wiener, author of *Cybernetics, or Control and Communication in the Animal and the Machine* (1948), was a lecturer at Ulm in the early 1950s, and Max Bense, with his theory of information aesthetics, taught courses when the school was in its infancy and resurfaced in 1965 with Abraham Moles's classes. Other subjects—topology with British designer Anthony Froshaug, modular geometry with Walter Zeischegg and operational mathematics with Georg Ritter—were considered valid methods for knowing and understanding design problems and applied to the formalisation of objects and systems.

The discipline of semiotics was taught at the HfG from day one thanks to Tomás Maldonado's theoretical classes. In this, as in other areas, the HfG Ulm was a pioneering institution. The posters designed in the early years convey simple messages of speed, danger, spirituality, etc., usually through photography, though this medium was exploited for its semiotic rather than artistic value. The Photography Department was one of the first to be created at the HfG as part of the core curriculum for all students. The workshop was directed by Christian Staub, who shared his interest in subjective photography and introduced students to the photography of the Bauhaus and the New Objectivity, as well as to the work of William Klein, Eugène Atget, Walker Evans and Bill Brandt.[9]

The relationship between design and art

The orientation of the Visual Communication Department was strongly influenced by the interests and skills of the professors who taught at Ulm. The students in this department received a constant stream of visual input through different channels: the influence of the Bauhaus via Max Bill and Albers and of concrete art through Max Bill and Tomás Maldonado, work on colour interactions courtesy of Josef Albers, the influence of guest lecturers, like the Swiss citizen Josef Müller-Brockmann, who showed them how to use Swiss typography and introduce the grid system in graphic design, the ideas of the Gestalt through Maldonado and concrete art, and the influence of subjective photography and the New Objectivity via the photography workshop teachers. Consequently, moving away from the art world was a challenge, to say the least.

This seemed to contradict the idea, defended by Aicher and the HfG itself, that the relationship between design and art should be more detached. While it is true that the school drank from the Bauhaus well, it always rejected the notion that design was related to any artistic form. However, many of the graphic designs produced by the Visual Communication Department and the actual praxis of designers like Aicher had to do with formal research. Products associated with poster art and photography, which might seem more closely related to the art world, undoubtedly had an element of continuous formal investigation derived from the teachings of Albers, Peterhans, Max Bill and concrete art, and the Gestalt. Aicher himself presented a photography show at the Ulm Museum and, at the same time, participated in a poster art exhibition at the MoMA in New York, the self-defined headquarters of modern art.[10]

Josef Albers was largely responsible for introducing the preliminary course at the Ulm School, modelled on the same course offered at the Bauhaus, which aimed to disabuse students of their preconceived notions about formalisation and give them a basic knowledge of morphology, proportion and colour. This introductory course, which might have been found in any type of art education programme, was taught consistently at the HfG Ulm until it closed in 1968, with some variations depending on changing trends.

The preliminary course that Albers brought to Ulm from the Bauhaus should be understood as purely abstract, not applied, training;[11] in other words, from a semiotic perspective, it was limited to the elementary, not applied, syntax of line, form and colour, allowing students to develop and understand their aesthetic capacity with these materials—line, form and colour—independently of any utilitarian or even artistic purpose. The goal of the aesthetic experience was to give students a set of tools—not inherited or learned, but assimilated tools—with which to tackle any design problem in any area of formalisation. Albers identified two concurrent process in the student: observation and formulation or vision and expression.[12]

This approach gave students a far more solid foundation than one based solely on a formalisation contingent on utility or social context, for when that context disappeared or the purpose of the object changed, they would be left with no formal resources for tackling new design problems.

At the Ulm School, Albers was highly respected by both Maldonado and Aicher. His systematic, coherent approach to educational research and elimination of the modish trappings in which his predecessors had shrouded the teaching of form—Moholy-Nagy and his exaggerated constructivism, Johannes Itten and his mystical expressionism—were precisely what distanced Albers from the aestheticist aspirations of which the HfG accused the Bauhaus. Albers's lessons focused solely on the syntax of formal elements—line, plane, matter, colour—whereas Itten and Moholy-Nagy's teachings addressed semiotic and symbolic elements: in other words, higher levels of formal language.

The morality of objects

Herbert Lindinger discussed the Hochschule für Gestaltung Ulm in a famous monograph about the school, subtitled

[9] Christiane Wachsman, Thilo Koenig and Michael Koetzle, *Objekt + Objektiv = Objektivität? Fotografie an der HfG Ulm 1953–1968*, exhibition catalogue (Ulm: HfG Archiv, 1991).

[10] Otl Aicher, 'Bauhaus and Ulm' in *The World as Design*, trans. Michael Robinson (Berlin: Ernst & Sohn, 2015), 85–93.

[11] Claudio F. Guerri and William S. Huff, 'El nonágono semiótico: un icono diagramático y tres niveles de iconicidad' (English version: 'A Comprehensive Treatment of Color Submitted to the Semiotic Nonagon') in *DeSignis*, no. 4 (2003), 157–174.

[12] Josef Albers, 'My Courses at the Hochschule für Gestaltung at Ulm (1954)' in *Josef Albers: Minimal Means, Maximum Effect*, exhibition catalogue (Madrid: Fundación Juan March, 2014), 274–277.

The Morality of Objects[13]—a very apt metaphor for the orientation that Aicher attempted to give the Ulm School. Indeed, an object cannot be moral in itself. We would never speak of the morality of a beautiful object designed at the Bauhaus. Yet a design approach to solving problems or concerns can be moral or immoral, right or wrong. This was the next great accomplishment of the Ulm School, which taught that design was a tool for solving problems, whether related to ergonomics, wayfinding, image or communication. In his own way, Aicher presaged the famous distinction that philosopher Bruno Latour made in 2008 between 'matters of fact' (focused on the objects that humanity needs) and 'matters of concern' (focused on the problems that concern humanity). In this, too, the school was a forerunner: design dematerialised, in the sense that it was no longer concerned with shaping objects but rather with solving problems, and consequently art, style and form were relegated to a position of secondary importance.[14]

Official guide and ticket to the inauguration of the 1972 Munich Olympics

Tackling complex issues
An anarchic designer

Otl Aicher was keenly aware of the need to confront the problems of the modern-day world. Therefore, his vision of design as a problem-solving tool and rejection of the aesthetic response were constantly explored at the school through mathematical and philosophical themes and resources.

One of the consequences of this vision was a preference for complex communication issues, such as signage in transport systems, corporate branding and technical communication. These interests were reflected in Aicher's involvement in the definition of Braun's corporate image and some of its industrial designs in 1955, and in the development of Lufthansa's corporate identity in 1962. Complexity required coordination and teamwork among several departments: Visual Communication, Industrial Design, even Industrialised Architecture and Information.

After the HfG Ulm closed, Aicher's commission for the Munich Olympic Games likewise involved communication at the service of urban planning and traffic flows. As part of this job, Aicher was also asked to standardise the image and signage of the Munich airport. The fact that architect Norman Foster made Aicher a regular collaborator and chose him to design the image and visual communication system of the Bilbao Metro is therefore entirely in keeping with the designer's professional preferences.

However, advertising and propaganda as such were not part of his professional production. Although his early posters, clearly influenced by concrete art, aimed to be persuasive, Aicher wanted nothing to do with persuasion and propaganda. The grim memory and long shadow of the heyday of National

[13] Herbert Lindinger, ed., *Ulm Design: The Morality of Objects*, trans. David Britt (Cambridge, MA: MIT Press, 1991).

[14] Bruno Latour, 'A Cautious Prometheus? A Few Steps toward a Philosophy of Design' in Fiona Hackney, Jonathan Glynne and Viv Minto, eds., *Networks of Design: Proceedings of the 2008 Annual International Conference of the Design History Society* (Falmouth: Universal Publishers, 2009), 2–10.

Socialism's persuasive propaganda forced him to remain radically opposed to such tactics.

Aicher did not ignore the drift towards propaganda and advertising in the graphic design profession throughout the second half of the twentieth century, as attested by the fact that the Ulm School programme included an Information Department which dealt with verbal communication in the press, television and advertising. The Ulm designer was clearly not oblivious to the characteristic that would eventually surpass graphic design, the dominance of the message. But despite its strong philosophical underpinnings, the school proved ill-prepared to meet the needs of capitalist consumerism; with the exception of Aicher's office, which held on to a fixed idea until the very end, the students were not equipped to face the advertising-dominated world that would become the norm in graphic design.[15]

In 1961, the writer Martin Walser invited Scholl and Aicher to contribute an article to the book *Die Alternative oder brauchen wir eine neue Regierung*? In their essay, the couple expressed their opposition to Adenauer's non-revisionist policy and reiterated their protests against the hollow consumerism of the neo-capitalist system which, ultimately, the Ulm School had helped to create.[16]

Aicher believed that technology and rational human action were the keys to achieving social welfare, a stance that was not incompatible with his rejection of the rampant, mindless consumerism that derived its strength from persuasive propaganda campaigns with little or no regard for functionality. This idea was reflected, though not without contradictions, in the efforts and aims of the HfG Ulm, particularly in its rejection of the growing desire of individual consumers to gain access to the world of decorative objects and the mastery that designers were expected to apply to the design of such objects.[17]

As a result, the professional career opportunities of Aicher's students were limited, though perhaps it would be more accurate to say that Ulm was not the right school for designers who wanted to find work in the advertising industry, because lies had no place at the HfG Ulm.

[15] Yves Zimmermann, *Del diseño* (Berlin: Gustavo Gili, 2002).

[16] Otl Aicher and Inge Scholl, 'Wohlstand ohne Konzept?' in Martin Walser, ed., *Die Alternative oder Brauchen wir eine neue Regierung?* (Reinbek: Rowohlt, 1961), 104–114.

[17] Eva Moser, *Otl Aicher: Gestalter* (Ostfildern: Hatje Cantz, 2012), 149.

braun

braun

industrialised construction system

In August 1960, during a summer sojourn at Tellaro, Otl Aicher invented an industrial building system: *entwurf eines mehrzeck - bausystems für ein - bis eineinhalbgesschossige bauten* [design of a multi-purpose construction system for one to one-and-a-half-storey buildings]. The document is illustrated with freehand drawings in black ink on parchment paper. It consists of 91 plates, each measuring 27 x 29.7 cm, and is filed in the Ulm archive under the consecutive reference numbers ai.p.512.1–91. It was clearly drafted with pedagogic intentions. The calculated synthesis of both the architectural components (22 elements) and typewritten information make it very easy to understand. Although this was a personal undertaking, unrelated to any particular commission, it was drafted in such painstaking detail that we can still assess and appreciate its construction.

Otl Aicher based this industrial construction system on the pavilions he and Hans Gugelot designed for Braun. In 1955, they worked together to design a system for indoor fair venues (Düsseldorf) and in 1959 they devised an outdoor version (Frankfurt). Looking at the project brief, we can see that this new multi-purpose system—published here for the first time—combines concepts and components of both Braun pavilions. With a limited number of elements (Düsseldorf 1955), Aicher devised a structure that could be expanded indefinitely in geometric order and sequence. Meanwhile, using the elements of the outdoor pavilion (Frankfurt 1959), he modified the horizontal and vertical planes to come up with new components and possibilities of growth. The system uses three modules: 3x3, 4x3 and 4x4. As the title indicates, it makes the most of the structure's relationship with the terrain, including basements for workshops or workspaces depending on the distribution and height in each case. The horizontal and vertical module system and the rhythmic sequences of the trim elements recall the order used by Max Bill at the HfG Ulm. The order of the storeys and the layout of the rooms foreshadow certain features of Aicher's architectural designs for Rotis in the 1970s.

Aicher may have drafted this project with the idea of presenting it to Braun executives, who at the time were considering building an employee housing development, the Siedlung Roter Hang. In the early 1960s, Dieter Rams was given the job of designing this estate in Kronberg im Taunus, modelled on the Siedlung Halen (Switzerland 1955–1961). When Gillette acquired Braun in 1967, the company decided not to build the neighbourhood, but it was eventually completed by the Polenzki & Zöllner construction company, using plans drawn up by an architect named Kramer from Königstein. Many Braun workers, including Dieter Rams and his wife Ingeborg, settled in this housing estate, which now has protected heritage status.[1]

[1] We are indebted to Prof. Klaus Klemp, who interviewed Dieter Rams on 24 September 2020, for this information.

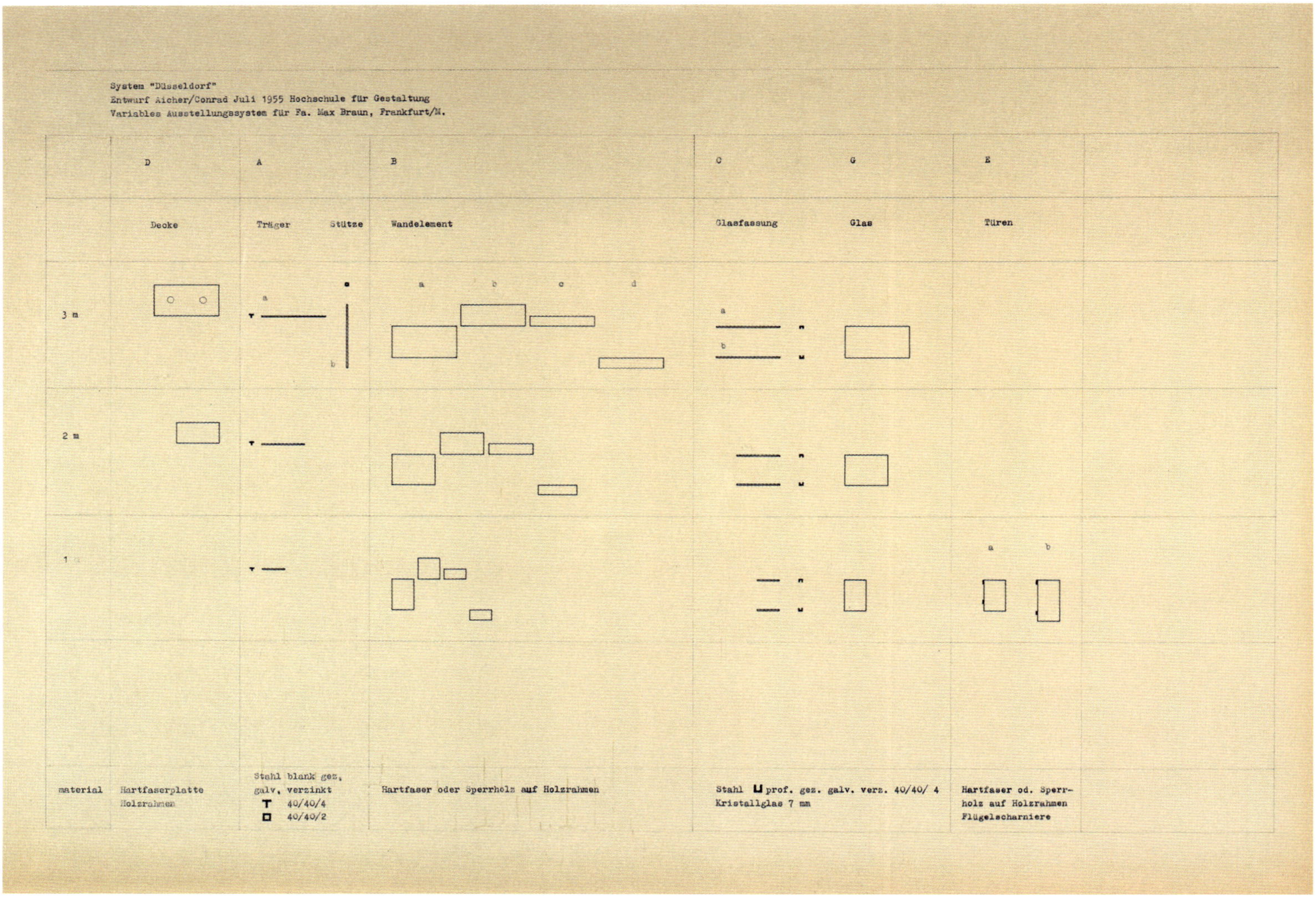

Hans G. Conrad. '"Düsseldorf" System / Aicher/Conrad Project July 1955 Hochschule für Gestaltung / Variable exhibition system for the Max Braun firm, Frankfurt/M.', July 1955. Black whiteprint on paper. 45 x 62 cm. HGC Collection, inv. no. P-61819

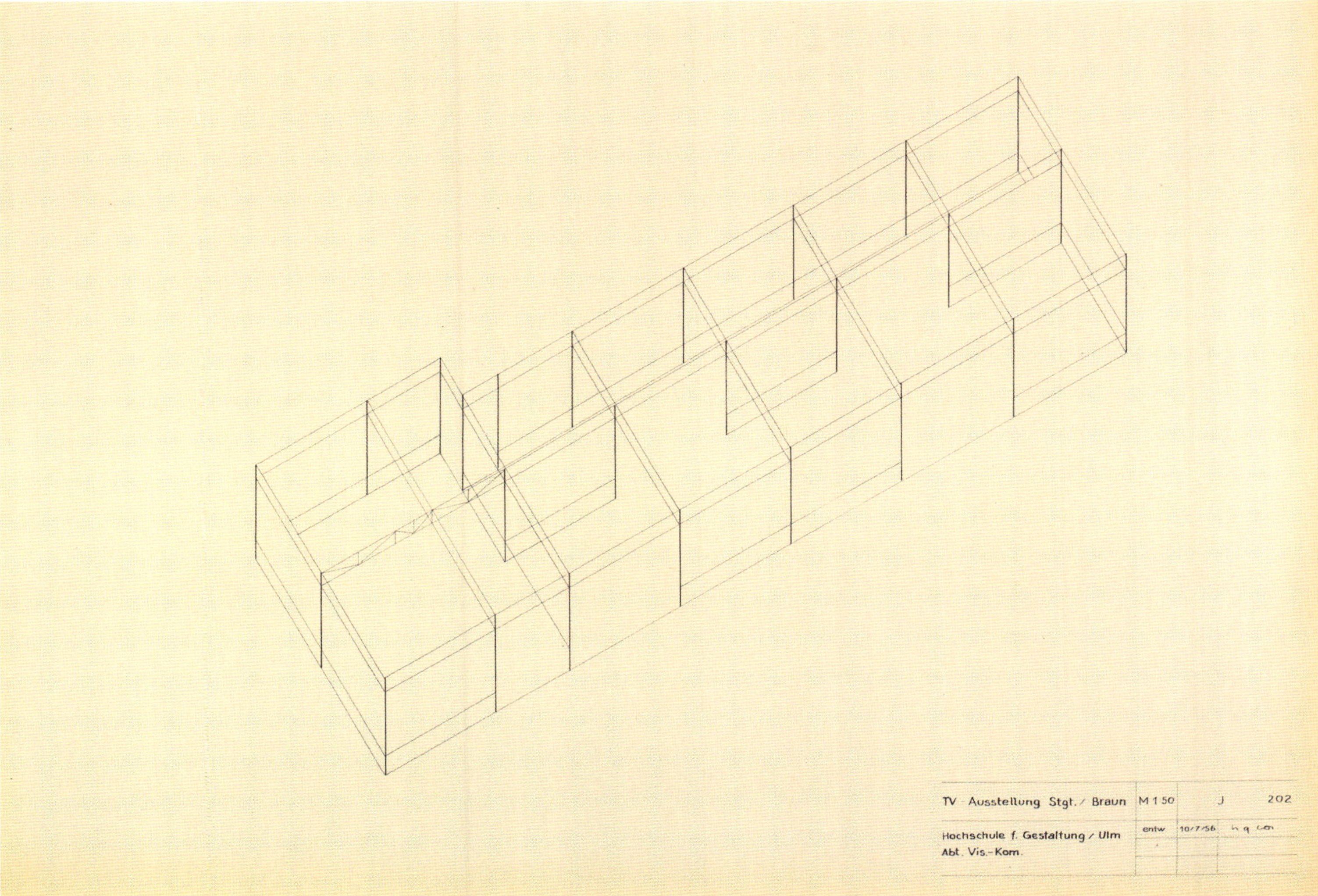

Hans G. Conrad. 'TV Stgt./Braun Exhibition', 10 July 1956. Positive photostat print on paper. 42.6 x 61.6 cm. HGC Collection, inv. no. P-61825

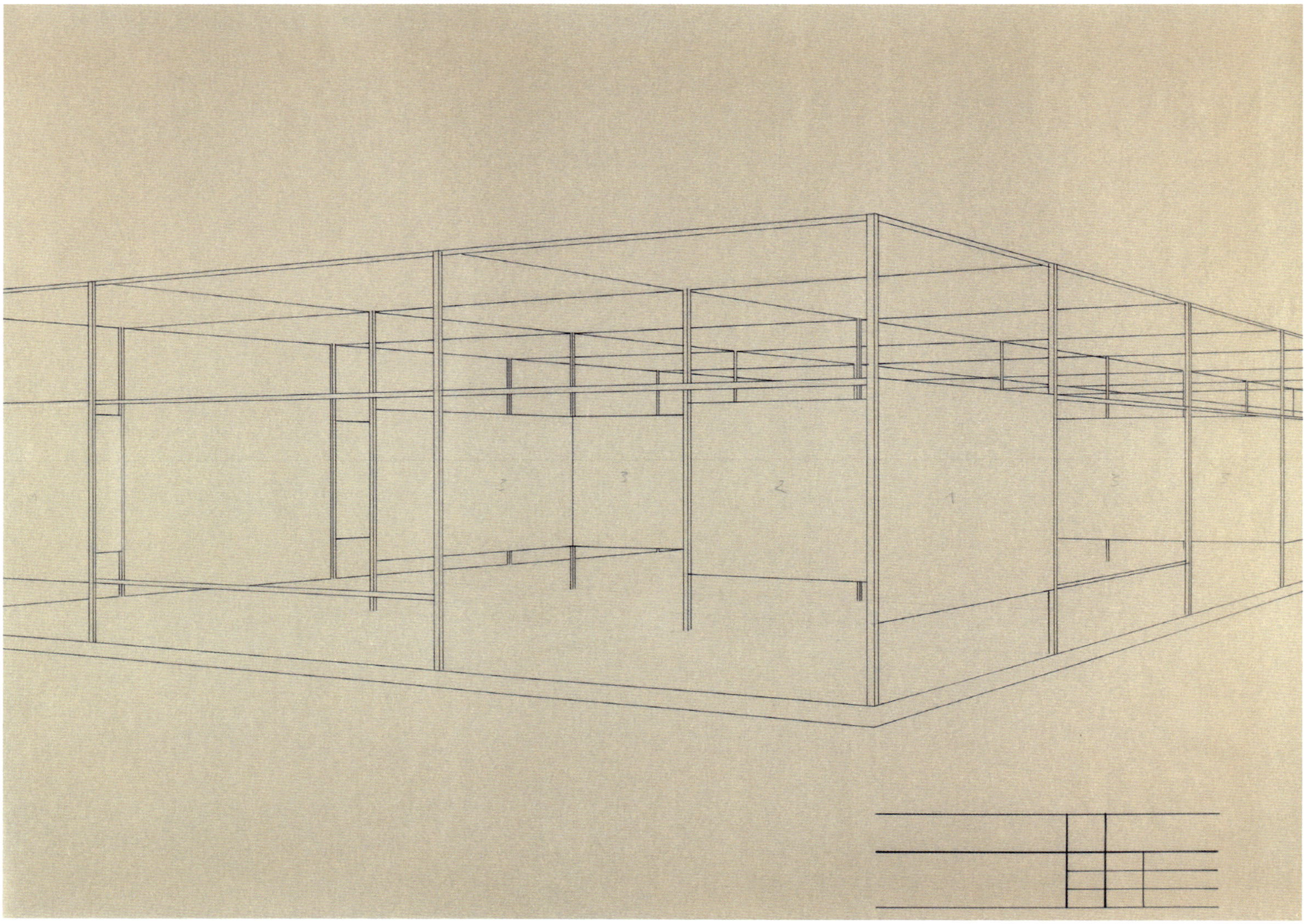

Hans G. Conrad. Sketch of the structure of the Braun Pavilion, c.1955–1956. Ink on paper. 44.9 x 62.3 cm. HGC Collection, inv. no. P-61929

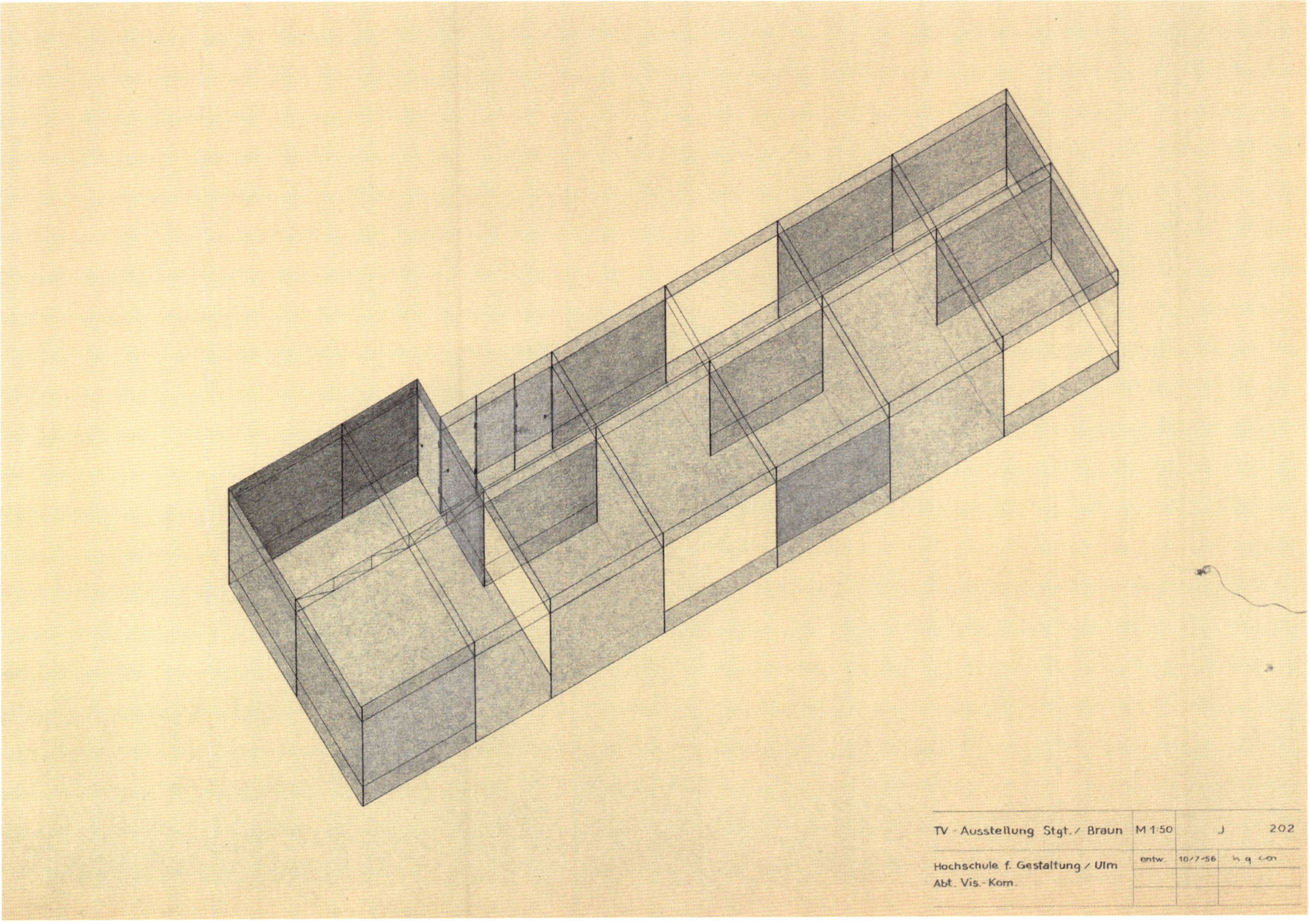

Hans G. Conrad. 'TV Stgt./Braun Exhibition', 10 July 1956. Blue whiteprint on paper. 44 x 60.5 cm. HGC collection, inv. no. P-61987

Otl Aicher and Hans Gugelot.
Braun Pavilion, Düsseldorf, 1955

Otl Aicher and Hans Gugelot.
Braun Pavilion, Düsseldorf, 1955

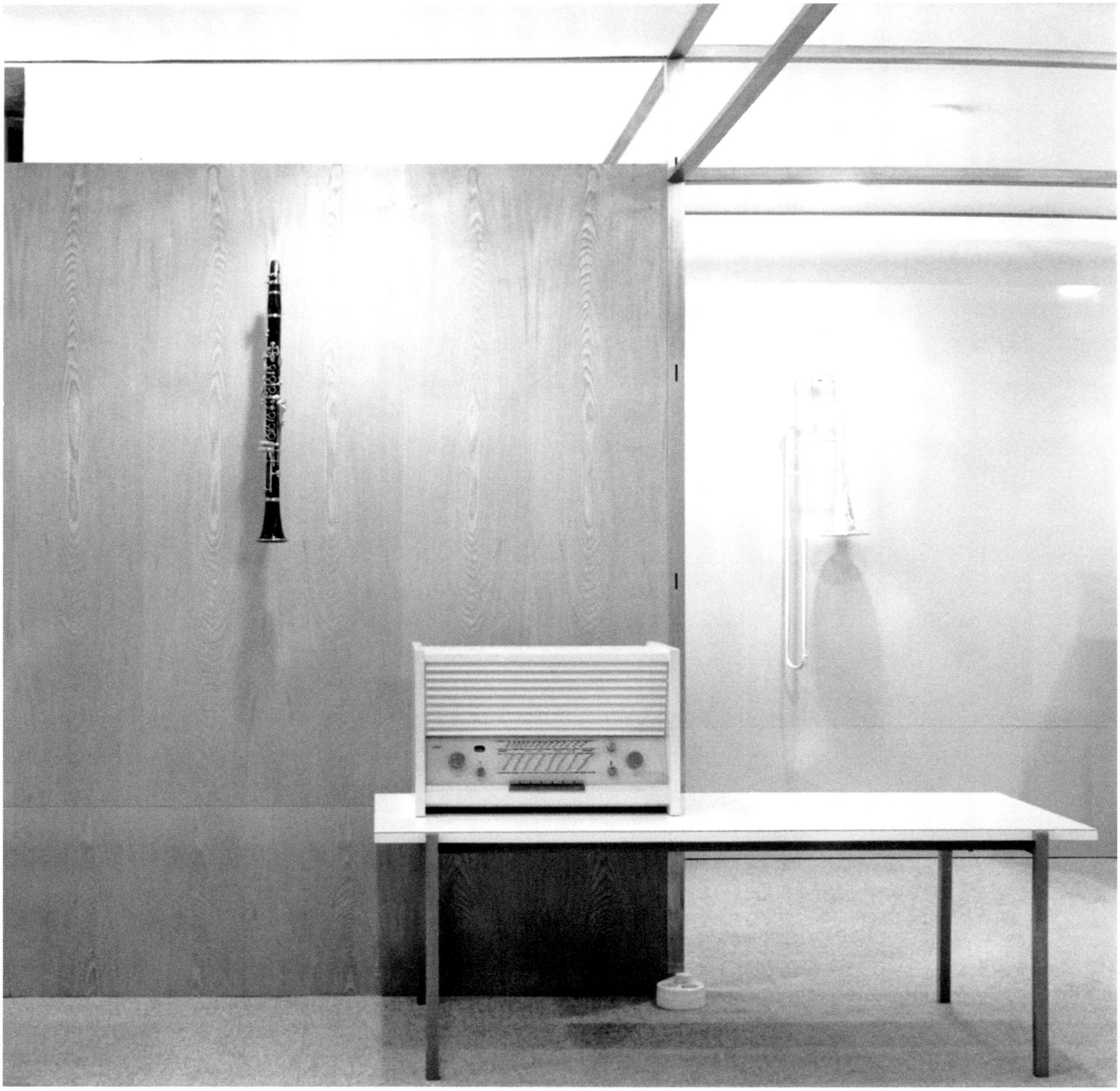

Otl Aicher and Hans Gugelot. Interior of
Braun Pavilion, Düsseldorf, 1955

Otl Aicher and Hans Gugelot.
Braun Pavilion, Frankfurt, 1959.
Photograph: Hans G. Conrad

Otl Aicher and Hans Gugelot.
Braun Pavilion, Frankfurt, 1959.
Photograph: Hans G. Conrad

Otl Aicher and Hans Gugelot.
Interior of Braun Pavilion,
Frankfurt, 1959. Photograph:
Hans G. Conrad

multi-purpose construction system

table of contents

mehrzweck-bausystem

inhalt

970 frankfurt pavilion
971 exterior view
972 frontal view
973 side view
974 interior view
975 vertical section
976 vertical section
977 general section
978 facade section

970 pavillon frankfurt
971 außenansicht
972 frontansicht
973 seitenansicht
974 innenansicht
975 vertikalschnitt
976 vertikalschnitt
977 gesamtschnitt
978 fassadenschnitt

910

<u>darstellung des prinzips</u>

strukturelle zellen aus zwei elementen:
stütze, träger.
orthogonales, räumliches fachwerk.
eingespannte stützen.
quadratischer (in ausnahmen rechteckiger)
grundriß.
erweiterungs- und anbaumöglichkeit nach jeder seite. der grundriß folgt im prinzip der konstruktionsstruktur.
auf die träger werden boden und decke aufgelegt.
zwischen die träger werden die wände eingeschoben. der träger ist so ausgebildet, daß dies auf einfache art ohne technischen aufwand geschehen kann (siehe konstruktion).
damit ist beweglichkeit in der innenaufteilung und anpassungsfähigkeit an wandelnde bauprogramme garantiert.

910

<u>description of the proposal</u>

structural cells consisting of two elements:
columns and beams.
orthogonal layout. embedded columns.
square (exceptionally rectangular)
floor plan.
possibility of expansion and growth in every direction. the floor plan follows the same principle as the building structure. the ceiling and floor rest on beams. the walls are inserted between the beams.
the beams are designed so that the construction process is simple, requiring no technical effort (see construction).
this ensures flexibility in the interior distribution
and the ability to adapt to changes in
the project.

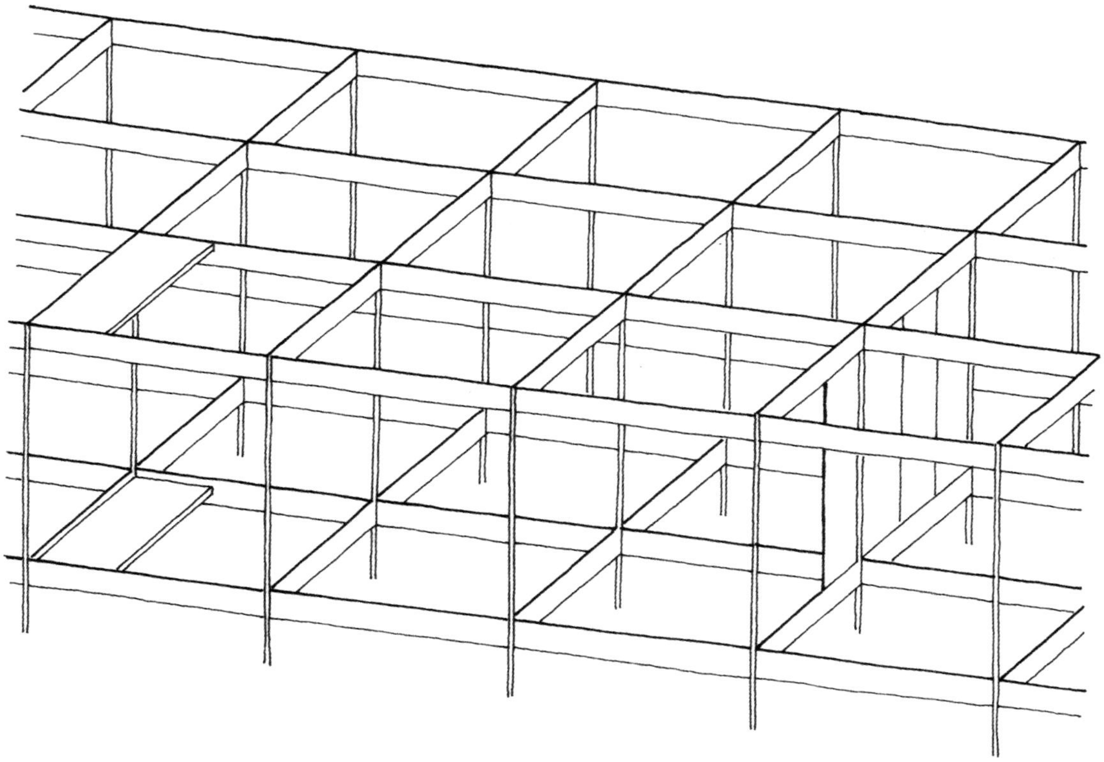

911

raumkombinationen

das system deckt die wohnwelt und den arbeitsbezirk durch die umkehrung der elementenanordnung.
wohnraum und keller (w + k) entspricht dem höheren arbeitsraum (A) mit oberlicht.

nicht neue elemente, sondern nur andere anordnung erfüllt den bedarf. reduktion der mittel und anpassung an den zweck durch änderung der kombination. erhöhung des variationsreichtums durch situierung.

aus dieser überlegung resultiert die fixierung des fußbodens für normale räume (höhe 2.50 m) auf der höhe von 1 m über dem erdboden. nichtunterkellerte bauten mit normaler raumhöhe stehen daher auf stützen. arbeitsräume sind prinzipiell ebenerdig.

911

spatial combinations

the system encompasses both living and working spaces
reversing the distribution of the elements.
the residence and basement (w + k) correspond to
the workspace, lit from above.

needs are met, not by adding new elements, but by rearranging existing ones. economising means and adapting to each purpose with different combinations. greater variety through strategic placement.

this idea inspired the decision to set the floor of the standard rooms (2.50 m ceiling height) 1 m off the ground. thus, buildings of standard height without basements stand on columns. in theory, workspaces are at ground level.

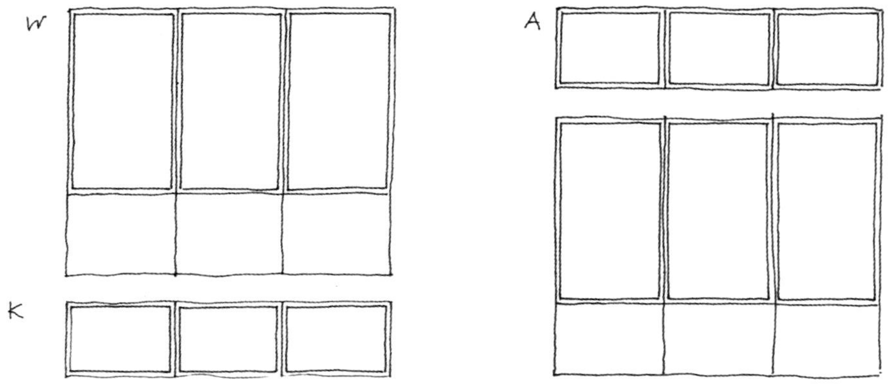
W
K
A

912

raumhöhen

1.
nicht unterkellert auf stützen
2.50 m raumhöhe
gesamthöhe 3.80 m
fußboden 1.00 m über erdboden

2.
unterkellert
keller 2.20 m   kellerfenster 0.70 m
darüber 2.50 m
gesamthöhe 3.80 m
fußboden 1.00 m über erdboden

3.
ebenerdig
raumhöhe 3.50 m
oberlichtband 0.70 m
gesamthöhe 3.80 m

4.
ebenerdig achsabstand 4 m
raumhöhe 3.50 m
oberlichtband 0.70 m
gesamthöhe 3.80 m

912
ceiling heights

1.
no basement, on columns
height 2.50 m
total height 3.80 m
floor 1 m above ground

2.
with basement
basement 2.20 m basement window 0.70 m
floor above basement 2.50 m
total height 3.80 m
floor 1 m above ground

3.
ground level
height 3.50 m
skylight 0.70 m
total height 3.8 m

4.
ground level, 4 m clear span
height 3.5 m
skylight 0.7 m
total height 3.8 m

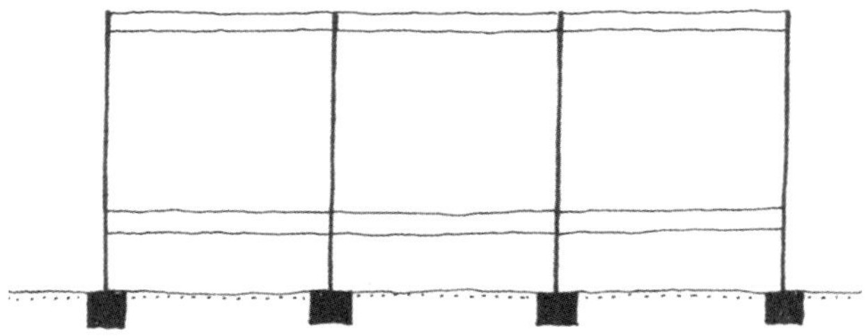

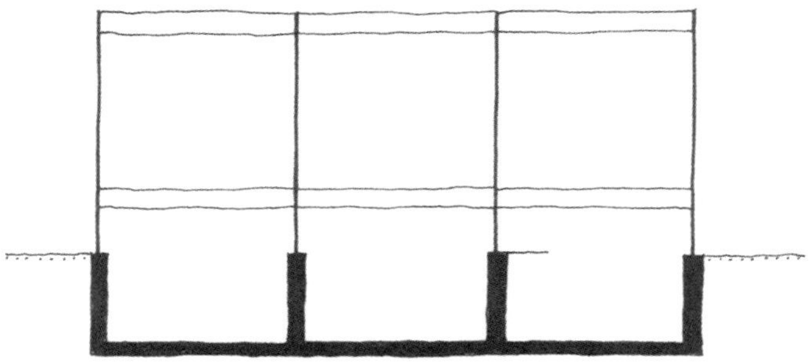

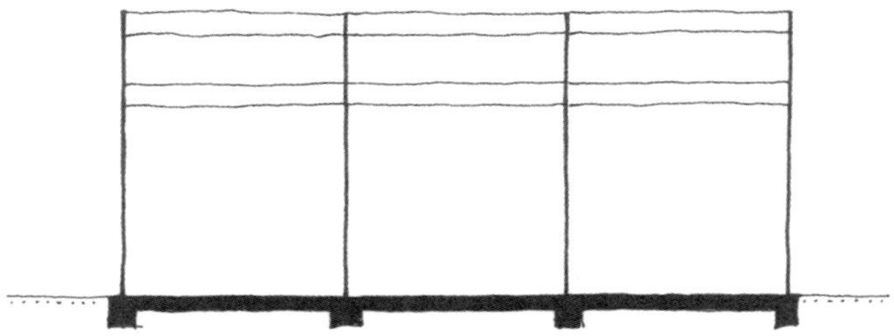

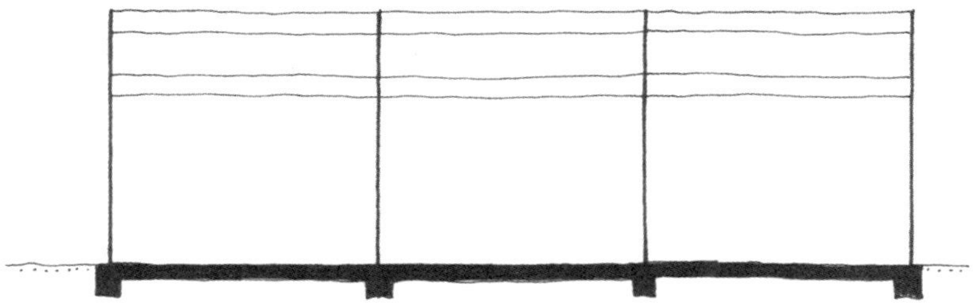

914

die elemente der normalzellen (3m)

1 stütze mit fuß

2 träger

3 regenwasserablauf
4 trichter groß
5 trichter halb

6 boden - deckenplatte

7 zwischendecke

8 türe innen und außen
9 fenster beweglich
10 fenster fest
11 wand innen
12 wand außen

13 fenster beweglich
14 fenster fest
15 wand innen
16 wand außen

17 isolierplatte
18 dachpappe
19 estrich für bodenbelag (einziges nasses material)
20 bodenbelag

21 kleine treppe
22 große treppe

914

standard (3 m) cell elements

1 column with footing

2 beam

3 rainwater drainage
4 large funnel
5 medium funnel

6 floor and ceiling panels

7 false ceiling

8 interior and exterior doors
9 moveable window
10 fixed window
11 interior wall
12 exterior wall

13 moveable window
14 fixed window
15 interior wall
16 exterior wall

17 insulation panel
18 roofing felt
19 screed for flooring (the only wet material)

20 floor

21 small stairway
22 large stairway

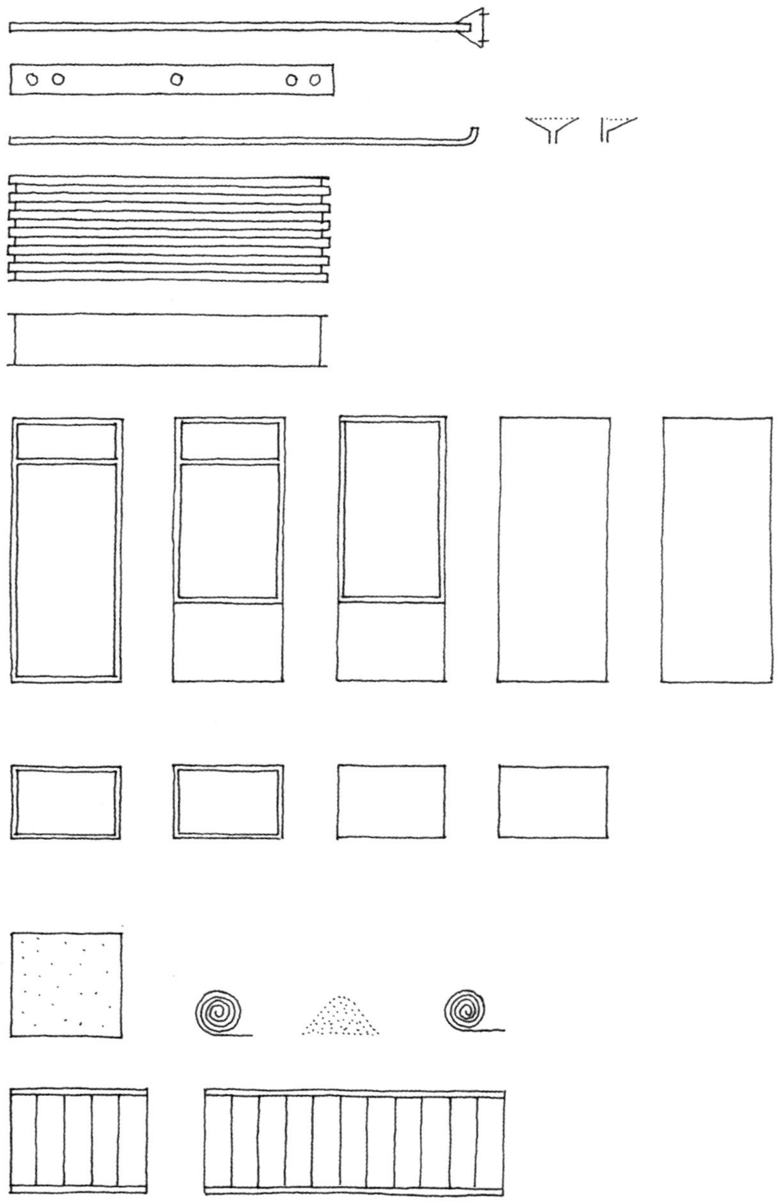

916

bauen in unvorhersehbaren etappen

(meiste planung ist pseudoplanung, weil sich das bauprogramm in der industriegesellschaft nicht vorausbestimmen läßt).

1962
kleines einfamilienhaus eines industriemechanikers

1964
ausbau einer kleinen mechanikerwerkstatt im keller
dadurch wohnterasse und notwendigkeit einer neuen innenraumaufteilung
neue fassade.

1966
aus eigener werkstatt wird eigener betrieb
bau eines werkstattgebäudes.

1968
erweiterung des wohnhauses. familie wird größer.
kleines büro
vergrößerung der werkstätte

1970
erweiterung des wohnhauses um büros. aus der werkstätte wird kleiner produktionsbetrieb.
verdoppelung der fläche.

usw.

916

building in unpredictable stages

(most planning is pseudo-planning
given that, in industrial society, it is impossible
to determine a work schedule in advance)

1962
small single-family home of an industrial mechanic

1964
extension of a small mechanic's workshop in the basement
a porch is created and the rooms
need to be redistributed
new facade.

1966
a home workshop becomes a home business
construction of a building to house the workshop

1968
extension of the house. the family grows.
small office extension of the workshop

1970
extension of the house with offices.
the workshop becomes a small factory.
the surface area doubles.

etc.

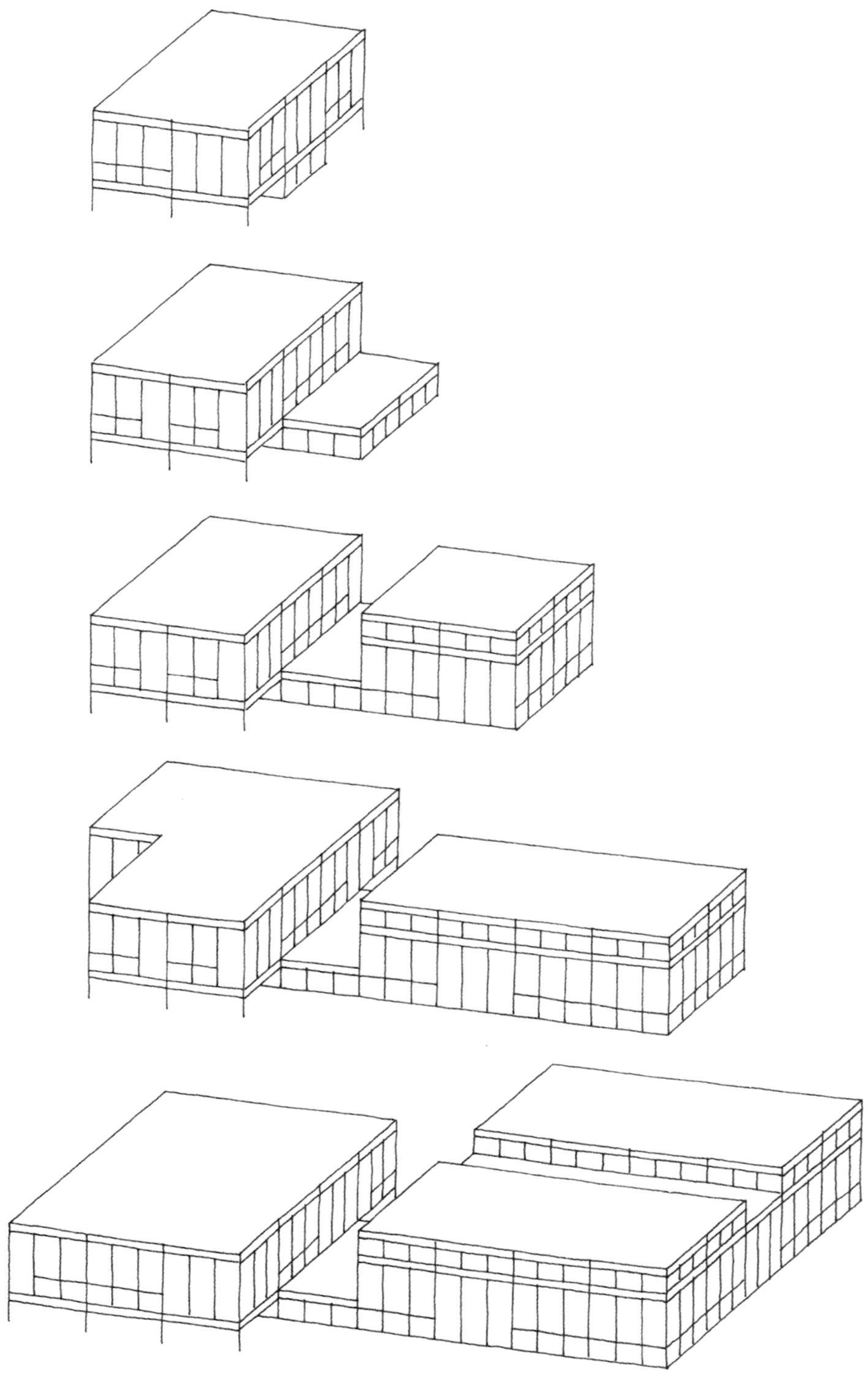

917

grundriß und konstruktionsraster

3 x 3 m
3 x 4 m
4 x 4 m

innerhalb dieser raster lassen sich so gut wie alle grundrißbedürfnisse realisieren.

917

floor plan and structural layout

3 x 3 m
3 x 4 m
4 x 4 m

this layout can accommodate all sorts of floor plan requirements

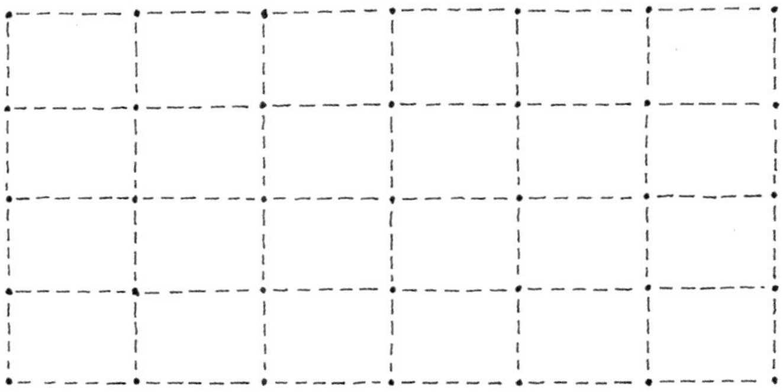

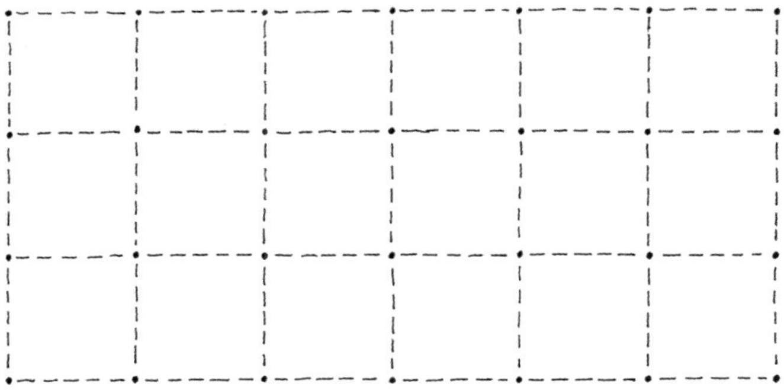

941
m 1:50

voll unterkellert
wohnungen
büro – geschäftsräume

941
scale 1:50

with full basement
residences
office – retail premises

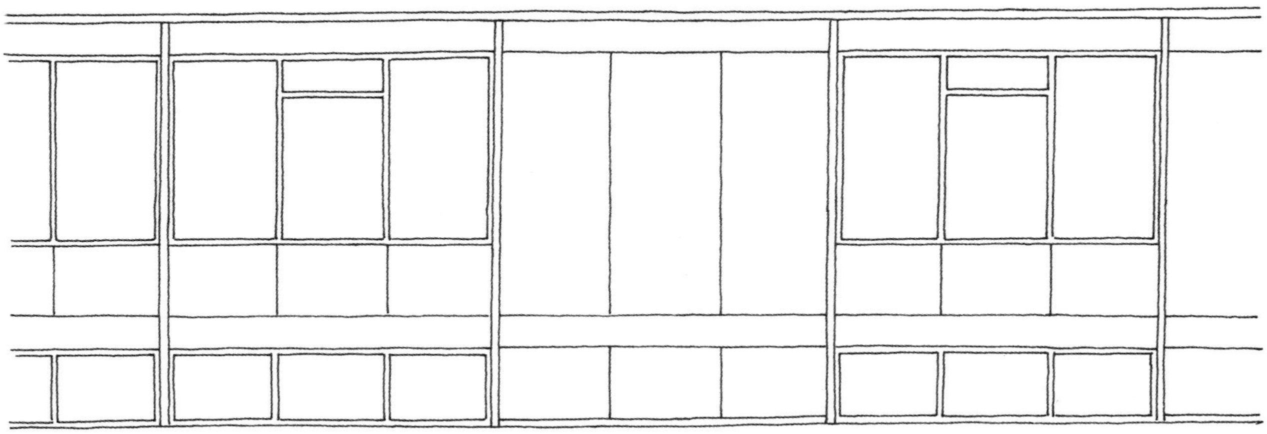

945

m 1:50

raumhöhe 3.50 m
schulen
arbeitsräume

945

scale 1:50

height 3.50 m
schools
work areas

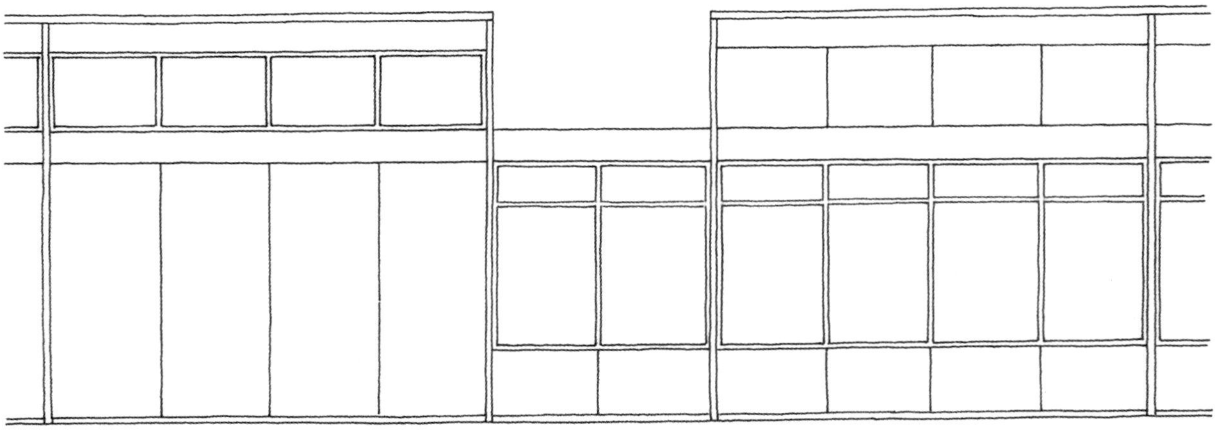

947
m 1:50

ladenstraße raumhöhe 3.50 m
davor überdachter gang 2.50 m hoch

947
scale 1:50

height on shopping street 3.50 m
covered walkway in front, 2.50 m high

coop
SPAR

948
m 1:50

tankstelle und waschboxe

948
scale 1:50

petrol station and car wash

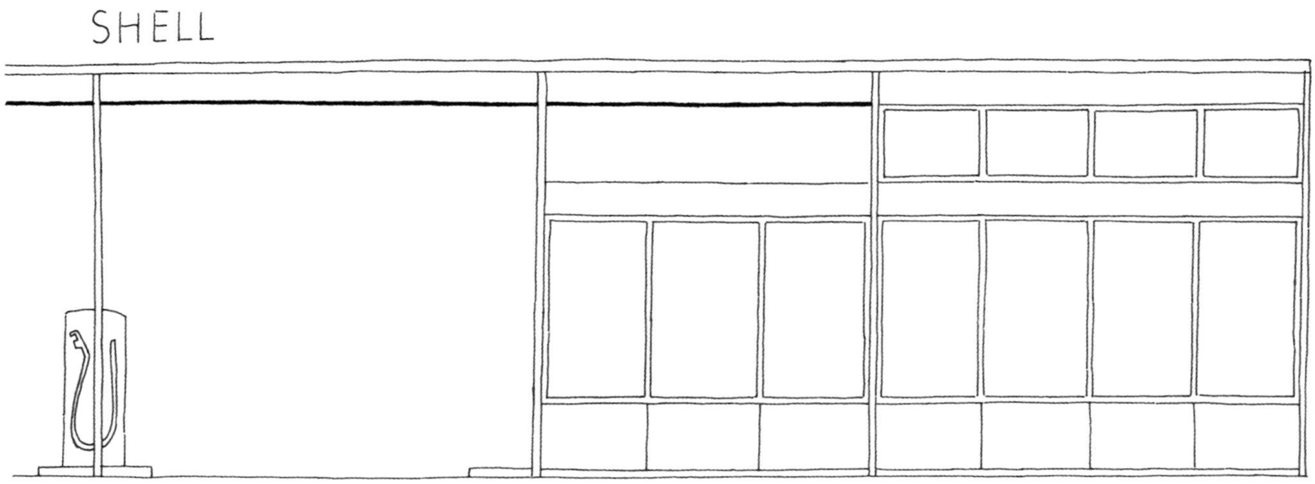
SHELL

951

grundriß
m 1:200

links unten kinderteil mit mädchenzimmer
rechts oben elternteil mit arbeitsplätzen
dazwischen gebäudeteil zum wohnen
und essen
rechts unten garage mit abstellraum

951

floor plan
scale 1:200

bottom left, children's area with domestic service room top right, parents' area with workspace between them, the living area and dining room bottom right, garage with storage room

955

ansicht des wohnteils
typ einer offenen fassade

955

view of the living area
open facade type

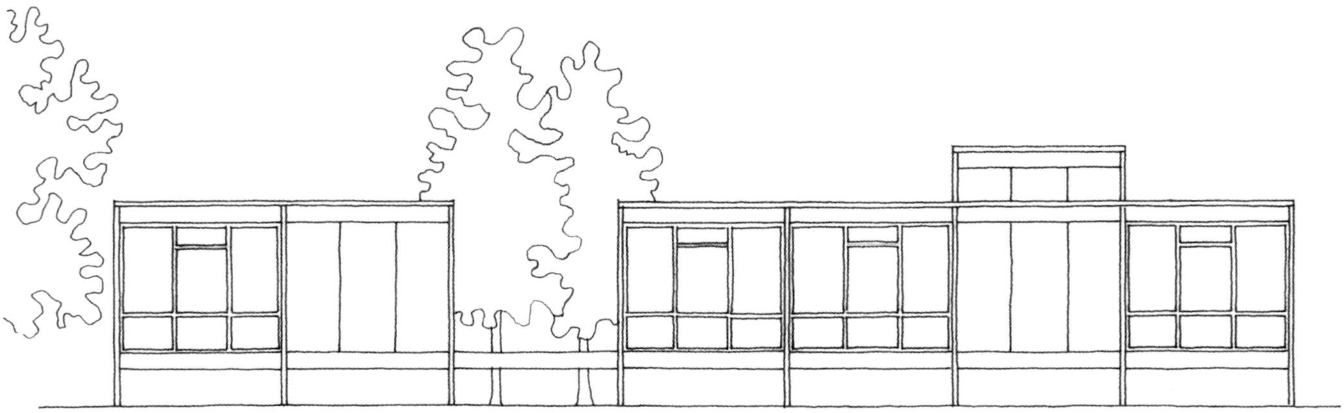

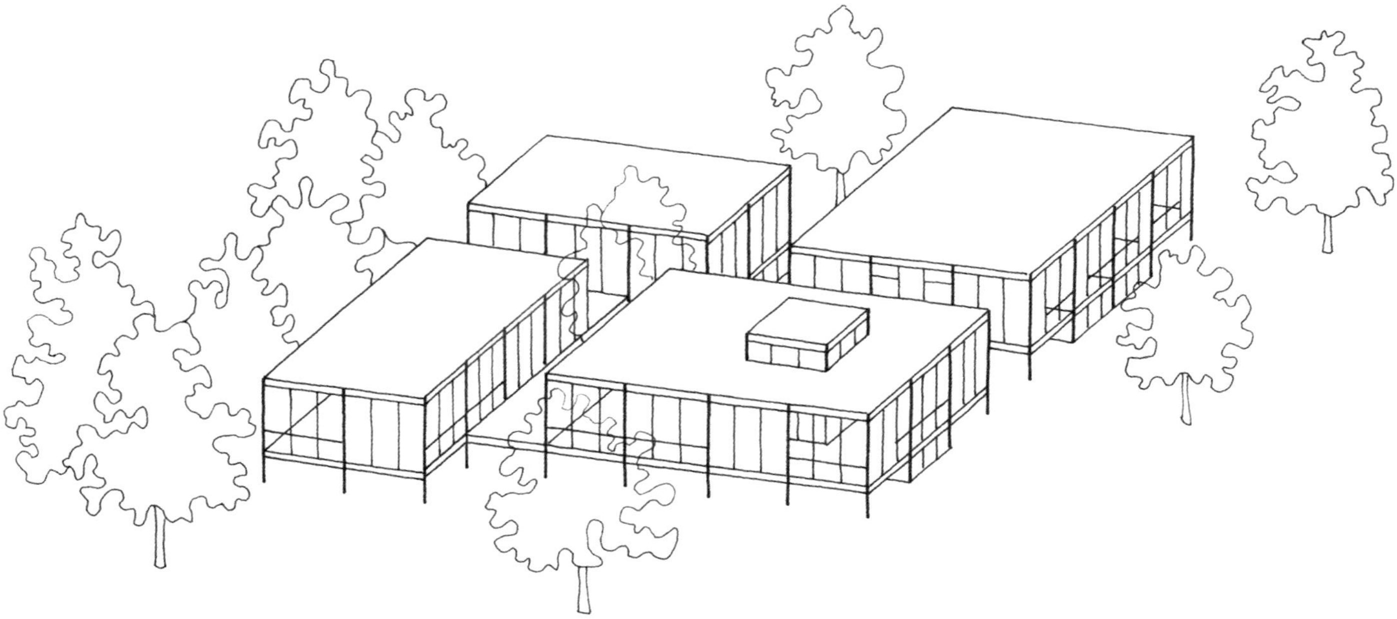

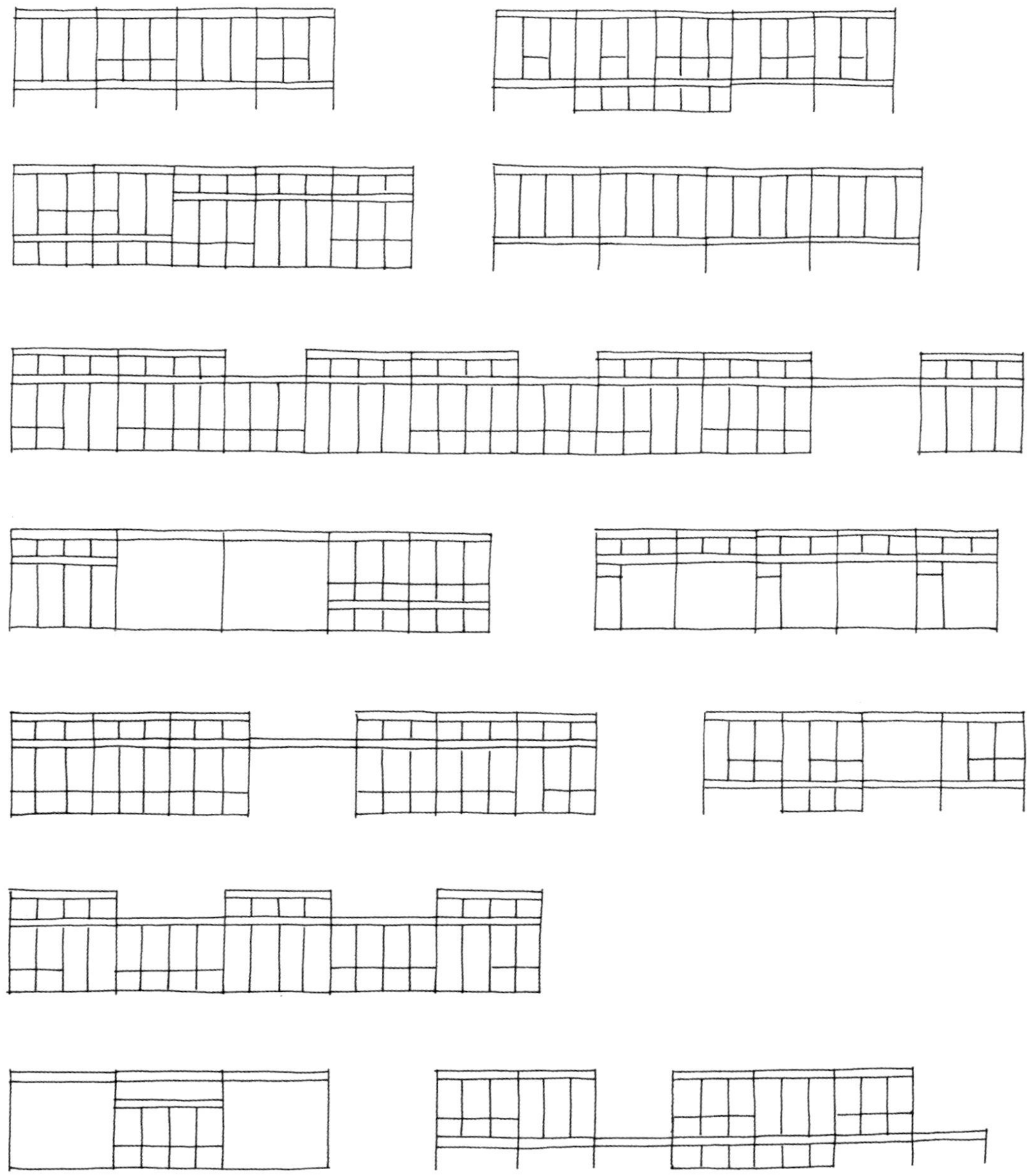

rotis

Ensemble of pavilions designed by Otl Aicher. From left to right: Aicher's photography workshop, power plant and studio. Photograph: Karsten de Riese

rotis:
an authentic place

florian aicher

Rotis mill house and saw shed, Leutkirch, c.1920. The ensemble of buildings would become Otl Aicher's studio from 1970 onwards

Construction of garage,
building 14, 1978

Location

Rotis, at 654 metres above sea level, is located in the Unterallgäu district, a land of gently rolling hills and flat elevations. Today the waterways flow north into the Danube. The Rotismühle or Rotis mill sits on the banks of the Iller, one of the region's major rivers. The village of Rotis is an ancient farming community with sterile soil on the valley floor and fertile fields on higher ground.

Border zone

The settlement was established in the period of Germanic occupation. Around the year 850, Rotis was on the eastern frontier of the lands controlled by the Abbey of Saint Gall. The river marked the boundary with the Princely Abbey of Kempten. The boundary remained, but the rulers changed: after 1150, Kempten seized the land from Saint Gall, and it later passed into the hands of the Leutkirch patriciate and Weingarten Abbey. Secularisation ushered in years of Habsburg and Bavarian rule, although after 1810 Rotis belonged to Württemberg.

Farming community

For centuries, Rotis had a subsistence economy revolving around the mill and two farms, which later grew to five. This changed in the nineteenth century when inhabitants began to exploit pasture lands, lairage and the dairy industry. The market economy became increasingly important, although the Rotis mill continued to grind grain until the mid-1950s (the sawmill remained operational until the late 1960s). More room was needed to accommodate grazing livestock, so existing facilities were enlarged and new ones added: four large new structures appeared in Rotis between 1901 and 1913. The need for labour also grew, a problem that was solved by farm electrification after the year 1900. Following the Treaty of Versailles (1919), industrialisation forcibly took over the markets. In the mid-twentieth century, commercial production became the norm, and by 2005 there were no farmers left in Rotis.

Mill

The earliest reference to the castle mill, from 1414, confirms that it stood by a ford which would later be spanned by a bridge. The first illustration from 1596 shows three buildings. A later print from 1716 presents a schematic view of the current layout: the stream flowing between woodsheds and the mill with its exposed beam structure, and another structure in one corner. The first property records from 1826 describe buildings clustered around a covered courtyard.

Later, in 1901, a decisive step was taken: farming was abandoned, the courtyard was opened up to the countryside, and a large barn (38 x 12.5 metres) was erected with what was then cutting-edge technology: a ground floor of masonry supporting an impressive column-free hayloft with wooden trusses and a tongue-and-groove ceiling. The barns with stone ceilings—arched over the horse stable and vaulted over the cattle barn—are an architectural expression of the importance attached to livestock. These constructions were made possible by families of builders who had been forced to leave their homes in northern Italy after the phylloxera plague wreaked havoc among wine growers.

In 1903 the mill burned down to the ground-floor walls, and a new one was built immediately. The extension added in the 1920s made it the house we see today. With a few sheds and other smaller outbuildings, the layout resembles that of a farm.

Different guilds and trades converged here: the sawmill stands beside the grain mill, and in 1924 the power plant arrived. A large orchard and garden appeared alongside the forest, pastures, meadows and grain fields, and cattle were joined by horses, pigs and poultry. Additionally, an independent cheese factory operated here for thirty years.

The cheese factory closed in the 1930s, the grain mill in the 1950s, agricultural operations in the 1960s and the sawmill in 1968, and in 1969 the Rotismühle property was put up for sale. It was purchased by Inge Aicher-Scholl and Otl Aicher.

Design enclave

After the Ulm School of Design closed in 1968 and his work for the 1972 Olympic Games in Munich neared completion, Otl Aicher began looking for a new place to establish his family residence. His holiday home in Allgäu since 1960, was unsuitable.

But the old rural mill house, with its multiple uses, was everything Otl Aicher had envisioned for his future enterprise. He wanted to bring together professionals from different disciplines in the field of visual communication, ideally working in independent studios. At first, he only ran his own studio; the photography workshop and printshop were managed separately.

From a spatial point of view, the property was restructured to make it an 'enclave'. The road (308) and country lane were moved to the outer limits to avoid vehicular traffic crossing the property. The plot was transformed into a park with extensive groves and an English garden designed by Günther Grzimek. The main buildings were modernised, and the outbuildings were replaced by new structures.

Erection of garage structure, building 14, 1978

Preserving the mill

The old mill house was, in all essentials, kept virtually intact: here were the bedrooms of the children and mistress of the house, the studio and the kitchen. The old mill itself was gutted. The three new storeys housed the library, the master's bedroom and the family living room. A three-flight staircase replaced the old service lift. The harmony of the space was enhanced by grey sisal fibre, thick fibre paper painted white, natural pine panelling, spherical light fixtures, white Formica tables with white steel frames, beige Eames shell chairs, chrome-plated adjustable table lamps placed here and there, and solid wooden furniture. There were no pictures on the walls; instead, they rested on the floor behind glass. At a later date, metal mesh was hung from the ceiling to support lighting rails. The only contrasting notes were the green carpet, the green chairs and the wooden railing in Inge Aicher-Scholl's studio.

Over time, the kitchen became the prototype for the Bulthaup kitchen still in use today. The old country kitchen became the model of the new 'kitchen for cooking', as indicated in the title of a book illustrating the Bulthaup concept. Another new feature was the sunny glassed-in porch with views of the countryside, Otl Aicher's favourite place to ruminate after work, converse or lunch with small or large groups of friends.

They also kept the original turbine from the watermill over the stream. One Kaplan turbine and one Francis turbine supplied exactly 17 kW of electricity. Although maintaining the power generating system was a constant struggle, at least the building had an independent supply of electricity. However, the voltage fluctuated depending on the water level. In the late 1980s, this problem was solved by a hook-up to the power grid.

Preserving the farm

The farm's crown jewel is the cattle barn, a structure of masonry walls with twelve sail vaults resting on six stone pillars. Stripped of livestock equipment, the white-painted room with a pine floor and a bar also made of solid pine, with tables and seats to match, became a rotisserie, canteen and events hall.

Beside the cattle barn is the horse stables, which housed a printshop for many years. After being moved in the 1980s, this place, slightly enlarged, was where they put the finishing touches to the Rotis typeface. The white walls and black-painted wood altered the structure's appearance.

The grounds, arranged like a park, needed improvements to replant the gravel surfaces where the sawmill lumber was once stored. Hundreds of autochthonous trees were planted in clusters that simultaneously beautify and divide the park from the surrounding fields. A new system of concrete blocks transformed the old orchard into an elevated garden, and fruit trees were planted in an orthogonal pattern beside it.

New buildings

New workshops were erected around the two main buildings, the mill and the farmhouse. The first to appear were Aicher's studio and the photography workshop, structures designed to promote creative concentration. In these buildings, the functional spaces were raised one storey above the ground. They have few windows but receive abundant sunlight thanks to the vertical skylights overhead, which give them their distinctive sawtooth outline. Each unit consists of a toilet, kitchenette and workspace (plus a darkroom in the photography workshop). The three or four shed roofs, with a 27-degree pitch, give the impression of a space with high ceilings.

A sober, functional atmosphere is created by the grey felt carpet, the tongue-and-groove wainscoting of untreated pine boards, the white-painted particleboard panels of the pitched ceiling, and the vertical window extending the entire width of the building. An ash wood staircase leads from this invisible core to the 'ground floor'. The last step off the metal grating platform leads to a concrete floor, the same size as the upper storey, that seamlessly segues to the surrounding meadows. From afar, a few slender columns provide a visual point of reference.

These columns—HEB 20 beams sunk into separate footings in a 4.2 x 5-metre grid—are the only structural elements made of steel. The rest of the building is made entirely of wood, solid pine. Between the longitudinal uprights, a framework of modular elements spreads like a sheaf of grain. The crossbeams, like the rafters, rest on brackets screwed to a number of soldered braces flanking the uprights. The ceiling rafters extend from the ridge to the eaves of the shed roofs. The spaces in between are uniformly insulated with eight centimetres of polystyrene, a popular construction solution in the 1970s. The smoothness of the polished interior cladding contrasts with the heavily textured exterior: a rough superimposed layer of vertical planks whose shadows are accentuated by the black paint. The roof slopes are covered by interlocking galvanised sheet metal, flaring out in the roof valleys to form deep channels. These drain into a rectangular gutter that runs along the eaves, with two downpipes between the flanges of the steel uprights, thereby eliminating any overhang.

These rooms are made liveable by a concrete energy station that houses the heating system, the fuel tank, workshops and access to the turbine. Shortly after finishing this structure, an adjacent hall was built. It serves no particular

Twice a week, the workers, including Otl Aicher, would eat together in the canteen of building 16. The tables and benches are Aicher's design.
Photograph: Karsten de Riese

The power plant and the photography workshop, building 18, in the background. Photograph: Karsten de Riese

purpose other than to provide protection from the elements, and inside the bare concrete frame is fully visible. Unlike in the wooden studios, here the webs of exposed beams freely embellish the spaces. This structure is covered with transparent polycarbonate sheets, between which the ceiling panels extend from ridge to eave. The hall also has a sawtooth profile, in this case formed by five roofs. There are no windows. Painted black on the outside, it and the studios form a homogeneous group. There are three doors on each of the narrow sides that can be folded outwards by means of a simple winch. Norman Foster called it the 'temple of Rotis'.

Years later, the old carriage house had to be replaced by a new space for vehicles. Reusing the building's sawtooth roof would have required a 90-degree change in orientation. For this reason, it was given a simple single-pitch roof facing the farm, similar to the other roofs in size and slope. Once again, steel columns and uprights support the upper storey, which houses studios, but in this case the space is framed by three wooden partitions, and sliding doors in the fourth wall lead to the new garages.

The series ends with a small 'pavilion', a wooden structure on a cement base that resembles a tool shed, sitting beside the orchard across the road and almost hidden by the hedges. This small black structure with a single-pitch roof might be mistaken for one of the studio units, if not for the fact that its walls do not touch the ground, making it look more like a simple hay shed.

References

Work began in 1970, and by the summer of 1972 the studios were ready to use. They were followed by the hall in 1973, the carriage house in 1978 and the small pavilion around 1985. The short period of time between the commission/design and the completion of the first iconic structures is explained by the fact that, years earlier, Otl Aicher had carefully studied and planned the construction of a studio building beside his holiday home, though it was never built due to environmental conservation concerns.

The notable quality of the work is evidence of the great strides being made in construction at the time. In addition to the Mayer structure and the Aicher & Schmid heating and plumbing systems, the project incorporated the remarkable woodwork of Redle, a carpentry firm in the neighbouring town of Ottmannshofen. A simple glance at the balanced design of the wall cladding gives us an idea of the level of skill involved. Without them it would have been impossible, as the project and site managers were in Munich, which was then several hours away.

People often ask why the studios are on the first floor. The reason is not to protect them from flooding; this might make sense for the studio closest to the stream, but not for the photography workshop, which stands on fairly high ground. Nor was it to provide covered parking spaces for employees beside their workplace, as cars were not allowed on the property. So why were they built this way?

Otl Aicher's preparatory studies and previous architectural training give us a clue. Some of the projects of the Ulm School of Design, like the City of Ulm pavilion in 1954 or the fair stand for Braun AG, included buildings raised off the ground, in the style of Mies van der Rohe's Farnsworth House. A seamless spatial continuum of interior and exterior was the ideal. The landscape of Allgäu had been a source of inspiration for Otl Aicher since his youth; he returned to it time and again, seeking ideas and solace in times of crisis.

Le Corbusier's Villa Savoye is the incunabulum of off-ground architecture. Otl Aicher admired Le Corbusier (even his 'Ronchamp aberration') for his *modernité absolue* and creative freedom. In order to burn bridges with the past, as he demanded, he transformed the image of the building by raising it off the ground and resting it on slender pilotis. Analogy: Rotis pilotis.

Yet the Villa Savoye is dazzling white, and Aicher's studios are black as coal. Why? On the one hand, we should recall certain modern post-war buildings in Munich, which occasionally contrasted traditional, white-plastered elements with dark, worn wooden surfaces, some of which were designed by Werner Wirsing, Aicher's colleague at the Ulm School of Design. On the other, in the 1960s people began to find a new appreciation for simple rural farm buildings: gloomy, dilapidated barns and haylofts. This new aesthetic was reflected in the impressive images that began arriving from across the Atlantic in the 1960s, such as Sea Ranch, a vernacular reinterpretation by MLTW (Charles W. Moore, Donlyn Lyndon, William Turnbull, Jr, and Richard Whitaker).

Farm buildings: Le Corbusier again. His Maison Ozenfant was modelled on the workshops of Parisian artisans that could still be found in the French capital at the time. Otl Aicher came from Söflingen, which in his youth was an industrial suburb of the imperial city of Ulm. The obvious contrast between the hard labour of one and the wealth of the other, between the workshop and the mansion, would mark his philosophy for the rest of his life.

Universe

A cluster of small black factories stand out against a sea of surrounding green. Are they satellites that have landed on slender pillars in virgin territory? Actually, each new building took the place of an older structure, and the spaces attest to a history of previous development: the studio replaced a woodshed; the heating system replaced the sawmill;

the photography workshop occupied the former cheese factory; and the garage was the old carriage house. The only structure that rests on the ground is the little pavilion where, in his final years of eagerly anticipated retirement, Aicher found the return to art that he had rejected his entire life.

Rotis is the universe where, over the course of nearly twenty years, corporate identities, signage systems, exhibitions, books, texts and, finally, three busts were created. In addition to clerical, cooking and maintenance duties, different jobs were carried out by three employees in the lean years and nearly two dozen in the years of plenty. The workday began at 8 am and ended at 5 pm, 4 pm on Fridays. The last hour on Friday afternoon was inevitably devoted to tidying up—making sure pencil and paper were perfectly aligned or, better yet, put away—to ensure optimal conditions for starting work on Monday morning.

When they finished, if everyone was up for it, the employees would have a beer together. They ate together twice a week, but otherwise their private lives were conducted off the premises, and they lived in neighbouring towns. Work was done in the studios, which were cold in winter and hot in summer. Badminton matches at midday, played outdoors or in the hall, provided a welcome break.

Industrious concentration? Rural retreat? Several crises had already occurred: lack of commissions, Inge Aicher-Scholl's dismissal from her teaching position at the Ulm Volkshochschule, accidents, plans to sell, etc. But life went on. Functionality demanded external changes. The advent of the digital era made a hook-up to the main power grid necessary, given the fluctuations in the self-generated electrical supply; and frames were fitted on the windows to support wooden lattices that would provide much-needed shade from the sun, reminiscent of the structures used in old farmhouses to ripen the fruits of their labour in the fields. At the new, more functional Rotis, this system was also installed on the north-facing windows.

Southeast view of the photography workshop, building 18, with pilotis, porch and window latticework formed of trunks and metallic frames.
Photograph: Karsten de Riese

A new path

In late August 1991, Otl Aicher was walking home from his solitary studio after finishing the busts of Hans and Sophie Scholl. He was struck by a motorcycle while crossing the street, and on 1 September he succumbed to his injuries. Suddenly, after 19 years, an entire era had come to an end. The first closures occurred before he was even buried.

Inge Aicher-Scholl survived her husband by seven years. She spent that time organising his legacy, now held in the archives of the Ulm School of Design. New uses were proposed for the property. For several years, the Rotis Forum, working with universities, held lectures, seminars and workshops on design which have been documented in various

Garage, building 14. It closes the ensemble to the northeast, separating it from the local road at the rear.
Photograph: Karsten de Riese

publications. The rural setting turned out to be an excellent source of inspiration. Concerts were given for the young people of the region. But none of it was enough to cover maintenance costs. The idea of selling part of the property gradually took hold and became a reality in the year 2000, with disastrous results. After that, Rotismühle sank into a deep slumber.

Materials began to decay and disintegrate from lack of use. After five years, a decisive intervention put an end to this situation, based on the conviction that there is a number inherent to every property, that of the people who occupy it. The goal was to bring the place back to life with the motto 'bake little buns instead of big cakes'. In practice, this meant settling the division of the estate, assigning responsibilities and opening up the property to people from outside the family. This was followed by a restructuring and complete energy overhaul of the main buildings: a system of low-energy heating panels optimised the running of the entire complex. At the same time, one of the studios and part of the hall were turned into residences, and today Rotis consists of five independent housing units.

A century of important changes: first, large new buildings; later, the decline of agricultural production; a beacon of design for more than two decades; and, for the past fifteen years, essentially a residential complex. Use calls for transformation: no building is 'original' anymore.

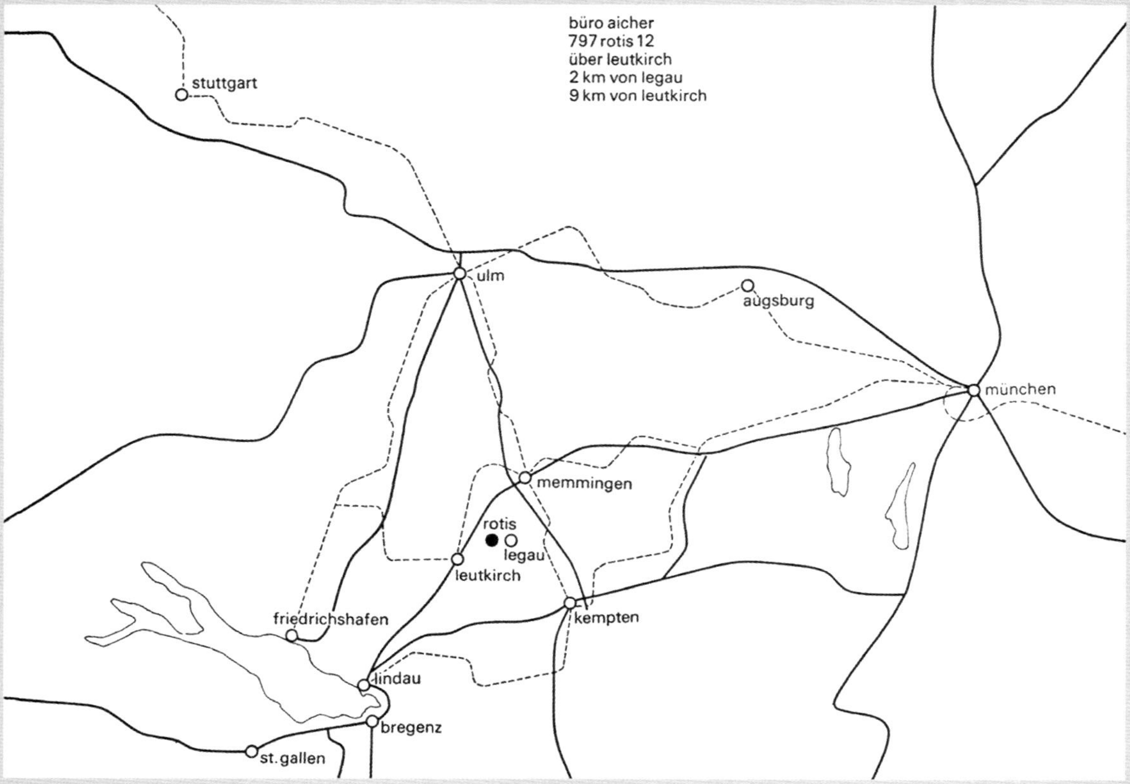
büro aicher
797 rotis 12
über leutkirch
2 km von legau
9 km von leutkirch
stuttgart
ulm
augsburg
münchen
memmingen
rotis
legau
leutkirch
friedrichshafen
kempten
lindau
bregenz
st. gallen

Otl Aicher. Bird's eye view sketch of Rotis (excluding buildings 14 and Y), c.1976. Ink on paper. 29.7 x 21 cm

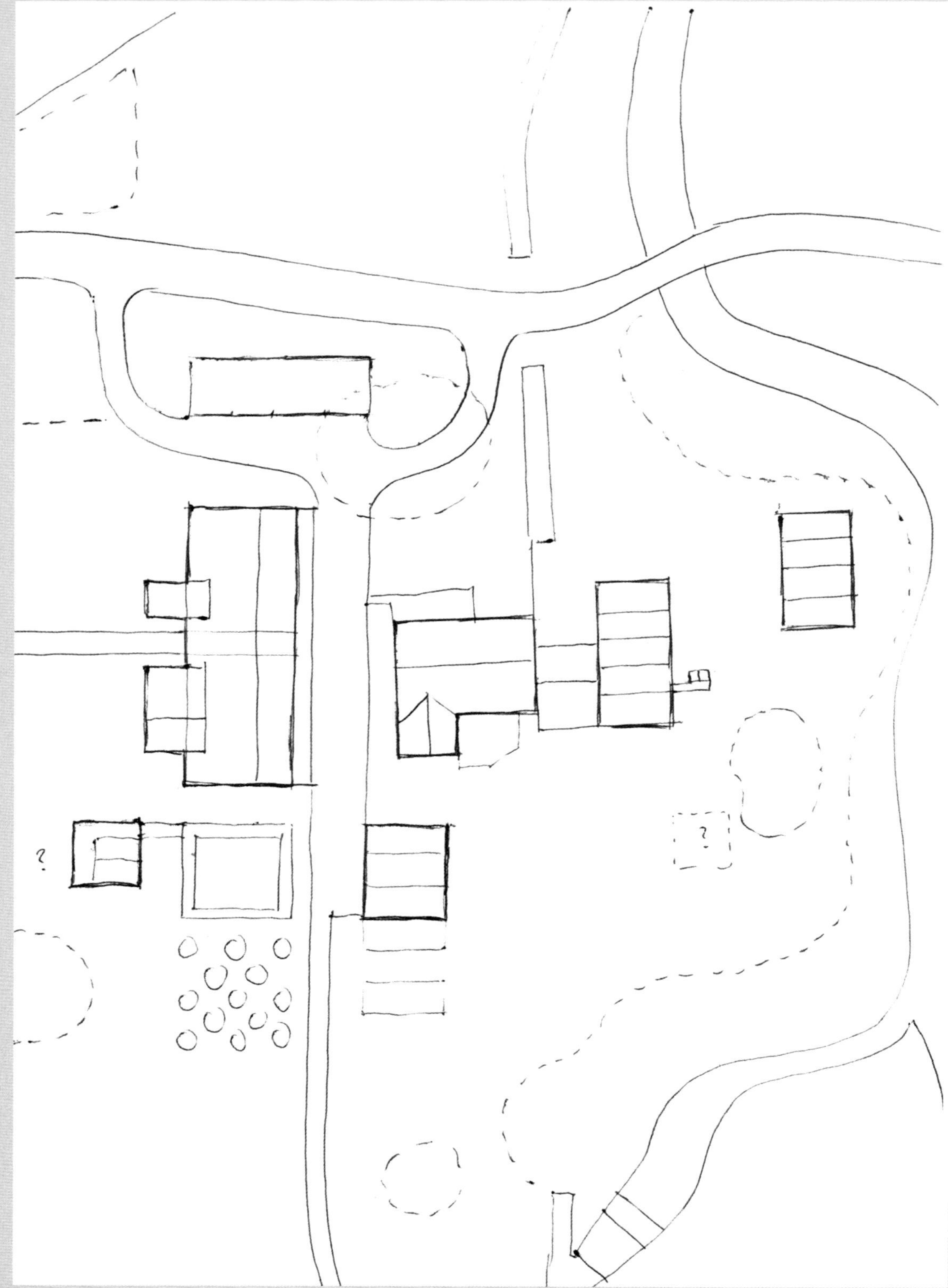

Otl Aicher. Sketch of Rotis site plan,
17 October 1976. Ink on paper.
29.7 x 21 cm

site

Otl Aicher. Sketch of the main building pergola, old mill, 10 October 1976. Ink on paper. 29.7 x 21 cm

5.a
Northeast elevation

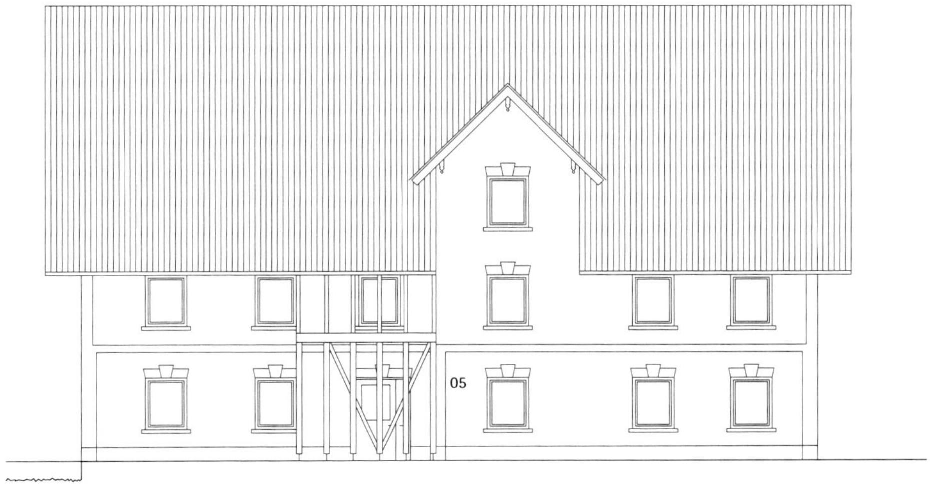

5.b
Ground floor

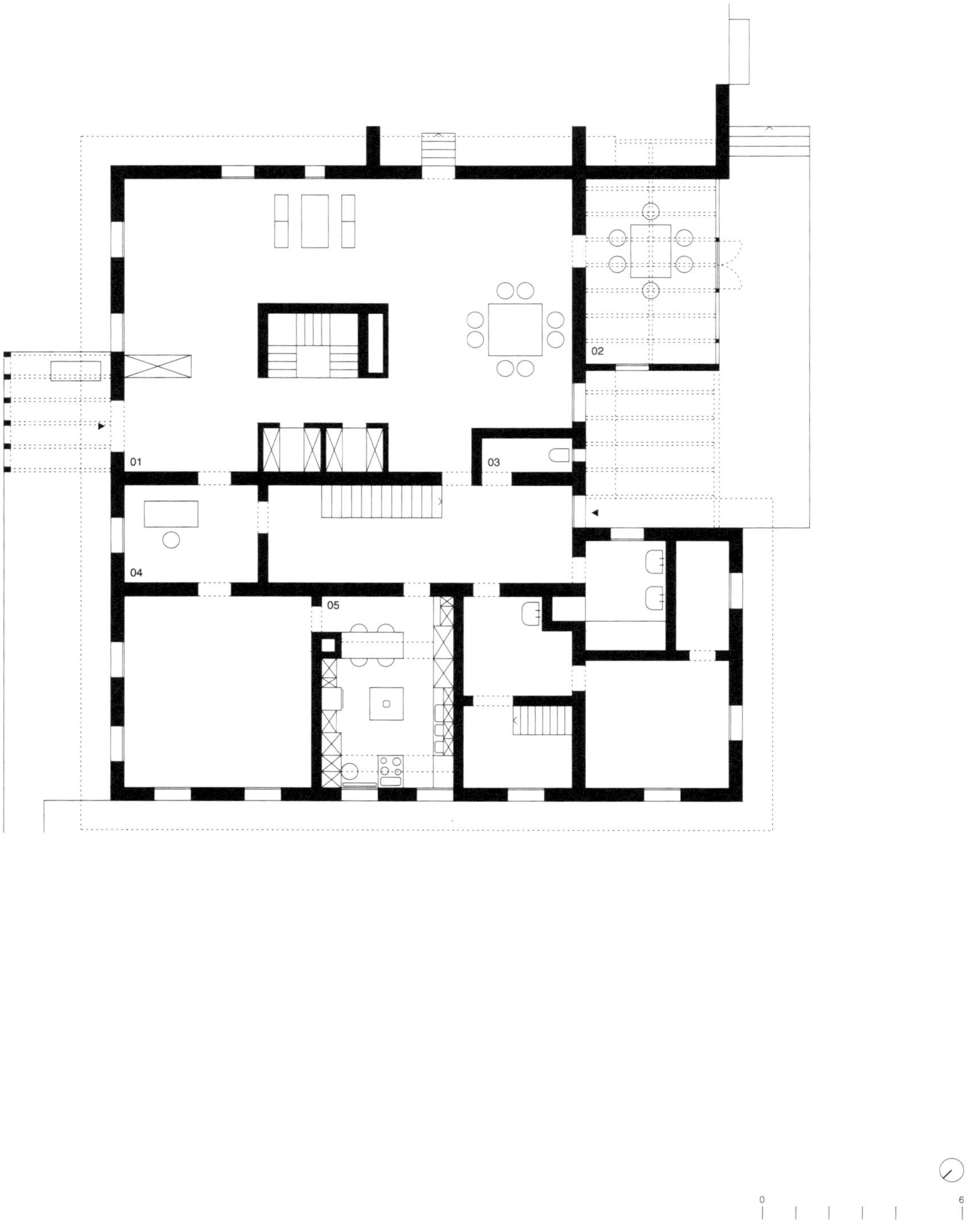

5.c
First floor

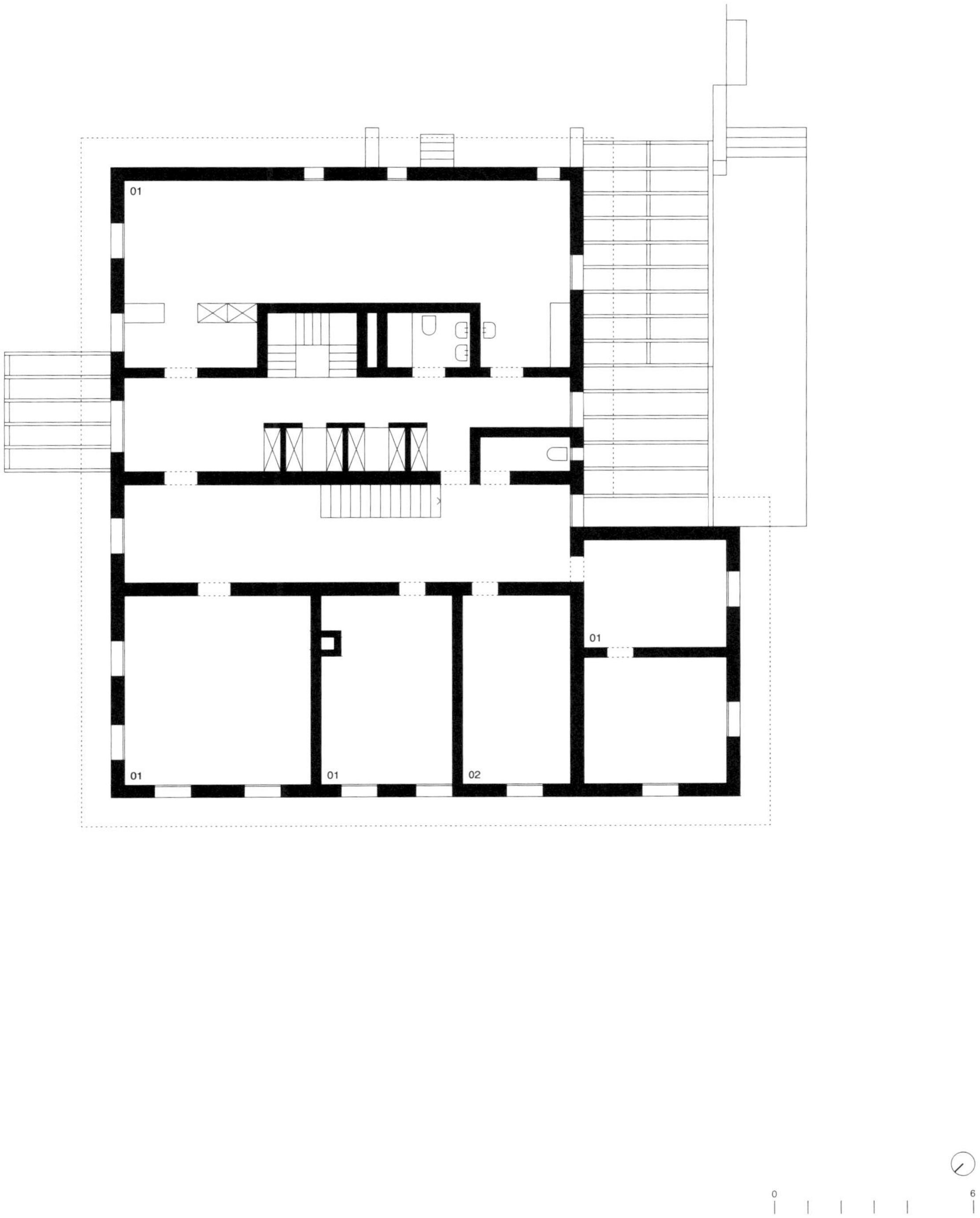

5.d
Second floor

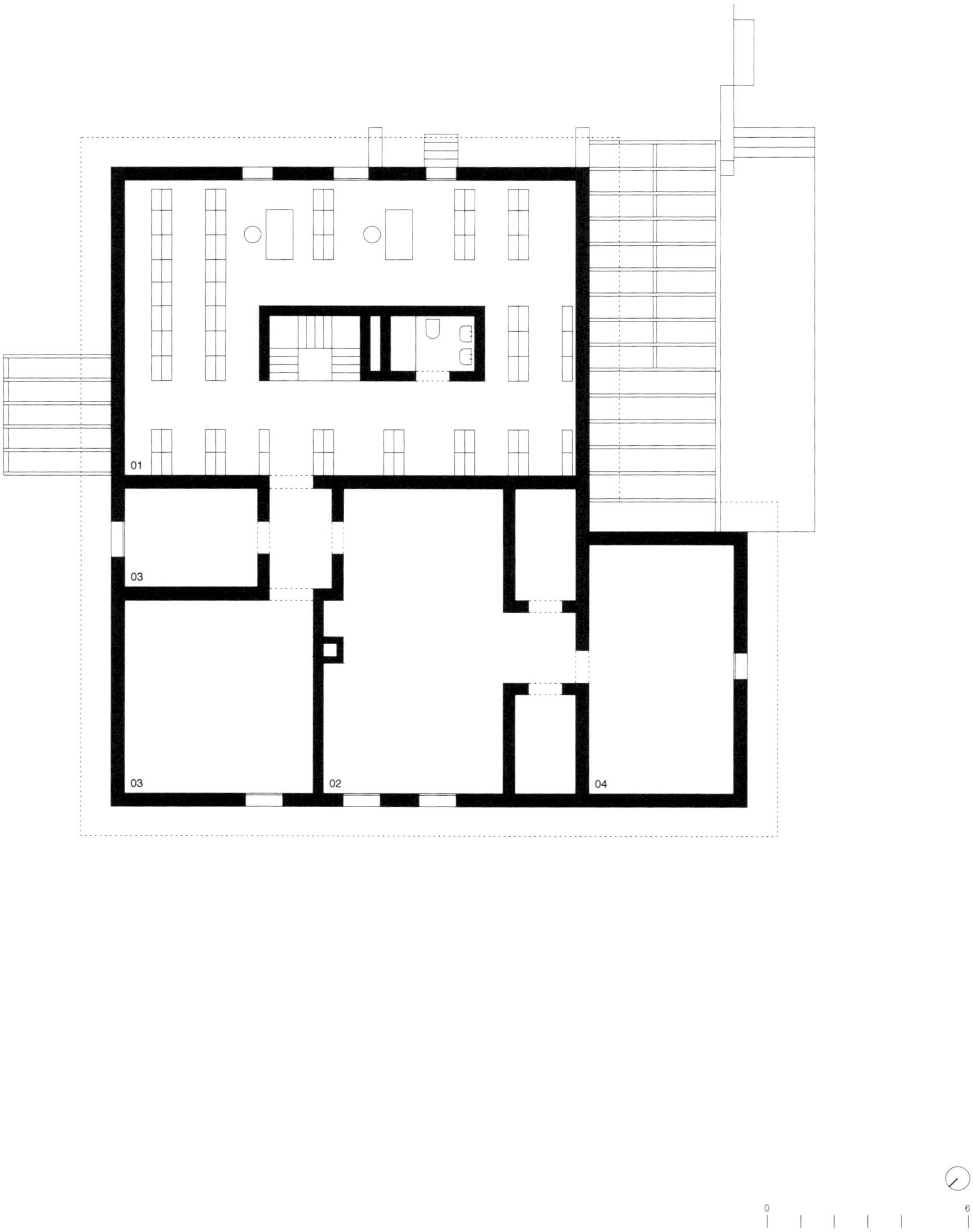

5.e
Northeast elevation

5.f
Southeast elevation

5.g
Southwest elevation

12.a
Northeast elevation

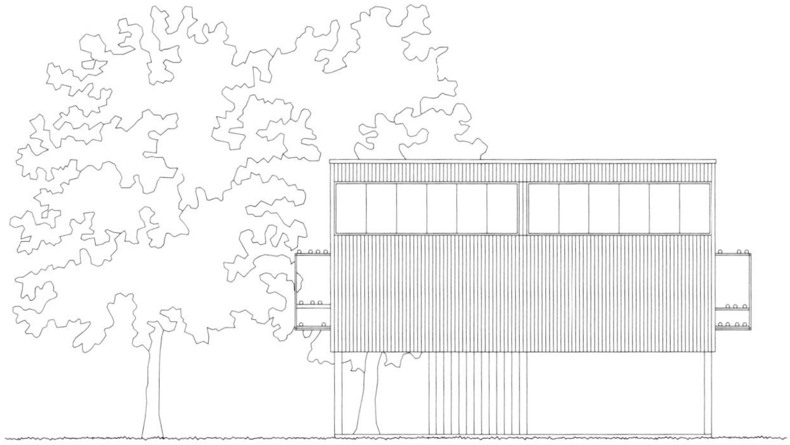

12.b
First floor

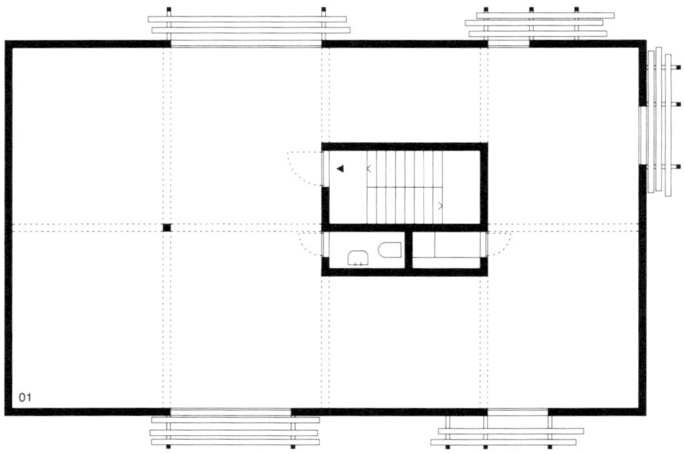

12.c
Ground floor

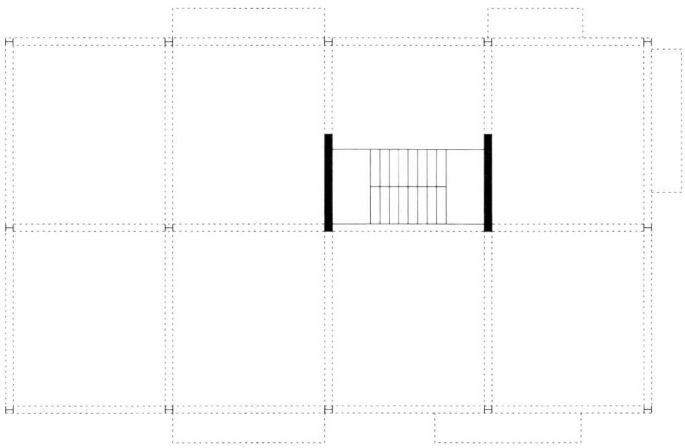

12.d
Southeast elevation

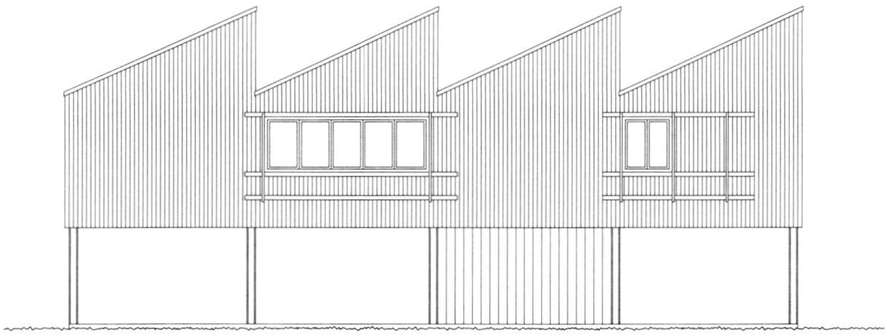

12.e
Southwest elevation

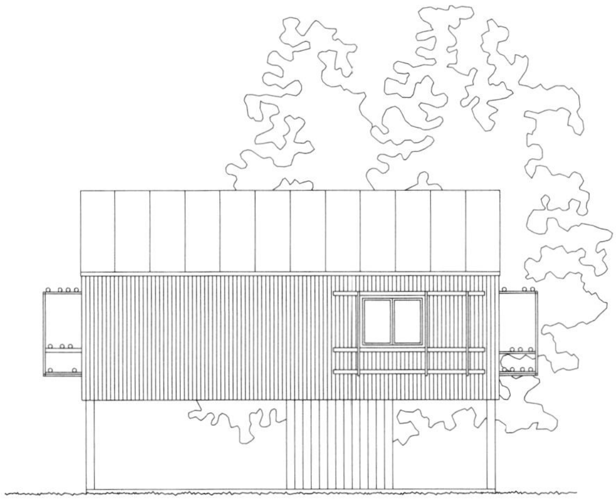

12.f
Northwest elevation

12

14.a
Northeast elevation

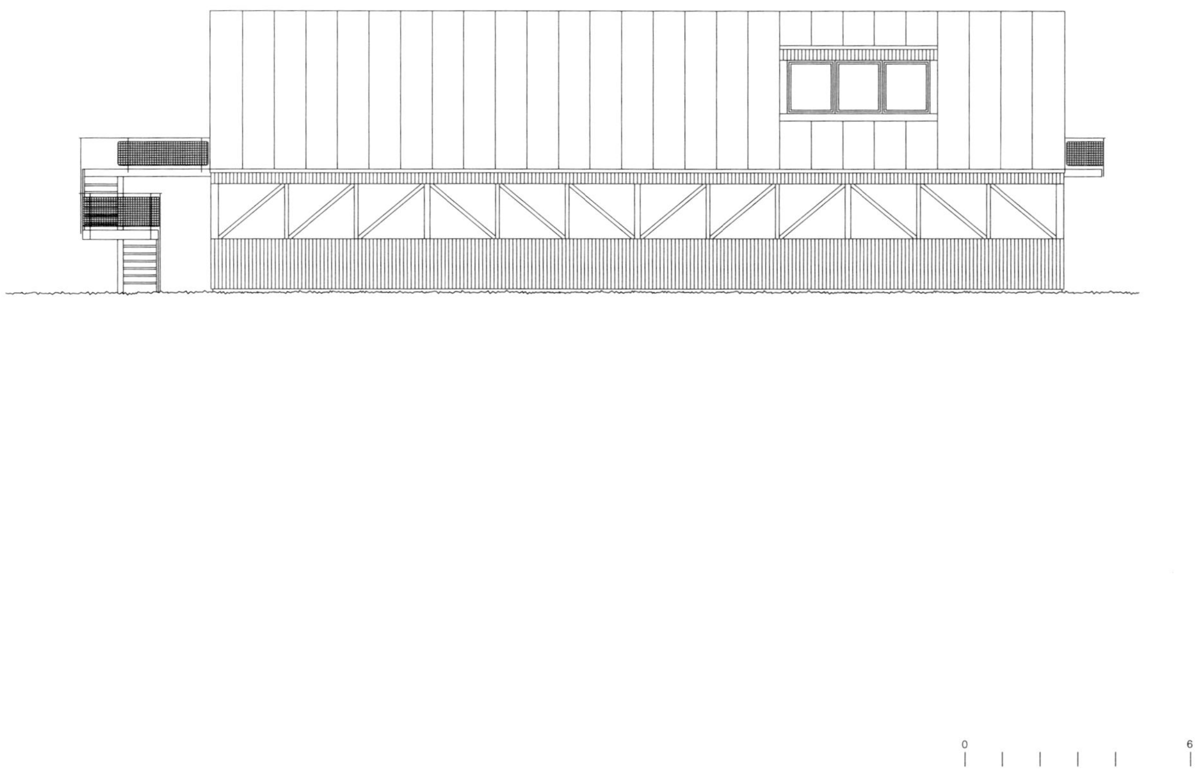

14.b
First floor

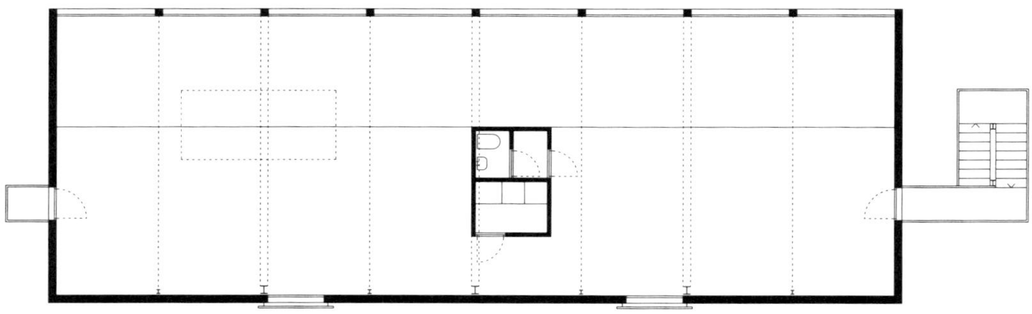

14.c
Ground floor

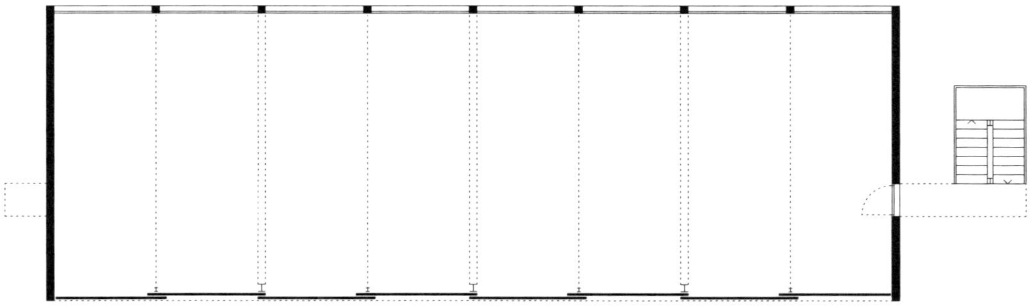

14.d
Southeast elevation

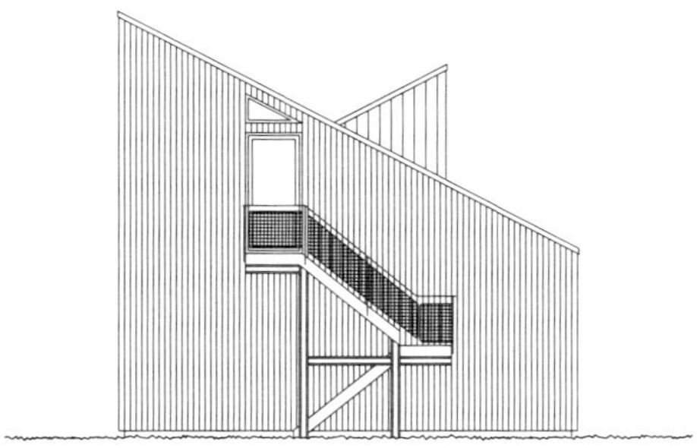

14.e
Southwest elevation

14.f
Northwest elevation

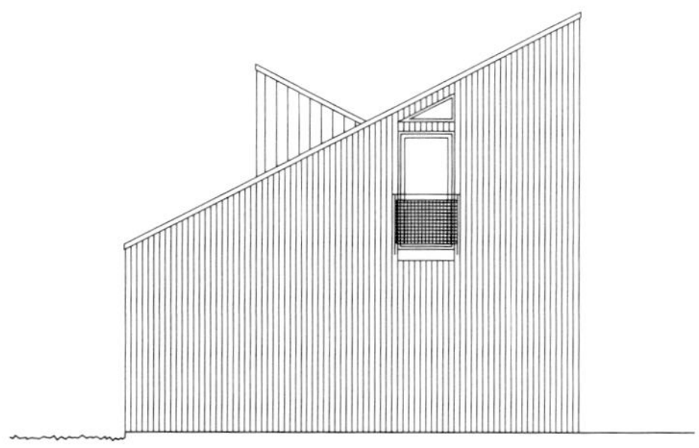

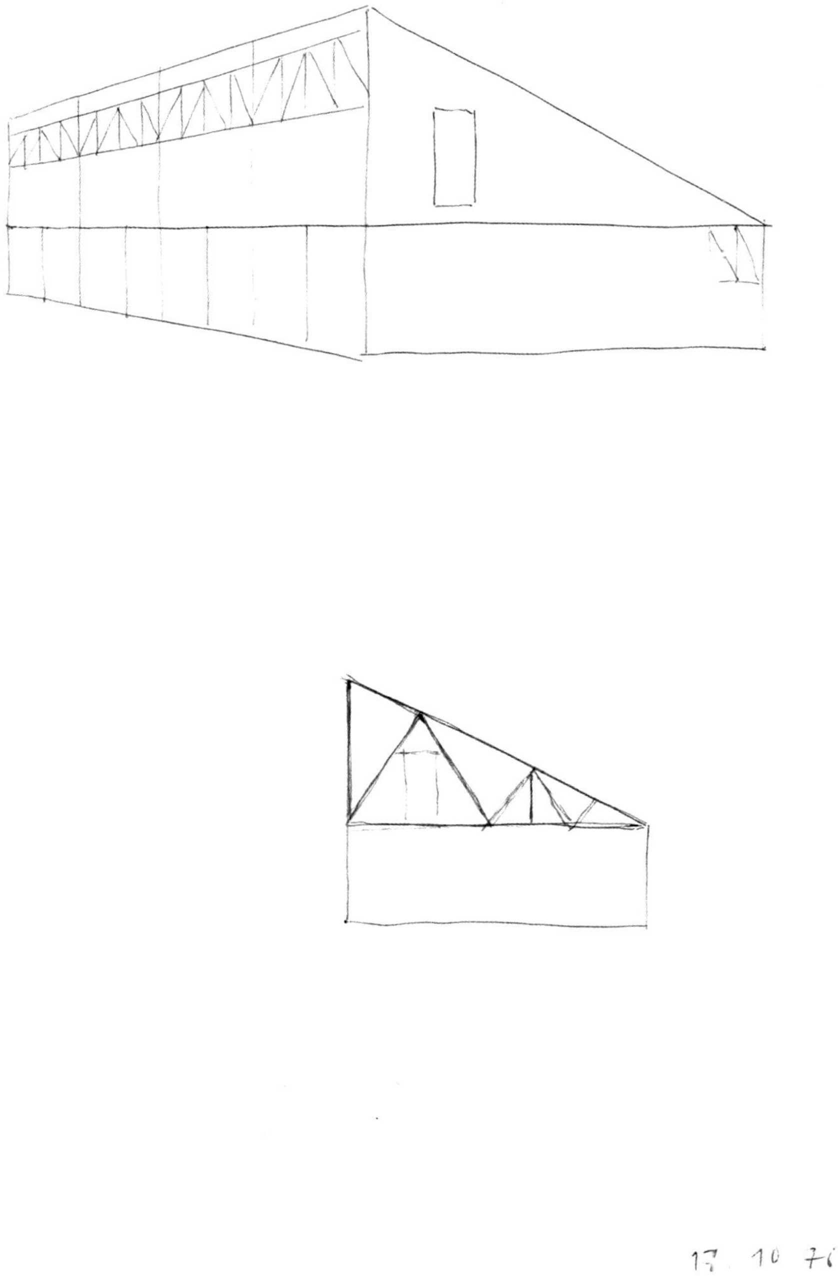

Otl Aicher. Axonometric
perspective and side elevation
of the garage, October 1976.
Ink on paper. 29.7 x 21 cm

1525

16.a
Northwest elevation

16.b
First floor

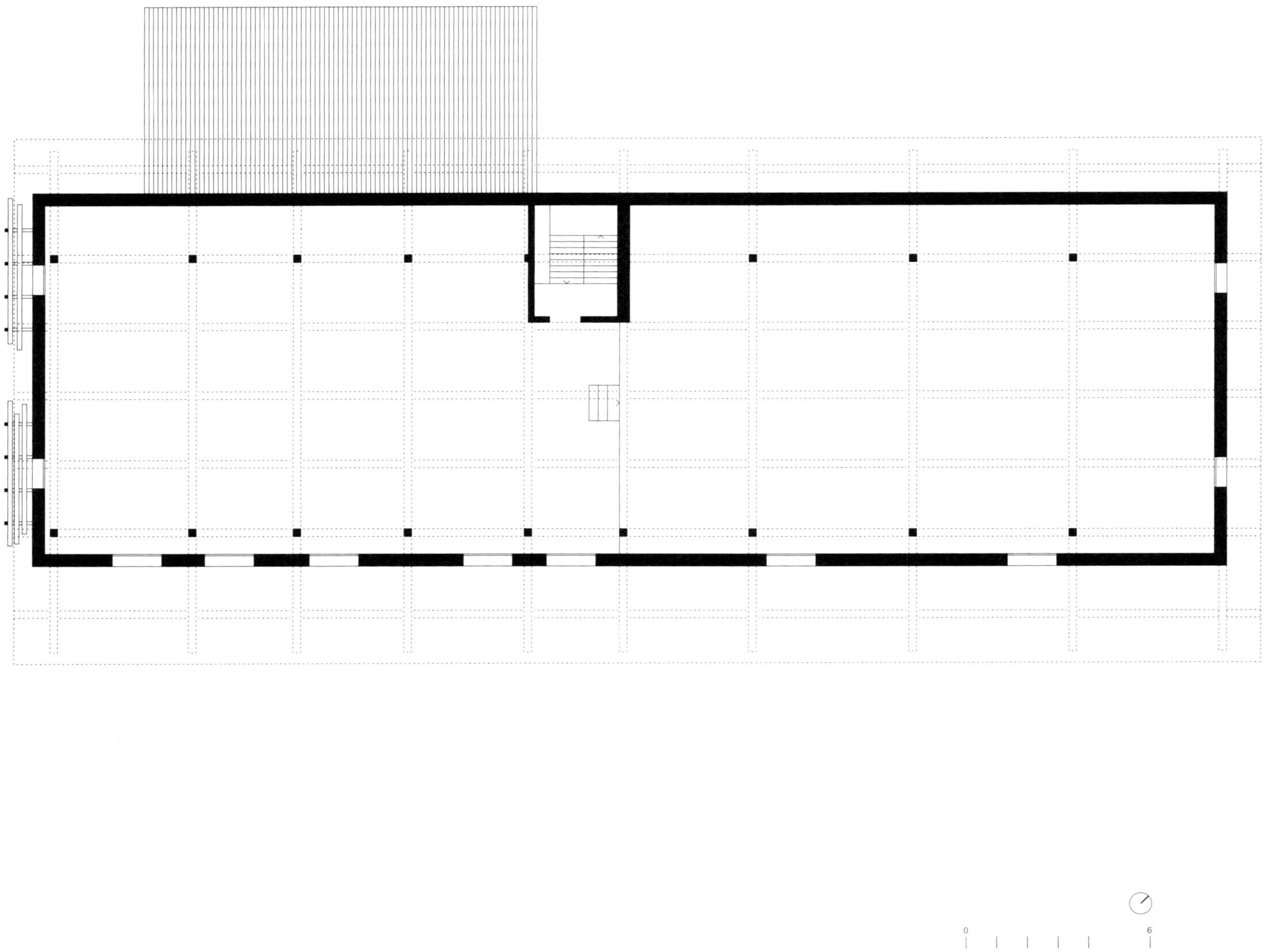

16.c
Ground floor

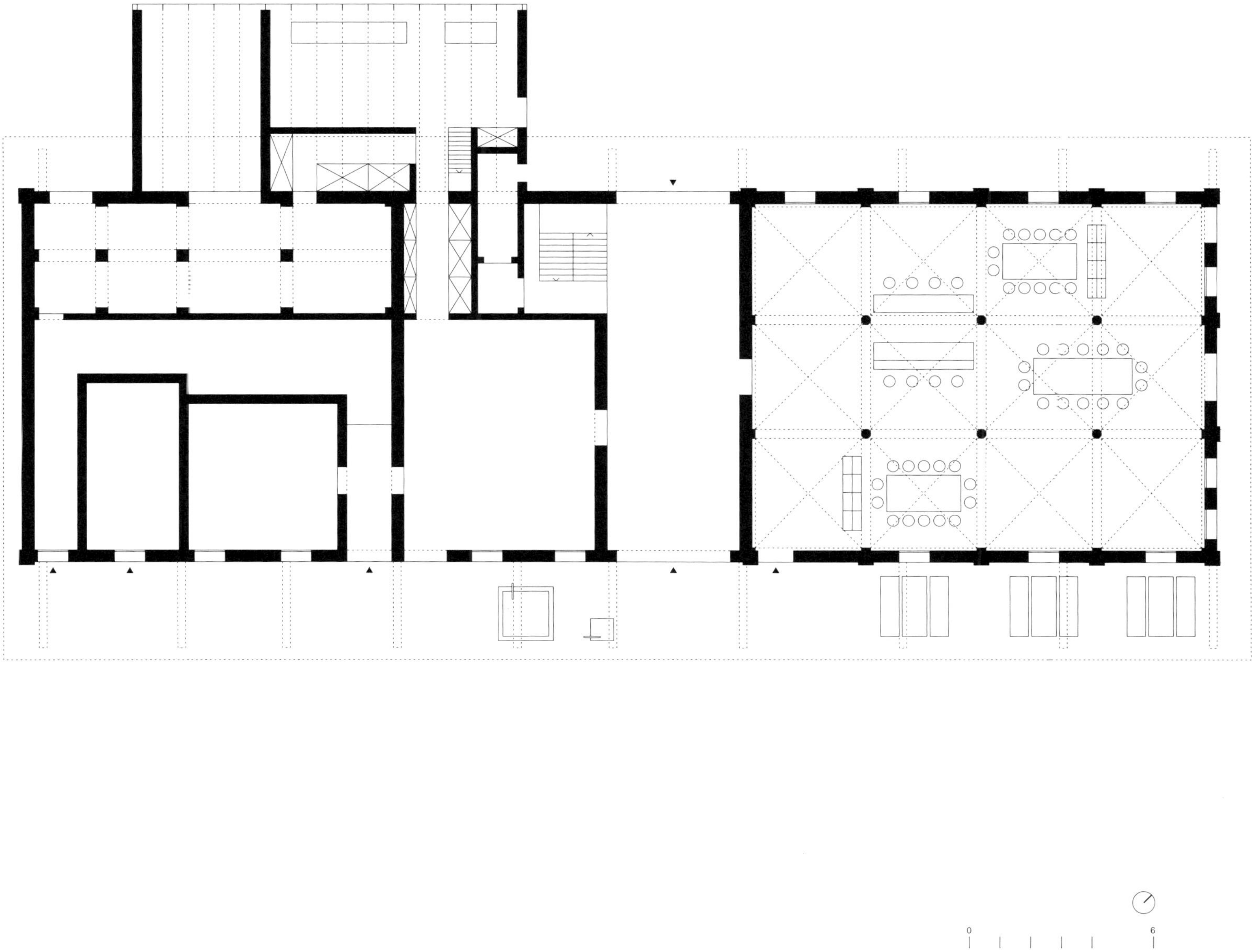

16.d
Southeast elevation

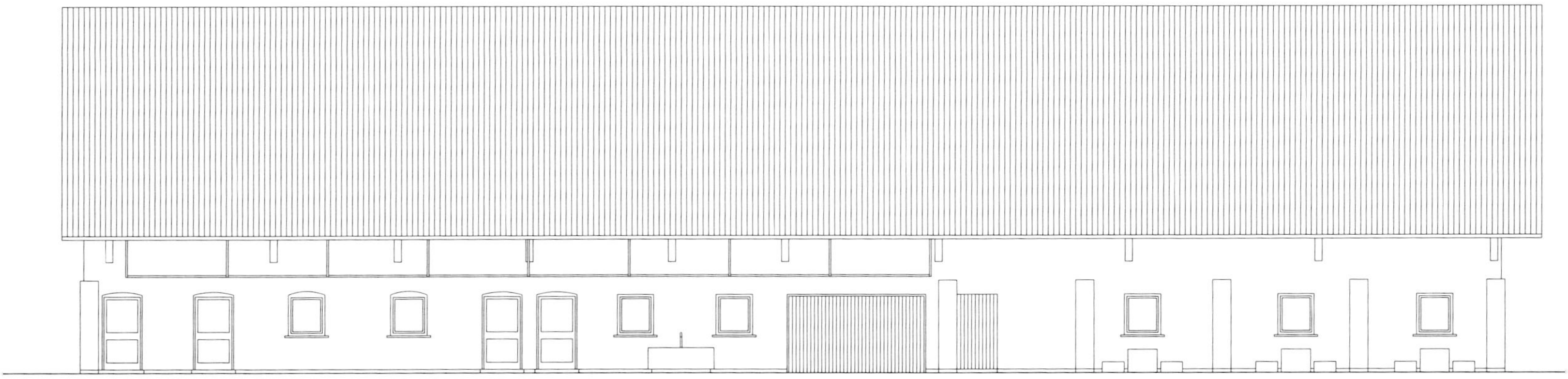

16.e
Southwest elevation

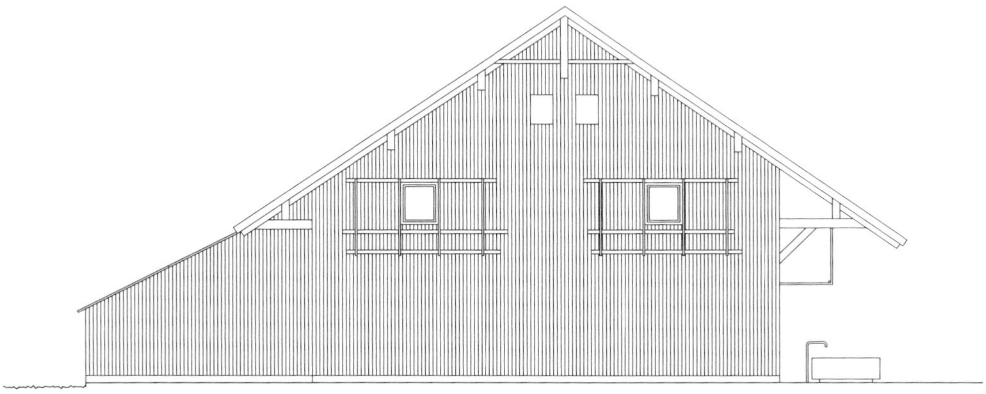

0 6

16.f
Northwest elevation

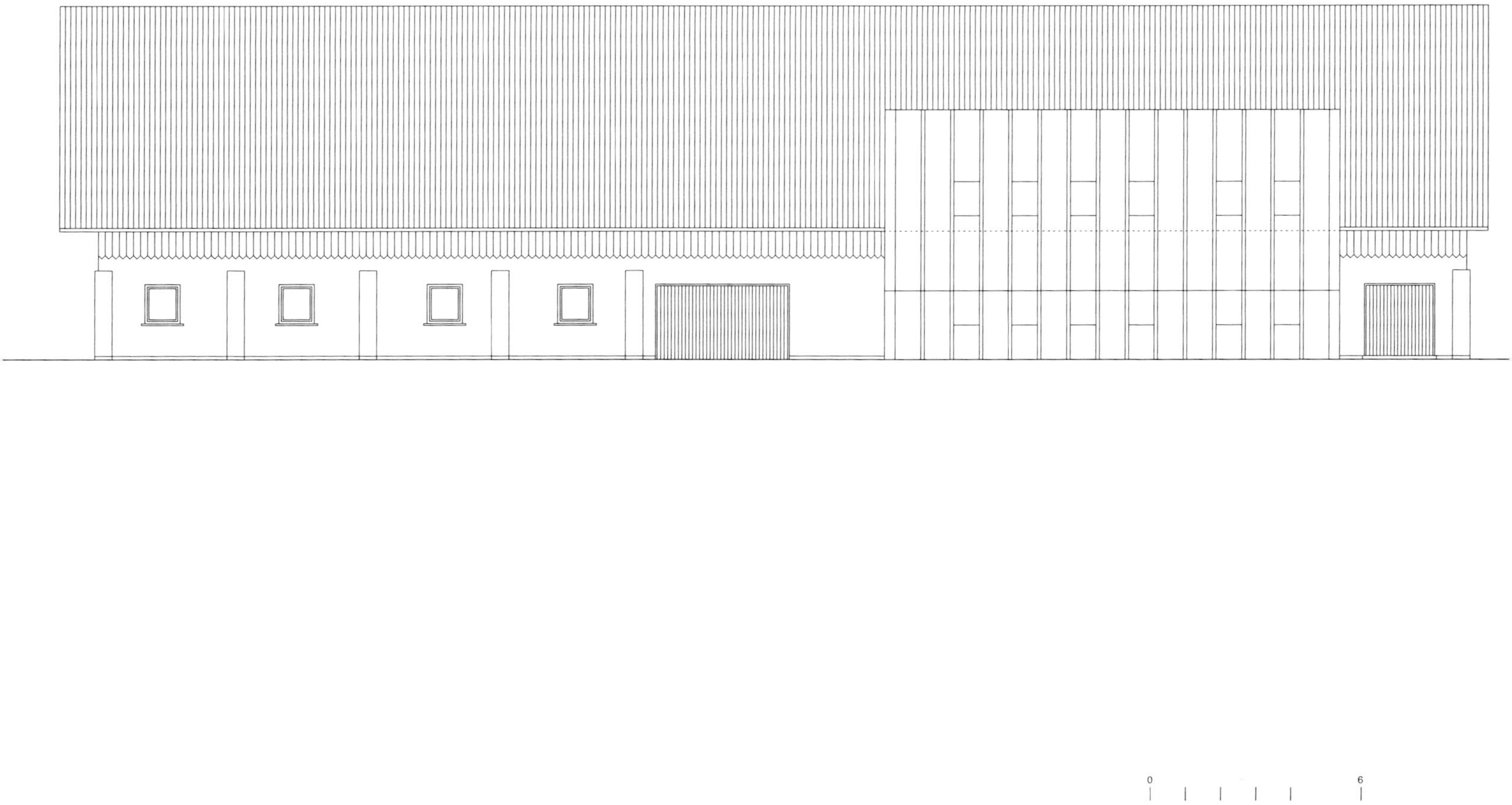

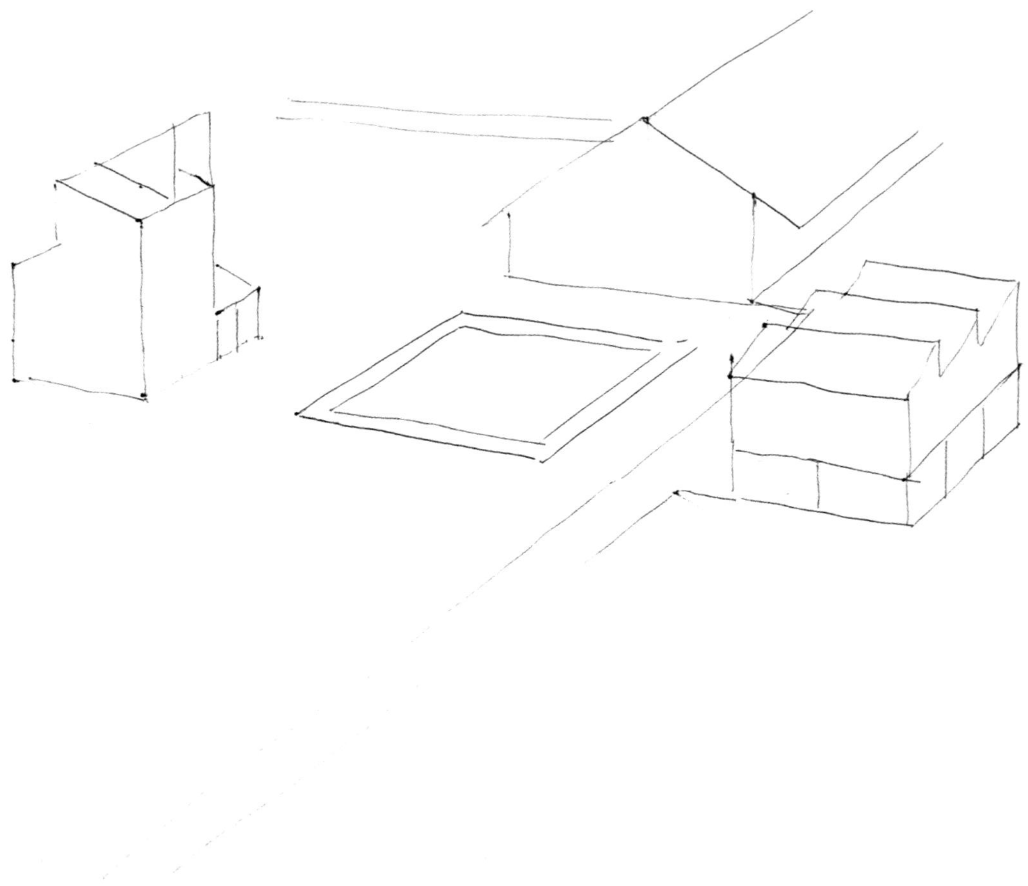

Otl Aicher. Bird's eye view sketch of buildings Y, 16 and 18, area surrounding the kitchen garden, c.1976. Ink on paper. 29.7 x 21 cm

building 17

17.a
Northeast elevation

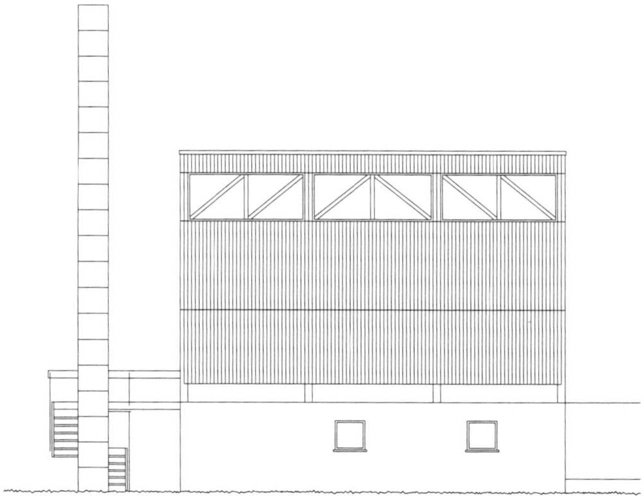

17.b
First floor

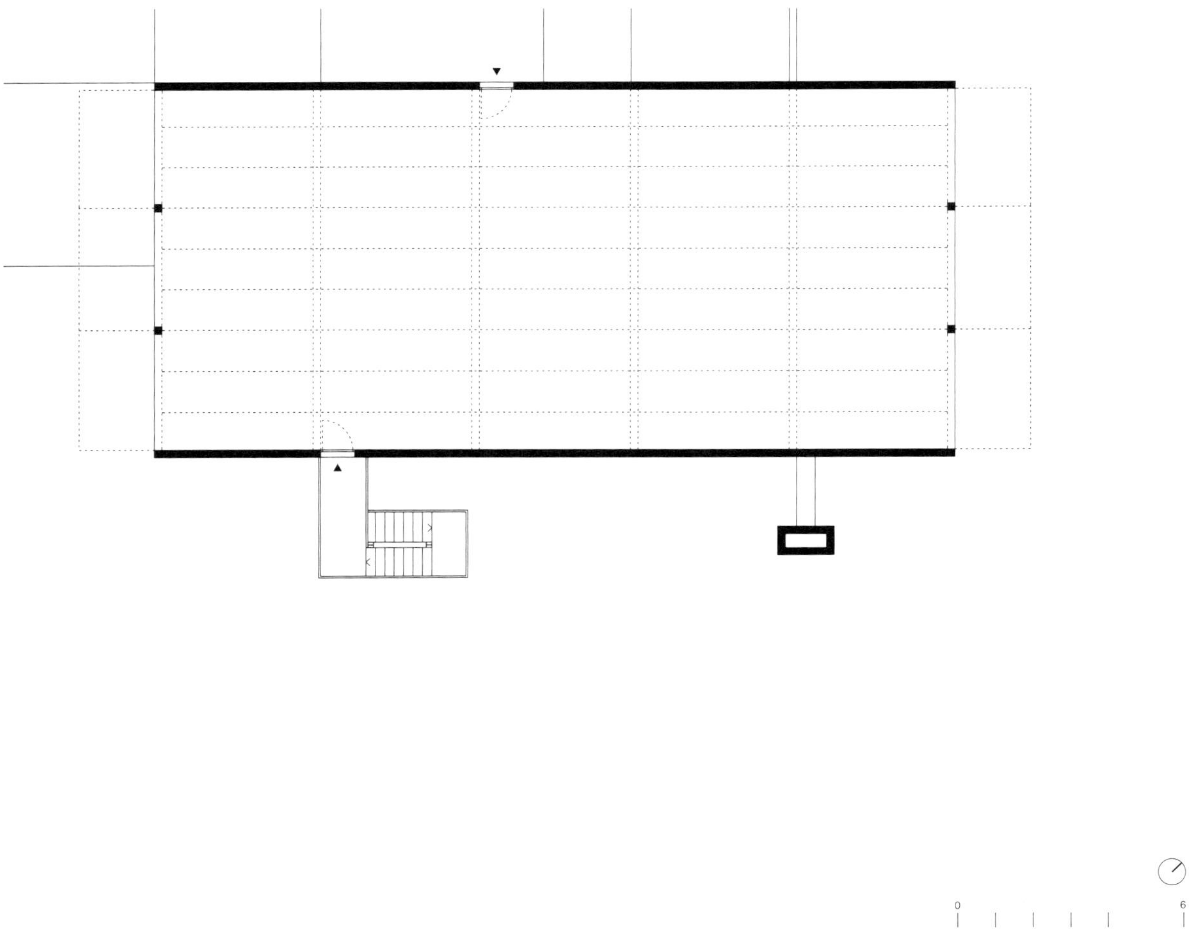

17.c
Ground floor

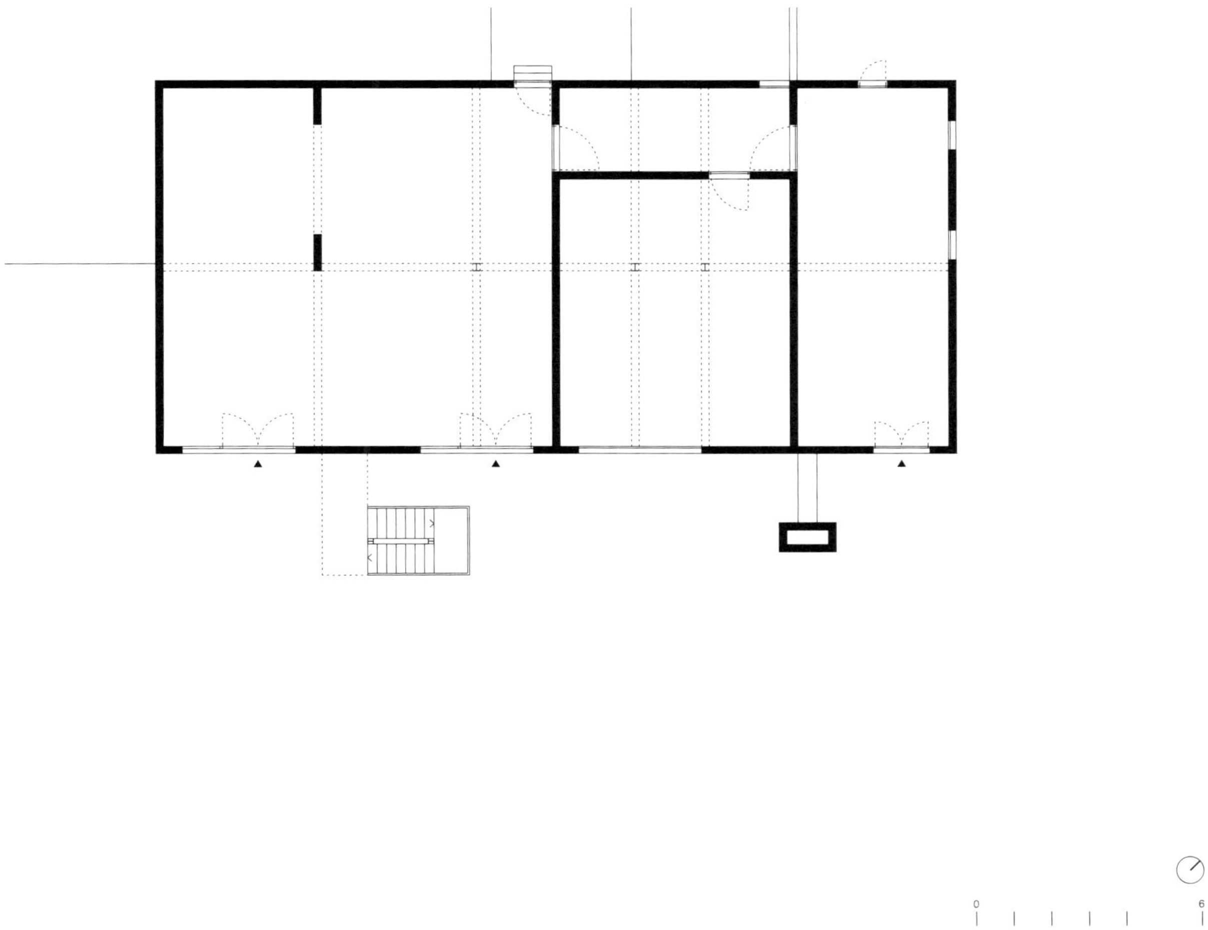

17.d
Southeast elevation

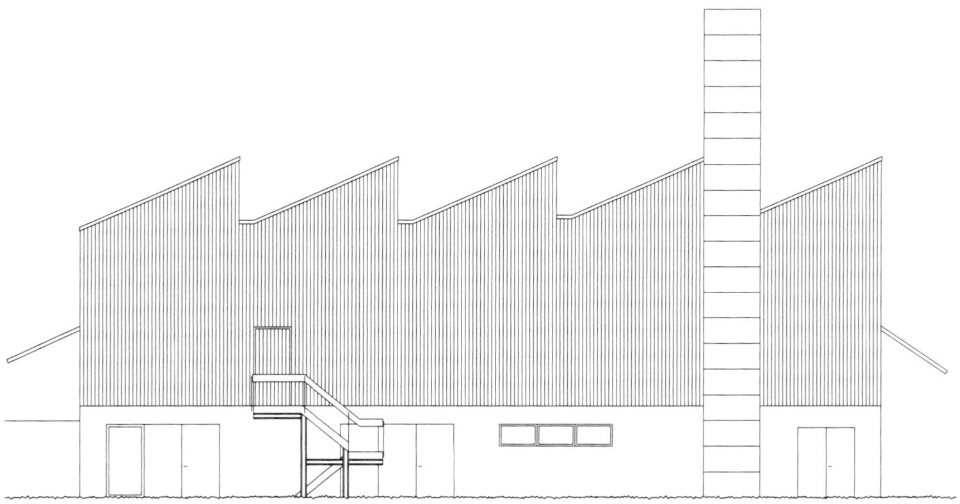

17.e
Southwest elevation

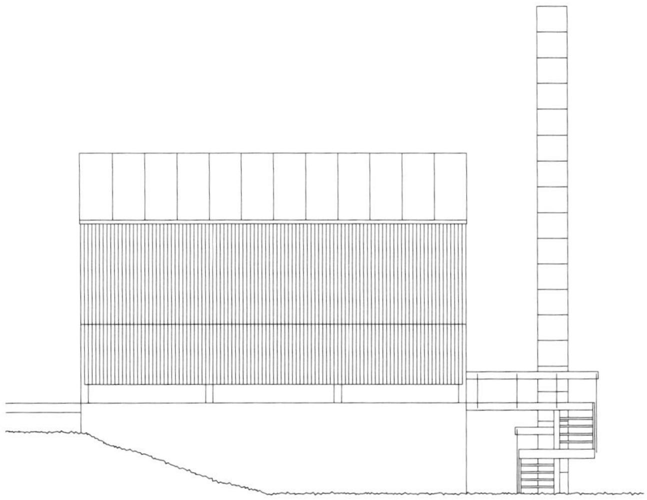

17.f
Northwest elevation

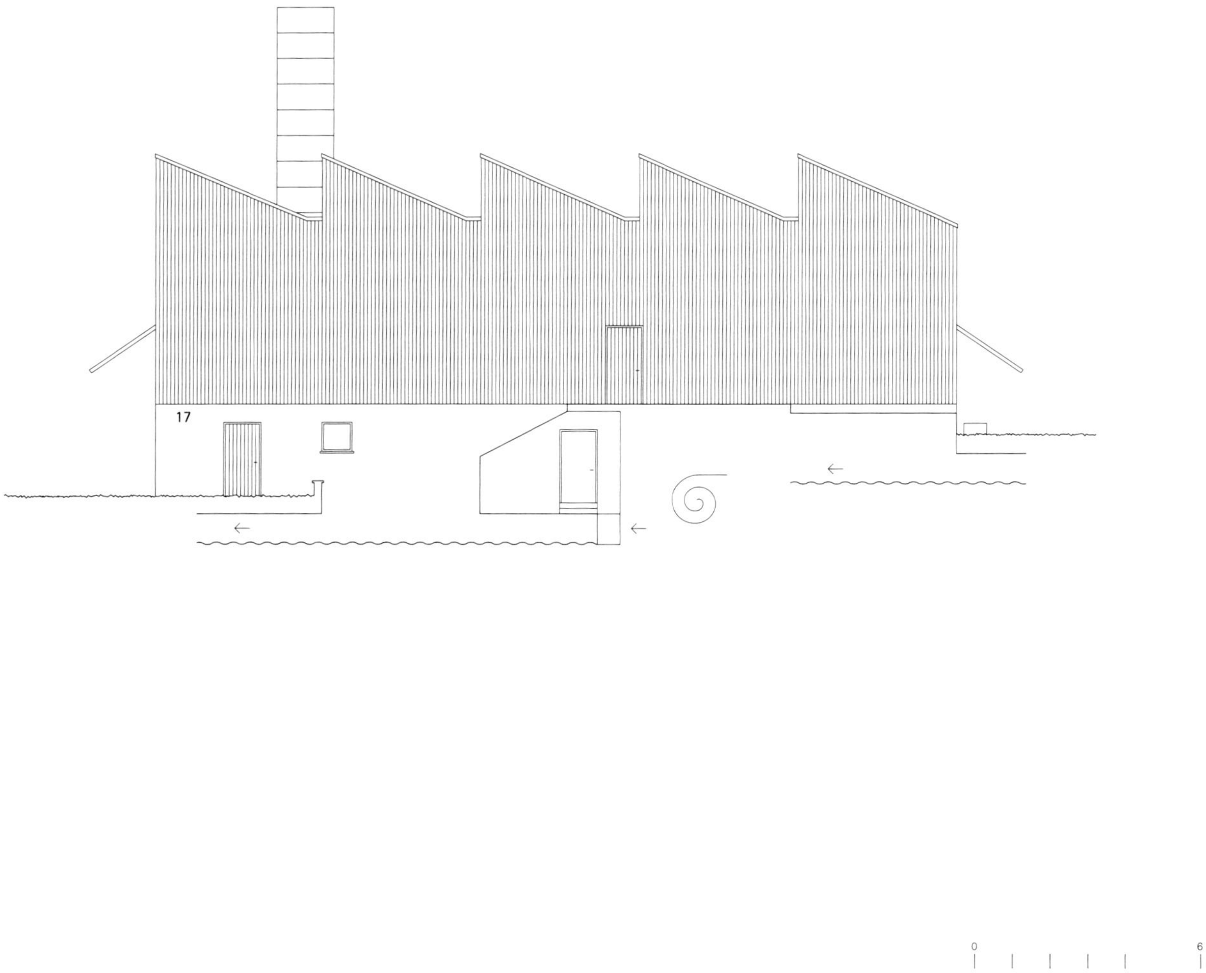

Southeast view of building 17. Lower floor used as a power and heating plant for the whole ensemble. The upper storey, with no specific purpose, is an open-plan area used for meetings and games. Photograph: Karsten de Riese

18.a
Northeast elevation

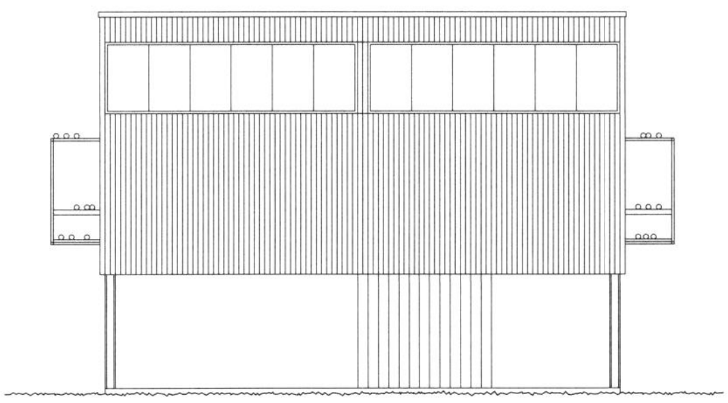

18.b
First floor

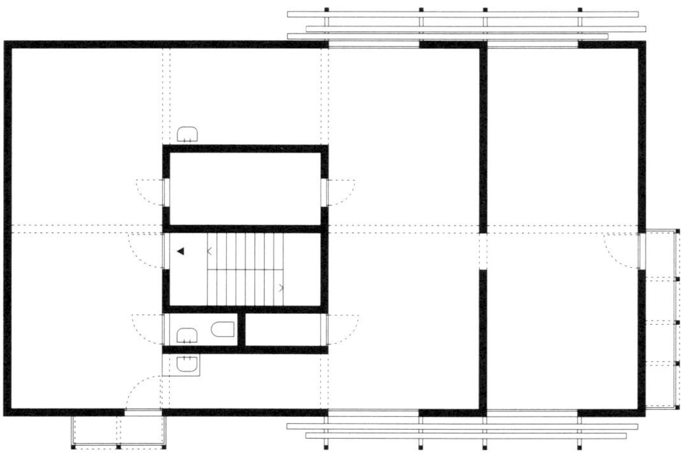

18.c
Ground floor

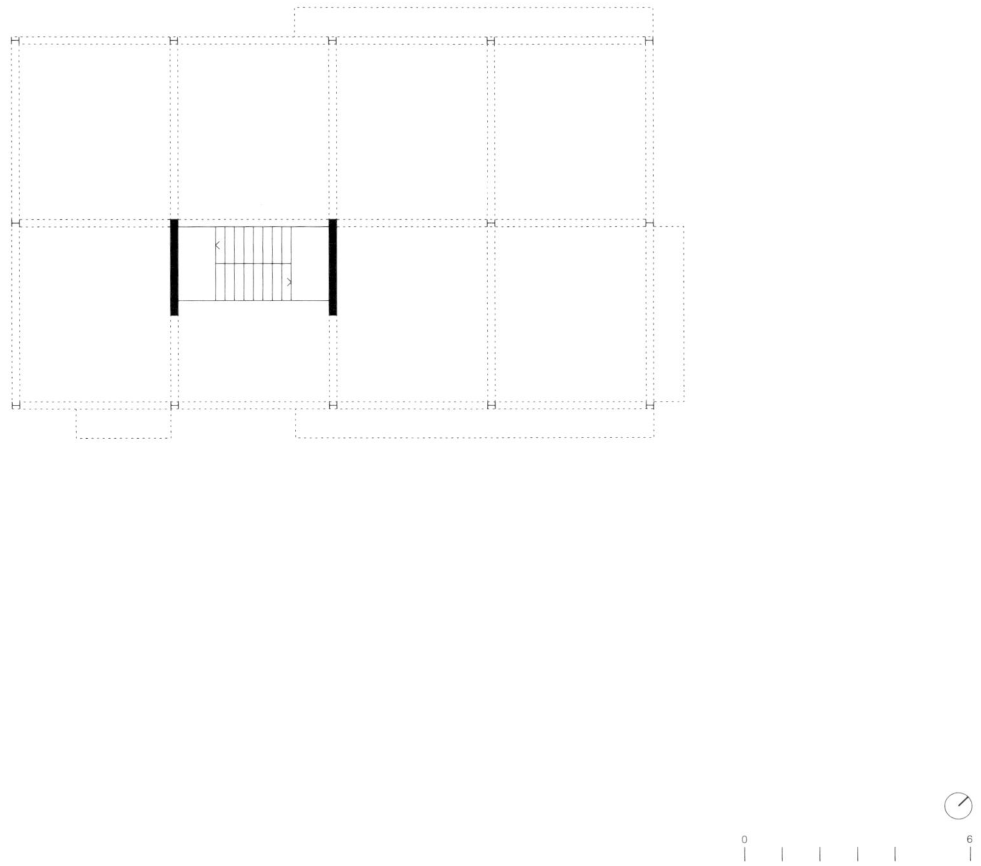

18.d
Southeast elevation

18.e
Southwest elevation

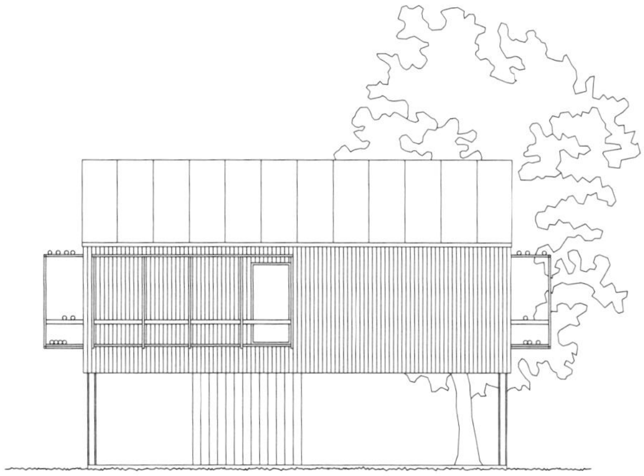

18.f
Northwest elevation

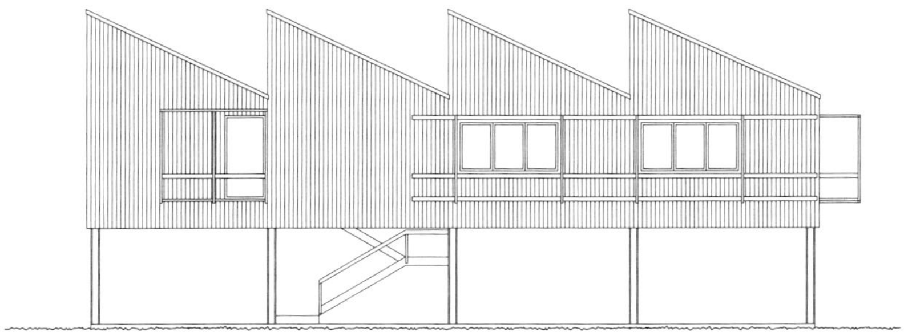

Otl Aicher in his sculpture atelier,
building X, modelling the busts of Sophie
and Hans Scholl, 26 August 1991.
Photograph: Hans Neudecker

x.a
Northeast elevation

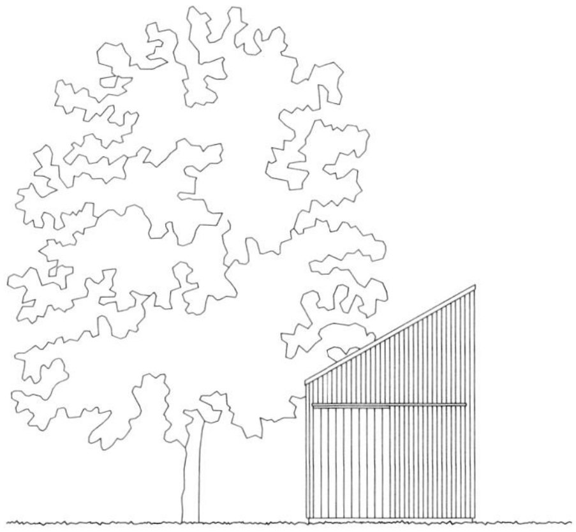

x.b
Ground floor

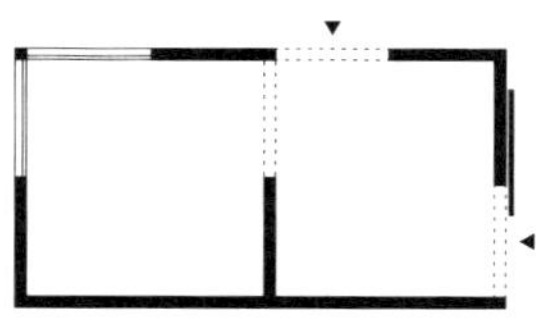

x.c
Southeast elevation

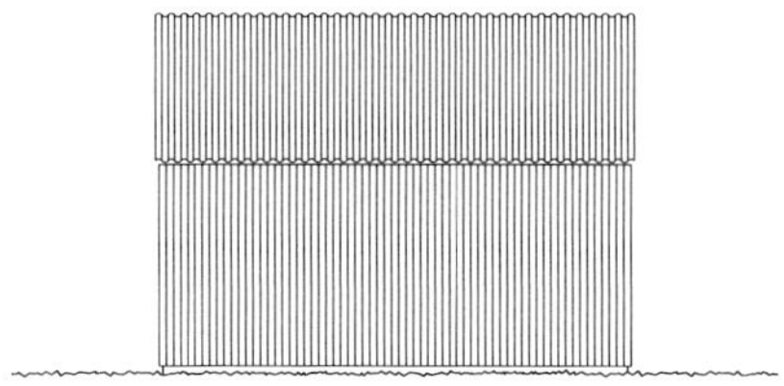

x.d
Southwest elevation

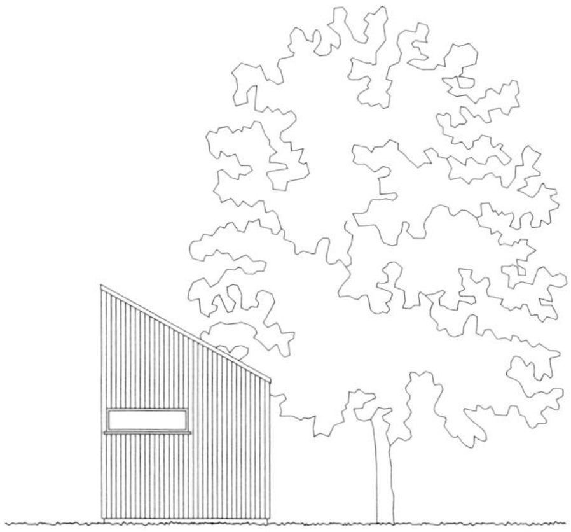

x.e
Northwest elevation

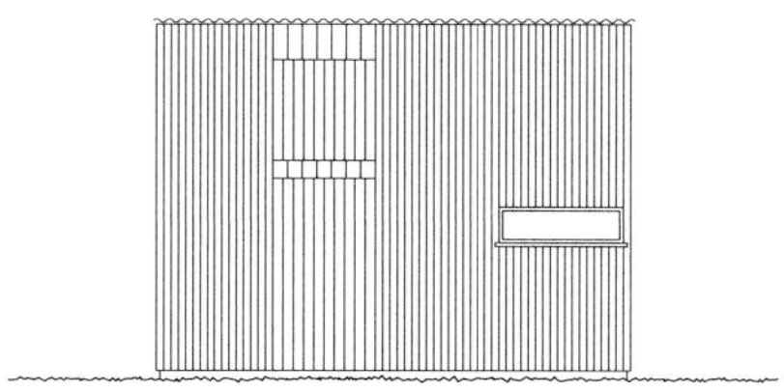

0 6

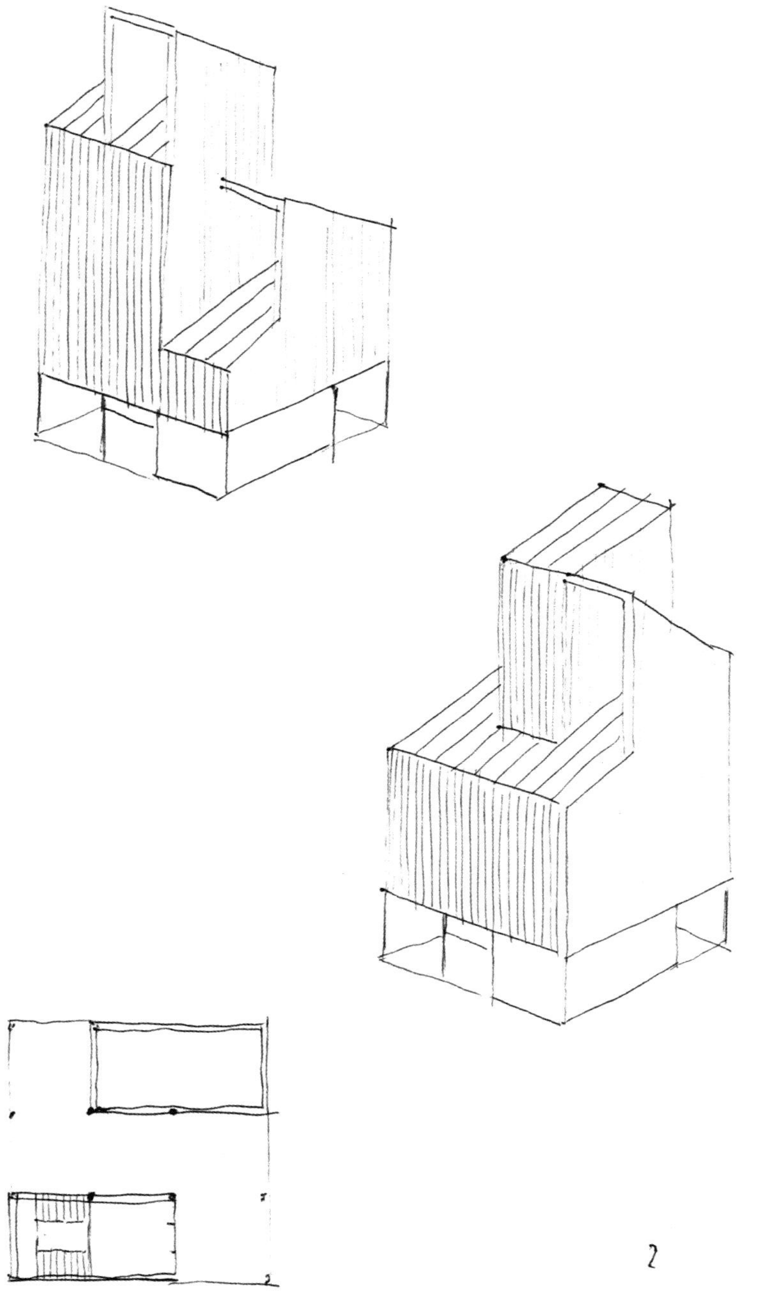

Otl Aicher. Project for a studio, 28 January 1978. Ink on paper. 29.7 x 21 cm

y.a
Northeast elevation

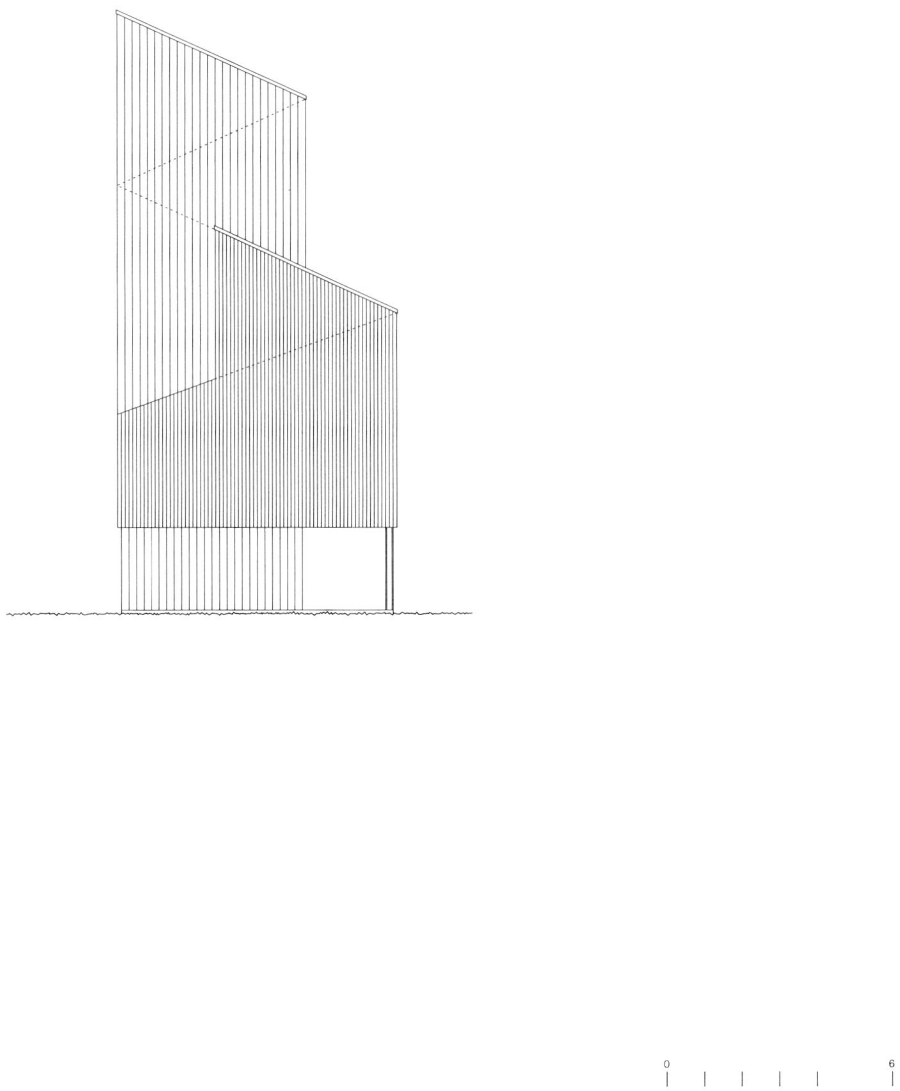

y.b
Ground floor

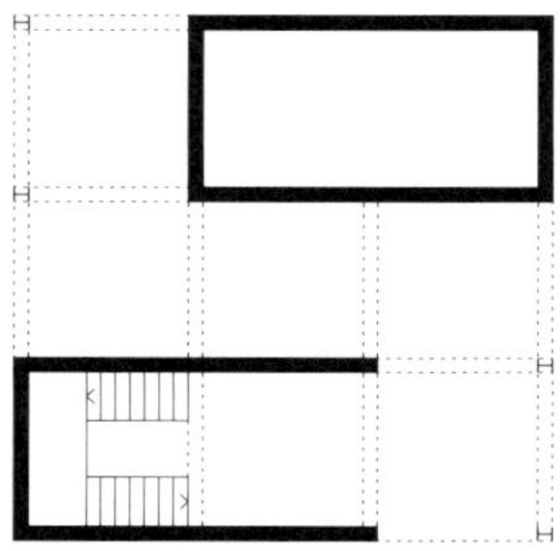

y.c
Southeast elevation

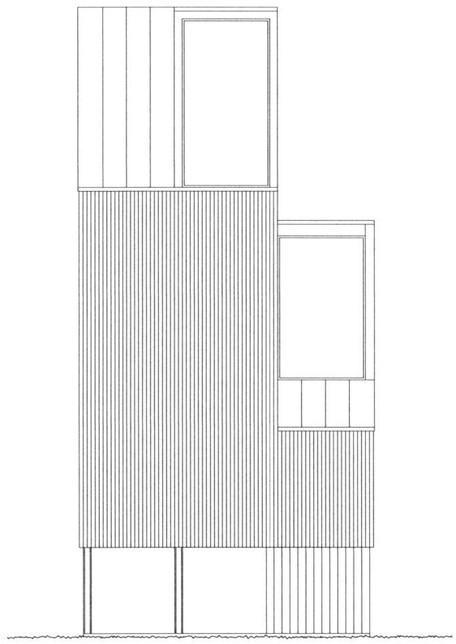

y.d
Northeast elevation

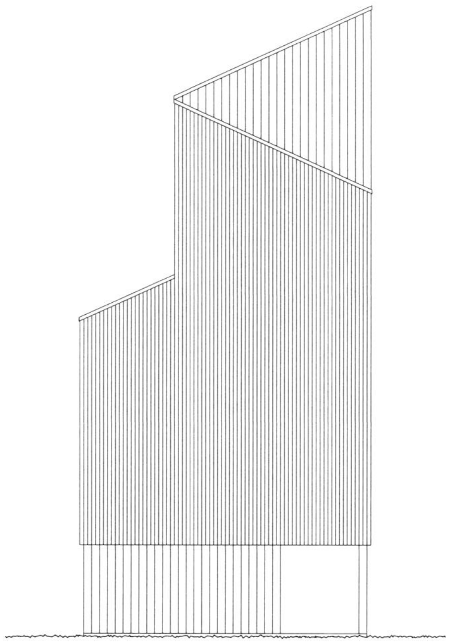

y.e
Northwest elevation

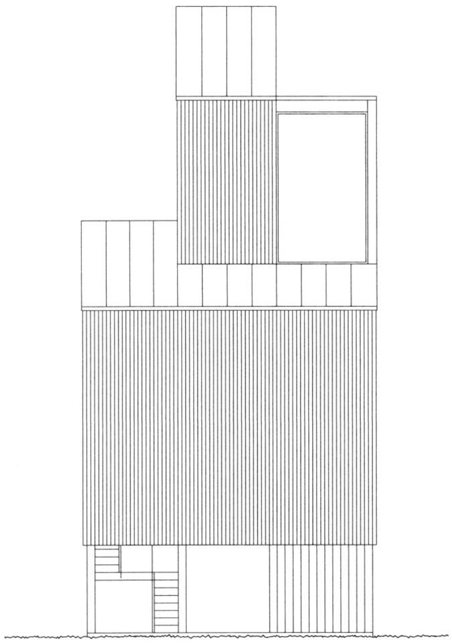

metro bilbao

was ist bilbao? otl aicher: architecture, landscape and world

gillermo zuaznabar

Axpe, La Naval, Serantes y Punta Lucero, c.1950. In Cándido Fullaondo, *La ría de Bilbao. Aspectos fotográficos* (Bilbao: Librería Arturo, 1966), no. 114

There is really no such thing as Art. There are only artists. Once these were men who took coloured earth and roughed out the forms of a bison on a wall of a cave; today they buy their paints, and design posters for the Underground.

Ernst H. Gombrich, 1950

was ist bilbao? asked Otl Aicher (Ulm, 1922–Günzburg, 1991) in the autumn of 1988 when he was designing a graphic system for the Bilbao Metro.[1] It was a useful question for figuring out what his project ought to reflect. Asking questions that challenged a project's central ideas was a common method for architects like Le Corbusier and Louis Kahn, and Aicher followed suit: What is Bilbao? What is a house? What is a kitchen? And a workplace?

A grave in London's Highgate Cemetery bears the following inscription: 'The philosophers have only interpreted the world, in various ways. The point, however, is to change it.' This quote makes a distinction between those who, like philosophers and theologians, interpret the world with and for language, and those who interpret it to effectively change it. Otl Aicher was one of the latter, as we shall see.

What is a Monument?

> here he [wittgenstein] is as bold as marx, who explains consciousness from the material culture of work, or the designer, who sees art as aesthetic metaphysics, and in designing does not turn to higher things, but to everyday use. the everyday is not a lower thing. 'the most important aspects of things for us are concealed by their simplicity and everyday quality.' we have to reveal them.[2]

On 22 February 1943, in an incredibly summary trial, the siblings Hans and Sophie Scholl and Christoph Probst were convicted of high treason and sentenced to die on the guillotine. Their crime? Taking on the full might of the Third Reich with nothing but their bare hands and a cyclostyle, copying and distributing leaflets that denounced Hitler and his warmongering. The Scholls and Probst belonged to the resistance group Die Wiese Rose (The White Rose), formed at the University of Munich in 1942. The group comprised a network of fellow students that included Alexander Schmorell, Heinz Brenner, Hans Hirzel and Franz Müller.[3]

Inge Scholl and Otl Aicher were introduced in 1939 by a mutual friend who also knew Inge's murdered brother and sister, and they developed a friendship that eventually led to their marriage in 1946. Wanting to preserve the memory of Inge's siblings and other fallen comrades, they sought a way to honour them. Inge Scholl, like Aicher, knew that there could be no more effective 'monument' than educating their neighbours who had been raised on Nazi ideology and, in many cases, had aided and abetted the persecution and murder of dissidents. Therefore, in 1946 they founded an adult education centre called the volkshochschule ulm (vh ulm).

Understanding that the vh ulm was not just a school but also a monument erected in memory of Hans and Sophie Scholl makes it easier to comprehend the ideological stance and method of action that Otl Aicher embraced as an activist, alongside Inge Scholl, throughout his life. It also sheds light on Aicher's own words in his 1987 article 'statt eines vorworts. nachdenken über ein denkmal' [in lieu of a prologue: reflections on the memorial].[4] The vh ulm offered adult literacy courses and classes on general culture, history, art and politics, imparting to local residents the political values that were persecuted from 1933 to 1946. The word used at the time to describe their activity was 'denazifying'.[5] The vh ulm was the first step, the foundation stone of a larger project and structure which, thanks to its efficacy and clear definition, would prove to be even more beautiful.

HfG Ulm

In May 1948, Inge Scholl and Otl Aicher travelled to Switzerland to attend a conference of adult education centre directors organised by the US government in an attempt to coordinate—and control—the various educational initiatives that were being launched in West Germany. Inge insisted that they take the opportunity to contact Bauhaus alumnus Max Bill and invite him to teach at the vh ulm.

After attending the Bauhaus for a year and a half, Bill had returned to Zurich in 1929. After the war he wrote a series of articles and organised exhibitions on art and industrial production, and in 1945 he published a book titled *wiederaufbau: dokumente über zerstörungen, planungen, konstruktionen* [reconstruction: documents on destruction, planning, construction]. Thanks to his involvement in the *USA baut* [USA builds] exhibition at the Kunstgewerbemuseum in Zurich[6] and the publication of his book on reconstruction, the American government invited him to travel across Germany as an expert consultant. The idea of reconstruction was also the driving force behind the HfG Ulm. Inge Scholl and Otl Aicher knew that this reconstruction had to be simultaneously physical and mental. This belief was conveyed with enthusiasm and determination in the first text they composed for that purpose, *studio null 16.6.1948 'fangen wir an'*, ['let's get started']:

> the new school should not be a business where everyone can buy their education as if shopping in a department store. it should be a community. with this school we want to begin to build a spirit of teamwork and spark the initiative that exists within every ordinary man. based on

[1] For Otl Aicher, and the generation of Germans born before World War II, Bilbao was probably little more than the quasi-onomatopoeic location of Bill's dancehall, 'the most beautiful on the whole continent. There you could get as rowdy as you wanted for one dollar.' *Der Bilbao Song*, lyrics by Bertolt Brecht and music by Kurt Weil, 1929 (English translation by Michael Feingold).

[2] Otl Aicher, *Analog und Digital* (Berlin: Ernst & Sohn, 1991). English edition: *Analogous and Digital*, trans. Michael Robinson (Berlin: Ernst & Sohn, 2015), 63.

[3] For more on the group and their activities, see Inge Scholl, *Die Weise Rose* (Frankfurt am Main: S. Fischer, 1982). After the execution of two of the Scholl siblings, the youngest brother Werner was sent to the Russian front, where he died, and the rest of the family—their parents Robert and Marianne and sisters Inge and Elisabeth—was arrested. The father also served an 18-month prison sentence for listening to the BBC. The National Socialist party leader in Ulm continued to hound the family, using press articles with headlines like 'Wie lange noch Scholl?' [How much longer (must we tolerate) the Scholls?] to campaign against them. The family left Ulm and sought refuge in the Black Forest, where they stayed until the end of the war. After the fall of the Nazi regime, on 7 June 1945 the allied forces made the father, Robert Scholl, mayor of Ulm. He remained in office until 1948.

[4] Published in Norbert Haase, *Deutsche Deserteure* (Berlin: Rotbuch, 1987), 7–13. In this text, Aicher analysed the reasons why no commemorative or funerary monuments from World War II were erected in the Federal Republic of Germany. According to Aicher, one was that there could be no heroes of a war which Germany had begun under monstrous pretexts. He argued that the only possible monuments would have to honour deserters, but such memorials would prick the consciences of citizens and politicians—some as relevant as Helmut Schmidt and Josef Franz Strauss—who, like the majority of German society, made excuses for their past by claiming that they were 'just doing their duty'. Public recognition of those who spoke out against Hitler and the war would speak loudly to those who supported and obeyed their führer.

[5] In the school's first curriculum. Inge Scholl and Otl Aicher, *Geschwister Scholl Hochschule: An Active School for Science, Art and Politics in Germany* (Ulm: HfG-Archiv, 1949).

this joint effort, a few years down the road we also want to give the 'new school' an external form. we want to start building. this learning institute must be engraved, even outwardly, on the image of the city, it must take shape. [...] we need to build our own cultural centre [...] the forms of the structures must express a new outlook on life. belief in the future, hope.[7]

Reconnecting with those who built the Bauhaus to draw on their experience for the Ulm project was Bill's primary task in 1950 and 1951. When drafting the curriculum, he sought the approval and advice of Bauhaus founders Henry van de Velde and Walter Gropius, telling them that the idea was to 'reopen' the Bauhaus in Ulm.[8]

In addition to his work, the mandates of the Geschwister Scholl Stiftung [Scholl Siblings Foundation] had to be considered.[9] At that time, Bill's interests and aims were not exactly aligned with those of the foundation. As mentioned, the Geschwister Scholl Stiftung was established as a political and cultural initiative to honour and preserve the memory of the Scholl siblings. Bill, considering this social dimension of the school, saw the project as an opportunity to build, putting all his theories about reconstruction and the modernisation of the concept of design into practice.[10]

New Colours

On 4 March 2011, a researcher met with Hans (Nick) Roericht, a student and professor at the HfG Ulm. The school had many guest lecturers. The most frequently mentioned in publications are former Bauhaus teachers: Josef Albers, Johannes Itten, Gropius, Hans Peterhans and even Mies. Among the guests were two unexpected—at least for the researcher—names: Ray and Charles Eames. Their presence in Bill's cold building and among the students must have surprised him. The researcher asked Roericht, 'What did the Eameses' visit mean to you?' Swiftly, spontaneously and without hesitation, Roericht replied, 'They brought us colour!'

This recollection of the Eameses' contribution says something very important about the American designers. If the Eameses brought colour, it follows that before they came there was no colour in the school or even in the city, or that the possibility of using colour, as a rationed, 'scarce commodity', was limited. Roericht's answer also reveals that colour is not a stylistic resource but an ideological statement.

How could the Ulm school students and professors, heirs to the Bauhaus legacy, and with a painter (Max Bill) at the helm, not be making free use of colour? The explanation may lie in the fact that these Bauhaus heirs, contrary to what English-language art commentators like to emphasise, did not simply pick up where that school left off; they were 'something else'. Looking back at the Bauhaus proposals, we find many multicolour[11] works with a predominance of primary colours—red, yellow and blue—and basic two-dimensional geometric shapes—circle, square and triangle.

Twenty years after that school closed, Max Bill, relieved of his directorial duties—by then the HfG was being run by Hans Gugelot, Tomás Maldonado and Aicher—distanced himself from the Bauhaus and any temptation to use artistic devices like those three recurring colours and shapes.

The HfG Ulm's rejection of the Bauhaus and the offer to use the same name for the new school[12] was based on two determinations:

I) Not to confuse design with art. Seeing the HfG Ulm's proposal, one deduces that the Bauhaus, as an applied arts school, was not overly concerned about this distinction. Artistic configurations like the *Triadic Ballet* are virtually inseparable from Wagenfeld's lamps or board games. Walter Gropius and Hannes Meyer tended to alternate between proposals, even contradictory ones, but they should be understood as configurations born of a need to break with academic tradition rather than parts of a single proactive or constructive project. Viewing the Bauhaus as a mould-breaking school—rather than a school that established the independence of design, which still resided in the hands and eyes of artisans and artists—makes it easier to comprehend its true contribution and position in the Europe of the 1920s and 30s.

> The visible is only the final step of a historical form. Its fulfilment. Its true fulfilment. Then it breaks off. And a new world arises.[13]

The alleged successors of the *neue bauhaus*, in their need to transform society and education, believed that the artistic had to be segregated from design. This division, defended by Adolf Loos as early as 1898, aimed to remove from the educational arena concepts related to artistic sensibility, taste or style, qualities and categories managed by the academy and the ruling classes which, consequently, had no place in a school established with a popular vocation.

II) To develop pedagogical methods that promoted democratic values. The goal of the HfG Ulm was to offer an education that would allow designers to learn and work with objectifiable processes that any student could grasp, with pedagogical parameters not influenced by either the background or social status of students—in other words, democratic parameters. This pedagogy yielded an education and products devoid of attributes and ornament, which were deemed unnecessary, again since Loos, in a modern society. The aim was not to contaminate the city with free or discriminatory resources. Rather, it was to economise production, forms and work. Scientific and democratic premises promoted efficacy in manufacture, usage and society itself.[14]

6 *USA baut.* Kunstgewerbemuseum, Zurich, 8 September–7 October 1945.

7 'die neue schule soll kein unternehmen sein, in dem jeder sich erziehung einkaufen kann wie in einem grosskaufhaus. sie soll ein gemeinschaftswerk werden. mit dieser schule wollen wir beginnen, ein gefühl für gemeinschaftsaufgaben und für die initiative zu wecken, die beim gemeinen mann liegt. aus diesem gemeinschaftswerk heraus wollen wir uns dann nach einige jahren daran machen, der "neue schule" auch eine äussere form zu geben. wir wollen bauen beginnen. dieses erziehungsinstitut muss sich auch äusserlich im bild der stadt einprägen. es muss gestalt annehmen, bild werden [...] wir müssen ein eigenes kulturelles zentrum bauen [...] die bauten müssten in ihrer forme in neues lebensgefühl zum ausdruck bringen. den glauben an die zukunft, die hoffnung.' Marcela Quijano, 'Programm der Geschwister Scholl Hochschule. Eine aktive Schule für Kultur und Politik, Ulm 1949–50' in *HfG Ulm: Programm wird Bau: die Gebäude der Hochschule für Gestaltung Ulm* (Ulm: Solitude, 2002), 20, note 5.

8 Letter to Gropius, Ulm, 22 November 1951 (Bauhaus-Archiv Berlin); and letter to Van de Velde, 26 June 1950 (HfG-Archiv, Ulm).

9 Geschwister Scholl Stiftung was the institution created in December 1950 to establish the HfG Ulm.

10 See Max Bill, *Wiederaufbau: Dokumente über Zerstörungen, Planungen, Konstruktionen* (Erlenbach-Zurich: Verlag für Architektur, 1945); Max Bill, *Moderne Schweizer Architektur, 1925–1945* (Basel: Karl Werner, 1949); *Die gute Form*, exhibition catalogue (Basel, 1949).

11 'Multicolour' was Walter Gropius's favourite colour as a child. Speech given on his seventieth birthday.

12 'When Walter Gropius made us the offer of calling the Hochschule für Gestaltung "Bauhaus Ulm", we refused.' Otl Aicher, *Die Welt Als Entwurf* (1991). English edition: *The World as Design*, trans. Michael Robinson (Berlin: Ernst & Sohn, 2015), 85.

13 Mies van der Rohe quoted in Fritz Neumeyer, ed., *The Artless Word: Mies van der Rohe on the Building Art* (Cambridge, MA: MIT Press, 1991), 326.

Otl Aicher. ERCO project, 1975

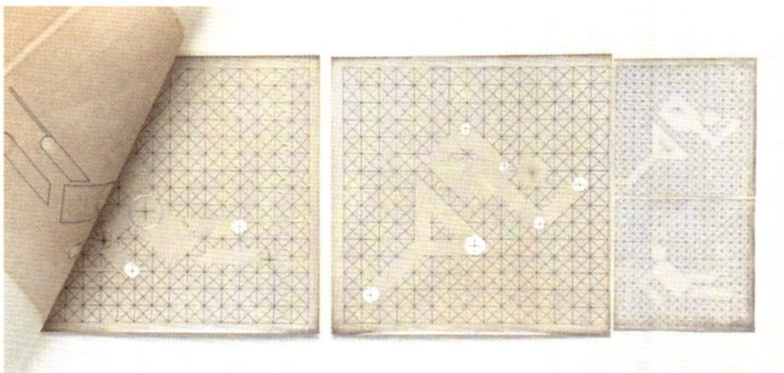

Gerhard Joksch. Original designs of the sports pictograms for the 1972 Munich Olympics. Photograph: György Kőrössy

Erasing Colours

Otl Aicher's best-known work is the system of pictograms he invented for the 1972 Munich Olympics and developed in 1975–1978 as a signage system for buildings and public spaces, still marketed today by the ERCO company.[15] Aicher devised his pictograms in 1967, building on Matsuri Katsumi's work for the 1964 Tokyo Olympics. Given the need to inform a large number of visitors with different cultures, languages and customs, Katsumi created a visual communication system based on easily decipherable signs and icons. For the 1972 Munich Olympics, Aicher revisited Katsumi's work and even met with the Japanese designer at his Roter Hof studio in August 1966, two months before the commission was officially awarded on 7 October. Aicher elaborated on the Tokyo '64 design but passed it through the filter of the grid, arranging it geometrically and minimising graphic resources in order to come up with more new icons. Trimming and simplifying Katsumi's proposal revealed its underlying structure, which he then used to design even more legible signs.

Both Katsumi and Aicher were indebted to the *Wiener Methode der Bildstatistik* (1925–1934) or Vienna Method of Pictorial Statistics invented by Otto Neurath, Marie Reidemeister and Gerd Arntz. This method aimed to present complex economic and sociological data and concepts in a way that less educated citizens could understand, using what were called Isotype figures, halfway between sign and picture.[16]

> The ordinary citizen ought to be able to get information freely about all subjects in which he is interested, just as he can get geographical knowledge from maps and atlases. There is no field where humanization of knowledge through the eye would not be possible. This is the goal of Isotype: to communicate knowledge by visual means as widely as possible and so help to reduce the gulf between nations and language groups.[17]

The last sentence of Neurath's definition of Isotype clearly sums up the goals for the Munich Games. However, upon examining Aicher's proposal for the Olympics, we are surprised by the unusual range of colours he used: yellow, green, orange, light blue, dark blue, grey and silver, combined in incredibly dynamic figures that avoid vertical and horizontal lines. This cheerful colouring—a far cry from the Ulm aesthetic—with photographs of 'messy' curved lines and diagonals, was employed to convey a dynamic image of the event and the country that was hosting the games for the second time. The colours were taken from the Olympic symbol, but Aicher deliberately avoided using black and red which, together with white and gold, had formed the dominant palette of German society in the 1930s and 40s and of the 1936 Berlin Games. The proposal for Munich '72 is even more striking when we

[14] In this respect, it is essential to review the ideas of Gui Bonsiepe, *Teoria e pratica del disegno industriale: elementi per una manualistica critica* (Milan: Feltrinelli, 1975).

[15] Otl Aicher and Martin Krampen, *Zeichensysteme der visuellen Kommunikation: Handbuch für Designer, Architekten, Planer, Organisatoren* (Stuttgart: Alexander Koch, 1977), 129–151.

[16] 'Isotype is the name of a visual language which Otto Neurath developed with his collaborators during the last 20 years of his life, and which we are now trying to develop further on the lines which we followed under his guidance. The name Isotype stands for "International System of Typographic Picture Education": if we want to make two visual statements about the same thing, we use the same symbol again for this thing. Thus Isotype follows certain rather strict rules like a language; on the other hand it is less rigid and less complete, as it is an educational tool and does not attempt to replace words entirely. Every Isotype chart uses words too.' Marie L. Neurath, 'Report on the last years of Isotype work' in *Synthese*, vol. 8, no. 12 (1950–1951), 22.

[17] Otto Neurath (1946) quoted in Friedrich Stadler, ed., *Arbeiterbildung in der Zwischenkriegszeit: Otto Neurath, Gerd Arntz* (Vienna: Löcker, 1982), 238.

Otto Neurath, Gerd Arntz and Marie Reidemeister. Isotype sports chart, probably created at IZOSTAT USSR, c.1930–1934

realise that the design strategy had a purpose: to omit the harsh lines and four colours that defined the darkest period in German and European history. The choice and treatment of images was objective, and the arguments were imbued with communicable logic. Randomness had no place in the designer's profession.

Inventing Colours

Forms and colours are signifying elements and therefore communicate values that affect people's lives. Their misuse can deteriorate a society and its culture;[18] but, when used properly, they can also be instruments of its recovery or progress. Aicher was aware of their impact on society and pondered them at length:

> i have invented a few colours in my lifetime. of course i did not invent them as such. all the colours that we see are there. but we only see those colours that we have in our consciousness, that we can name. we see only that which we know and can name communicatively as an object of information. the colour turquoise has existed only since the empire. it was not known in the middle ages, even though matthias grünewald almost achieved turquoise in the halo of the risen christ. in the field of grey we have invented two colours. one went into the language of colour as greige, and is used in department stores for things like describing the colour of women's stockings. it is a mixture of grey and sand colour. there are countless colour shades in the field of grey, more than among the bright colours. you can get enthusiastic about it, and you do not have to be afraid of disrespectful bleak and dreary grey. the other grey is called vlau. the word has not yet become established. i am certain that it will come, as this colour is the most exciting colour in the late twentieth century.[19]

Thinking about colours, imagining them, naming them, understanding them as territories that must be formed through language to organise the world and make it liveable—that is the designer's task.

was ist bilbao?

> *Desordenada selva roja, blanca y verde,*
> *con trozos de páginas*
> *que arrastra el viento hasta más allá del horizonte,* [...]
>
> Blas de Otero, 'Desde el fondo', 1968

Aicher began each project by reading up on the history and values of the company or society in which his work would be

Ian McLaren and Margarete Bodarwé working on colour studies for the 1972 Munich Olympics

[18] A good example of cultural deterioration due to the poor use of forms and colours is provided every weekend in Basque-Spanish society at *pelota* matches, in *trainera* regattas and even on the gear worn by many amateur cyclists and mountain climbers.

implemented. This research process enabled him to choose the most suitable forms for the project. In Bilbao, the design of a corporate identity for the Metro was also a product of analysing the city's history, geography and culture. Aicher read books and visited the city to study the heraldry and forms of Bilbao. After sketching some initial ideas for the competition that Norman Foster won in the spring of 1988, that autumn Aicher prepared a document detailing and justifying his proposal. This study, consisting of approximately two hundred illustrations and three briefs, was finished in December 1988. Aicher referred to it as his 'complementary study'.

> red is the predominant colour of the metro.
>
> red is the predominant colour of the city of bilbao (red and white) and of the flag of the basque country the colours that stand out are (red, green and white). It seems important that the metro colours should be rooted in those of heraldic tradition to maintain the region's identity in the future.[20]

The designer did not draw on a blank page, nor deploy his purported creativity on a memory-less map. Cultural and economic conditions were a motivating factor and integral part of the design. The designer separated the gratuitous, the noise that disturbs life, from the elements that helped him to define the identity of users and of the city.

Three sets of documents can be distinguished in the 'complementary study'. Each set represents a 'qualitative leap'[21] in the project.

'Complementary study' for Bilbao: Three 'qualitative leaps' in the Metro design

The first 'leap' is the group of diagnostic drawings. Aicher identified and streamlined historical and contemporary forms using a language that allowed him to devise a new iconography. Along with green and white, he analysed and gauged reds, greys and blacks.

> the bilbao metro is the backbone of the technical plan for the bilbao bay area (bilbao estuary). therefore the visual attributes of the metro should assimilate the visual attributes of the region, its ancient heraldry as well as its new signs. as the metro's attributes develop, so the region's symptoms should also take shape. the beginning of a modernisation and updating of heraldic signs, as well as the development of new symbols for the region's content. These signs will be components of the metro communication system for both the maps and the information panel.[22]

The second 'leap' is a set of images that represent Bilbao. Aicher prepared an extensive photographic report to get a panoramic view of the city. From above, he illustrated and listened to the heartbeat of Bilbao and its offshoots. He needed to reconnoitre the context in which the city was inserted.

> This study attempts to prove that the appearance of the new Bilbao Metro requires a new structure.
> In the design competition in the spring of 1988 the Metro was envisioned more as an underground vehicle for connecting the suburbs to the city centre.
> However, Bilbao has clearly expanded into a larger region, in which the city is only one part of a greater whole. The advantage of regional planning is that it allows the mutual sharing of civilisation and nature, urban and recreational contents. That region requires a new awareness of itself, as well as new contents. The Metro thus becomes the backbone and ligament. It becomes the symbol of renewal.[23]

The 'third leap' is another group of images representing Bilbao. But here the images show how the city would change when the Metro was completed. This group imagines the city that Aicher and Foster envisioned and that the Metro could bring. The Metro is revealed not only as a mode of transport or a great engineering feat, but also as a structure and a language that would lead to transformation thanks to a new relational network linking citizens, the public space, the estuary and the landscape. Aicher suggested—and, in a way, conditioned—the nature of that transformation.

The images of the three 'leaps' are accompanied by notes, instructions and reflections that helped to define the project brief and its final outcome. Each 'leap' encompasses the three tenses of the images: past (history), present (1988) and future. Three presents converged in the body of his work: a present with memory, a contemporary present, and a present pregnant with the future. By integrating these three times in his information system, Aicher allowed them to flow in the continuous present which any project that aspires to endure must seek.

Bird's-eye views

In autumn 1988, Aicher spent several days flying over Bilbao to obtain 'bird's-eye view' photographs of the city. Aicher was already quite familiar with this method of representation. The famous aerial photograph of the brand-new HfG Ulm, with the cathedral spire rising above the city in a dense halo of misty shadow, was taken by Aicher from an aircraft in 1955. In the 1960s and 70s he designed campaigns and

[19] Aicher, 'Appearance' in *The World as Design*, 160–161.

[20] Otl Aicher, 'Complementary Study' in *Bilbao*, Rotis, 1988, no. 25, HfG-Archiv, Ulm.

[21] Sergei Eisenstein used this term when analysing his films. It is used here because the images and layout of the 'Complementary Study' make it a visual territory comparable to Eisenstein's montages. On this term, see Paulino Viota, 'El trampolín del salto' in *La herencia del cine: escritos escogidos* (Madrid: Ediciones Asimétricas, 2019), 49–61.

[22] Aicher, *Bilbao*, no. 22.

[23] Aicher, 'preliminary remarks' in *Bilbao*, no. 2.

publications for Lufthansa.[24] Although the pictures he took of Bilbao might make us think they served the same purpose as the photograph of the HfG Ulm or the Lufthansa images, the aerial views of Bilbao are in fact radically different. From the sixteenth century to Le Corbusier and Lufthansa, bird's-eye views had served to identify, glorify or obtain the profile of a city, river or coastline, but in 1988, thanks to existing records, Aicher was already perfectly acquainted with the outline of Bilbao. He must have been looking for the opposite of its outer limits—in other words, the inner limits.

was ist bilbao? Ground-level images provided no answers. Aicher manipulated the photographs and turned them into something else. He eschewed the enveloping light, the colours, even the very idea we have of photography, associated with technical resolution or a supposedly 'objective' document. Aicher did away with what one expects to see in a photograph: brightness, colour, precision ... He went in the opposite direction, eliminating those attributes and reducing the photographs of Bilbao to grainy, low-resolution smudges of black, white and grey. This alteration penetrated the city's skin, making his aerial views look more like X-rays. And what better than an X-ray to diagnose and prescribe treatment for an ailing subject? Aicher was able to test how his graphic language should work inside the body of the city, where the maladies—congestion, pollution, violence, lack of light and air—that defined Bilbao's identity in the 1940s, 50s, 60s, 70s and 80s were plain to see. With the Metro, Aicher and Foster teamed up to treat these ailments. Red lines stretch across the 'X-rays', standing out sharply against the blacks and greys. The lines, including those drawn by Foster, have a calculated organic quality. They look like blood vessels snaking across a section of closed tissue. By structuring and defining its parts, the city could be 'cured', among many other things, thanks to the colours and graphic information deployed in the Metro.

> speed, air, light
> Aicher reflected on the logo:
> The semantics of the symbol recall moving wheels, speed, dynamics and movement.
> The same goes for the tubular shape of the tunnel and the technical functionality of the station.[25]
> (25) [...]
> 1 City
> 2 Port, shipyards, industry
> 3 Riverside
> The signs appear on the vehicles, on printed materials and as symbols at the station entrances. It is also recognised as a two-dimensional sign in a nearly 360-degree field of vision.
> (26) The tunnel
> The wheel
> Repetition
> Perspective
> (27) single chain with three parts
> Unity
> Hand in hand
> Independence and unity[26]
> the colour of the bilbao metro company is vermilion red. additional colours range from light to darker greys with a slightly reddish tinge. in exceptional cases pure black and white colours will be used.[27]

His words and the symbol highlight the industrial history of the city and of the client to whom the 'complementary study' is addressed.[28] But the goal of the new machine was to break away from the nineteenth-century city that Bilbao still was, in some respects, even in 1988. Like Wright and Le Corbusier, Aicher and Foster knew that the machine could save the city and architecture could save it from the evils of that machine. The new machine and the new language that came with it had the opposite effect of the nineteenth-century machine. Whereas the old machine congested and destroyed, the new one would decongest and structure. Whereas the old was inorganic, the new had to be organic. Whereas the old destroyed, the new should build. Whereas the old aligned, the new had to combine. Whereas the old exploited workers, the new ought to serve them. Whereas the old closed, the new was called to open.

The three rings, designed between 1988 and 1991 and adopted in 1995, according to Aicher, evoke the tunnel, wheels and speed, as well as the three zones of the metropolitan area that the Metro would connect: city, industry and riverside. However, the symbol devised to both inform and form the new city also had to reflect the flip side of the machine—the Metro. Today, twenty-five years later, we can see that the concepts the symbol conveys are the antithesis of the old world: speed, air, light. Isn't oxygen, clean energy, distributed via electrical impulses, the cure for an ailing city? And isn't it exactly what the circulatory system of a living organism distributes—also via electrical impulses—to stay alive? Now that we know what Bilbao was and is, we can better appreciate Aicher's design. Thanks to the fragmented composition, to photography and film, we can also see three instants, three snapshots of a ring which, depending on its thickness, seems closer or further away, carried and carriers of light. This was not the first time that Aicher used font weight to represent light. In 1975 he designed the logo for ERCO, then a small business dealing in light fixtures. By giving each letter a different weight, the logo conveyed the idea of moving from lesser to greater clarity, like a light turning on or off.[29] In Bilbao, where the darkness had to be shattered, black was only used in the process of designing the rings and otherwise reserved for exceptional situations, as indicated in the project brief. The idea was to make the rings white if printed on a red ground, and vermilion if printed on

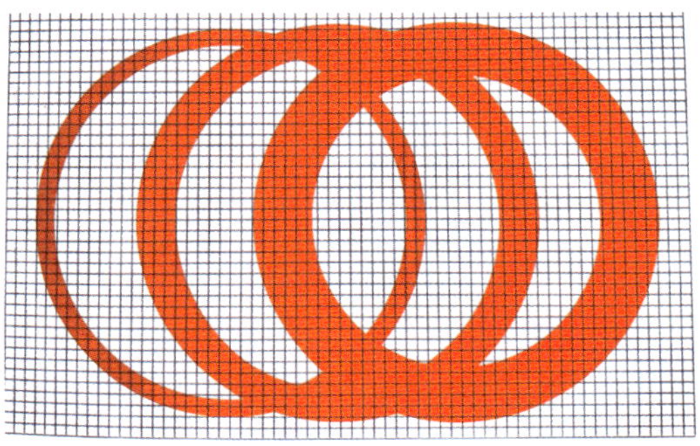

Otl Aicher. Metro Bilbao project, autumn/winter 1988

[24] Rudolf Sass and Otl Aicher, *Flugbild Deutschland Lufthansa* (Gütersloh: Heinz Peter, 1968); Rudolf Sass and Otl Aicher, *Im Flug über Europa. Lufthansa* (Salzburg: Otto Müller, 1974).

[25] Aicher, 'Complementary Study' in *Bilbao*, nos. 25–27.

[26] Aicher, 'Complementary Study' in *Bilbao*, no. 26.

[27] Aicher, 'Style Book' in *Bilbao*, no. 1.

[28] Based on correspondence from July 1990, it appears that Aicher had a contract with the developer IMEBISA, whose offices were on the 5th floor of number 4 Plaza España, Bilbao.

[29] See the essay by Yves Zimmermann in this volume, where he analyses the ERCO logo.

white. In both versions, white and red, the Metro brings light, and the sequential rings bring air. The light of each version is different; they represent opposite times and worlds. In white, the symbol is cold, clean, electric. In red, the circles look like fiery red rings, forged in the bubbling steel cauldrons of smoke-belching, coal-fired factories. One hails from the past, while the other ushers in the new world. When the underground tunnels were dug and the Metro arrived, the city would have space, air and light steeped in memory. The Metro promised to structure and define the city. What would the result be? Aicher drew that, too.

The third set of images, here referred to as the 'third qualitative leap', consists of drawings that show the city with the Metro in operation. The Bilbao we see here is the antithesis of the X-rayed city depicted in the 'second qualitative leap'. To make the Metro visible, this new panoramic picture was drawn at ground level, with Bilbao's identifying buildings and landscape features rising above: Abando [district], Arriaga [theatre], Altos Hornos [blast furnaces], Puente Colgante [suspension bridge], Portu Zaharra [old port], Punta Galea [cape]. The old city has disappeared. In its place we find white paper and the landscape lines that Aicher had retrieved from historical records and his 'X-rays'. In order to streamline and define the city, Aicher used a method scorned by draughtsmen but which enabled him to transform the world: tracing. With this 'inferior' technique, he carefully went over the image before his eyes, separating the essential from the superfluous. Tracing let him analyse reality, but the intention behind this act of copying was not to embellish or glorify the original image. Quite the opposite: tracing allowed him to build or alter the world before him, as the represented world was profoundly affected by the clear, orderly, elementary images that Aicher produced. He appropriated the world, sharing its virtues and thereby making it possible for those who studied his drawings. The paper showed what life would allow; outside lay the world that would have to be transformed over the years to make it happen. For Aicher, tracing was an analytical method that helped him to imagine and envision a landscape, a house or a kitchen.

A house and a kitchen

After the Olympic commission was made official on 7 October 1966, Aicher worked with his collaborators in Ulm, Munich and occasionally at Roter Hof, the farm where he and his family had been spending their holidays since the 1960s. With the closure of the HfG in 1968 and the Olympic job nearing completion, the Aicher-Scholl family began looking for a new place to live and work communally. One hour outside Ulm, though not on any map, and equidistant from Stuttgart, Munich and Zurich, Rotis was a small village whose economy revolved around agriculture, animal husbandry and the timber industry of the Allgäu region. In 1970, Aicher and Inge Scholl bought an old mill with four hectares of land that included a canal, a lovely three-storey house and a large stable.

> Approaches to Rotis,
>
> Rotis is an old mill in Allgäu, situated at an altitude of 652–655 metres above sea level, between what were once the free imperial cities of Memmingen, Kempten and Leutkirch.
>
> Rotis considers itself an Independent Republic consisting of six buildings (four of them are studios) and three inhabitants (one being Otl Aicher). Rotis is, first and foremost, an independent (and even obstinate) mindset, ideology and attitude towards life, free of the pressures and strictures of systems and doctrines, with no uniformity and no state titles or measures.
>
> The life of Rotis and at Rotis is a life of action. Not of action for action's sake, nor of action for productivity's sake, but of action to discover oneself and find one's own way of life.
>
> The action has meaning in and of itself. With the method comes knowing. Output comes from input. The outcome is inferred; moreover, it is not sought.[30]

The farm stood in a large field, with the mill canal and a country road cutting across it lengthwise. These lines and the northeast-southwest orientation of the plot and buildings conditioned the new architecture that Aicher himself would design.

> my office is a three-dimensional garden with various levels, separate workplaces. the dividing walls have fallen. the various activities take place on various platforms. but the space is an open structure. you can see the people you want to see and hear the people you want to hear. general and public things take place on the lower level. here there are drawing tables, desks, telephones and computers. special things develop on a higher level. here there are ordinary tables, pencils are enough. there are books, everything that you need for thinking.[31]

The title of the article from which this excerpt was taken, written around 1990, declares, 'My Workplace Does Not Yet Exist'. But if we compare this statement with the structural drawings created specifically for this publication, we find it easier to understand the architecture and Aicher's words: 'my office is a three-dimensional garden with various levels, separate workplaces.'

Steel rings made at a foundry in Bizkaia. Photograph: Bloomberg

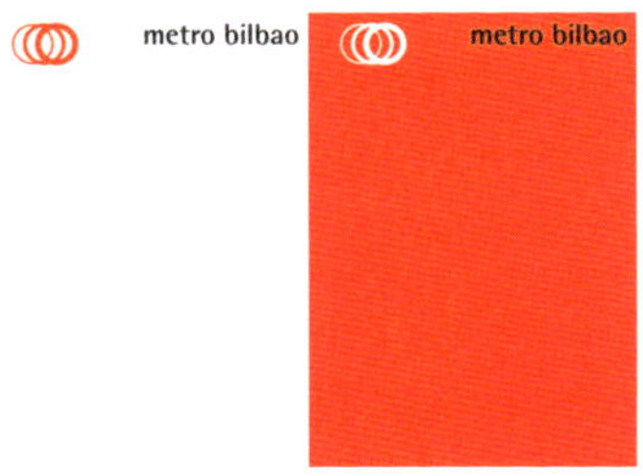

Otl Aicher. Metro Bilbao project, autumn/winter 1988

[30] Aicher, 'Complementary Study' in *Bilbao*, cit. R255.

[31] Aicher, 'My Workspace Does Not Yet Exist' in *The World as Design*, 142.

Looking at the general ground plan, we see that what was once farmland has now become a property whose primary purpose is to be seen and roamed. The four-hectare plot is divided into one hectare of buildings, two of open fields, and one of wooded land. The new buildings rise above the meadow. The nearest views are of grassy meadows, but in the distance to the northeast and to the sides, oak and pine groves rise up, concealing the road. To the southwest, the prospect marches over a wide open field, interrupted at various intervals by small stands of oak trees that act as screens or backdrops to create a sense of depth and balance between the steady flatness of the meadow and the tree clusters that mark the boundaries of the domain.

Aicher eliminated barriers. He diverted the road, moving it off the property so that people could move freely among the different structures. Between 1971 and 1991, he designed a complex in which he set his own house (5) and the studios he needed to work. He placed the printshop on the southwest side of the stable (16), and the other half of the building—the colder but more impressive northeast side, which originally housed cows—was turned into a canteen for collaborators and social gatherings. He erected a new pavilion atop the walls of the old mill (17). The ground floor housed the hydroelectric machinery and heating equipment, but the upper level had no specific use and remained empty. Aicher made the most of the existing foundations. He built four new structures of his own design: first his own studio (12) and the photography workshop (18), and later a pavilion for the archive (14) and a cabin (x). He also designed a tower with a zigzag roof (y), intended as another studio but never actually built. Life, work and energy independence in contact with nature were the ideas that underpinned the entire complex.

Aicher's interest in architecture was nothing new. At the HfG Ulm he had worked with Hans Gugelot on the design of the Braun pavilions, proposing two systems: one for indoor exhibitions (Düsseldorf, 1955) and another for outdoor use (Frankfurt, 1959). Using the components of the 1959 pavilion, while on holiday in Tellaro in August 1960 he came up with a project—*entwurf eines mehrzeck - bausystems für ein - bis eineinhalbgesschossige bauten* [design of a multi-purpose construction system for one to one-and-a-half-storey buildings]—which he used to design everything from a bedroom to an entire estate, complete with homes, shops and workplaces. The memory of those earlier projects lives on in architecture of Rotis, in its distribution and how the different units are interrelated. We might say that several different memories converge at Rotis. The floor plans of the house and stables recall the aforementioned compositions designed in 1960. The history of the place is present in the farm and mill, where the main buildings or the foundations of old structures determined the size and position of the five new additions: Aicher's studio (12), the mill room (17), the

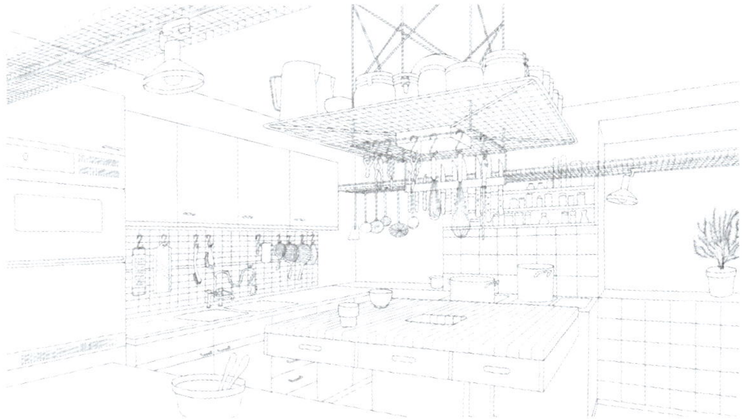

Plan and drawing for the Bulthaup kitchen prototype. In Otl Aicher, *Die Küche zum Kochem. Das Ende einer Architekturdoktrin*, (Munich: Callwey, 1982), 66 and 46–47.

Kitchen of the Rotis house, March 2020. Photograph: Gillermo Zuaznabar

photography workshop (18), the archive (14) and the cabin (x). Grouped around the family residence (5), the order of the buildings forms an urban-density cluster. The new structures contrast with the traditional architecture. Both Aicher's studio and the photography workshop sit 2.26 metres above the ground, resting on widely spaced metal columns that form a sequence of four 4.5 x 5 metre bays. This grid creates a porch (10 x 18 metres) without dividing walls. The roof with its vertical skylights, facing northeast, has a sawtooth outline. The industrial look of the pavilions is at odds with their structure and the black-painted wood exterior. The pilotis and floors at a height of 226 centimetres are testaments to Aicher's admiration for Le Corbusier.

> it is perhaps scarcely possible to understand what an effect it could make when someone came across the first volumes of le corbusier's work. a bookseller i was friendly with had them hidden in his cellar. i have never had a book in my hand that was as important for me politically as le corbusier's work. here freedom was not an abstraction. it manifested itself in realizations. what for most germans is only a way of thinking was demonstrated as behaviour here.[32]

The kitchen

In the early 1980s, a kitchen outfitter came to Rotis and hired Aicher to design a corporate identity for his small firm. Aicher asked about his products. After he was shown some examples, Aicher told the man, 'First you have to make good kitchens. If you don't know how to make kitchens, I can't design your corporate identity.' End of meeting. Two weeks later, the man returned. He apologised and asked if Aicher would help him to create 'good kitchens'. Aicher decided to conduct a historical, functional and aesthetic investigation into what a kitchen is, in order to understand what the new mid-century kitchen should be. He traced country kitchens, medieval kitchens, kitchens in bourgeois restaurants devoted to *la grande cuisine*, Ernst May's Frankfurt kitchen, the Munich kitchen designed by Robert Vorhoelzer and Walther Schmidt, and the objects and fabrics used to outfit them. This research, documented in the book *Die Küche zum Kochen: Das Ende einer Architekturdoktrin* (1982), yielded the now-famous Bulthaup kitchens.[33] Meanwhile, Aicher and the outfitter made alterations and created a prototype in the designer's own home. Aicher traced and retraced his own kitchen until it looked exactly like the drawing on pages 46 and 47 of the book. Heavily reliant on the world, Aicher proved that if the eye were willing to explore and refine it, the result would be an orderly world, good as new and uniquely personal.

Across the road

The last structure Aicher designed and occupied was a small cabin (x), quite similar to Le Corbusier's Cabanon. It was built at a distance from the main complex, across the road beside an orchard. This unit represented a departure from the general order and from what Aicher had always publicly defended since Ulm: the segregation of design and art, considering the latter a bourgeois expression of contemporary society.[34] On the opposite side of the road and of his own professional life, Aicher built a studio where he secretly practised the art of sculpture, keeping his hobby hidden for years, even from his own family. But a graphic record of his activity survived. On 26 August 1991, Aicher invited his collaborator, photographer Hans Neudecker, to take pictures of the busts he was modelling of Hans and Sophie Scholl. They were nearly finished, and he wanted to visually document the heads before taking them to be cast. The photographs were taken, the workday came to an end, and he headed for home. While crossing the road that separated the cabin from the complex, he was struck by a speeding motorcycle. Six days later, on 1 September, he died from his injuries in Günzburg hospital.

Canal by the Rotis studio and Rotis farm with the studio in the distance, March 2020. Photograph: Carlos Gonzalvo

[32] Aicher, 'Architecture as a Reflection of the State' in *The World as Design*, 106.

[33] The title in English would be *The Kitchen for Cooking: The End of an Architectural Doctrine*. In German, the subtitle was later changed to *Werkstatt einer neuen Lebenskultur* [Workshop for a New Lifestyle Culture].

[34] 'Anyone who has nothing to communicate looks for style, anyone who lives by materialism honours the spirit, anyone who does business is furthering culture.' Aicher, 'Bauhaus and Ulm' in *The World as Design*, 88.

vorbemerkung

diese Studie will die unterlagen des wettbewerbs für die metro bilbao vom märz 1988 erweitern und ergänzen. sie will belegen, daß das erscheinungsbild der neuen metro ein neues, erweitertes bezugsfeld braucht. im wettbewerb frühjahr 1988 wurde die metro primär verstanden als u-bahn der stadt und als anbindung der vororte an die stadt.
es zeigt sich jedoch, daß bilbao heraus-gewachsen ist aus dem stadtbereich und inzwischen eine großregion bildet. die region hat den Vorzug, daß zivilisation und natur, urbane inhalte und solche der freizeit aufeinander bezogen sind. eine solche region benötigt neue inhalte, ein neues selbstbewußtsein und ein neues selbstverständnis. die metro wird zum rückgrat und zum bindeglied. sie wird zum symbol der erneuerung aus einer ökonomischen und ökologi-schen krise.

die wölfe aus dem wappen von bilbao bieten sich an, ein hauptmotiv der visuellen sprache der großregion zu werden. wenn man sie von historischen zufälligkeiten der alten heraldik befreit, gewinnen sie eine starke visuelle wirkung. insgesamt wäre die historische heraldik zu einer neuen zeichensprache der region weiterzuent-wickeln. die umsetzung in eine heutige ästhetik ist zu verstehen als initiative der erneuerung.

Preliminary remarks

The present study proposes to complement and expand on the documentation submitted to the March 1998 Metro Bilbao competition. The study attempts to prove that the image of the new Metro requires a new structure. In the March 1988 design competition, the Metro was primarily envisioned as an underground system for connecting the suburbs to the city centre. However, Bilbao has clearly spread beyond its metropolitan area and become a greater region.
The advantage of the region is the convergence of civilisation and nature, urban and recreational facilities. Such a region requires new contents and a new awareness of itself. The Metro thus becomes the backbone, ligament and symbol of recovery from an economic and environmental crisis.

The wolves on the Bilbao coat of arms present themselves as the central motif of the greater region's visual language. Freed from the historical vagaries of ancient heraldry, they have a strong visual impact. In short, historical heraldry must become the new symbolic language of the region. Its adaptation to today's aesthetics should be seen as an initiative of renewal.

vorbemerkung

diese studie will die unterlagen des wettbewerbs für die metro bilbao vom märz 1988 erweitern und ergänzen. sie will belegen, daß das erscheinungsbild der neuen metro ein neues bezugsfeld braucht.

im wettbewerb frühjahr 1988 wurde die metro primär verstanden als u-bahn der stadt und als anbindung der vororte an die stadt

es zeigt sich jedoch, daß bilbao herausgewachsen ist aus dem stadtbereich und inzwischen eine großregion bildet. die region hat den vorzug, daß zivilisation und natur, urbane inhalte und solche der freizeit aufeinander bezogen sind. eine solche region benötigt neue inhalte, ein neues selbstbewußtsein und ein neues selbstverständnis. die metro wird zum rückgrat und zum bindeglied. sie wird zum symbol der erneuerung aus einer ökonomischen und ökologischen krise.

die wölfe aus dem wappen von bilbao bieten sich an, ein hauptmotiv der visuellen sprache der großregion zu werden. wenn man sie von historischen zufälligkeiten der alten heraldik befreit, gewinnen sie eine starke visuelle wirkung. insgesamt wäre die historische heraldik zu einer neuen zeichensprache der region weiterzuentwickeln. die umsetzung in eine heutige ästhetik ist zu verstehen als initiative zur erneuerung.

1.

colours heraldry history

FBB Bilbao

die dominierende farbe der metro ist rot.rot ist die dominierende farbe in den stadtfarben von bilbao (rot und weiß) sowie die dominierende farbe in der flagge des baskenlandes (rot, grün und weiß). es erscheint wichtig, daß die farben der metro sich auf die heraldische tradition beziehen und damit die identität der region auch für die zukunft sichern.

als emblem der metro kann ent-weder der entwurf des wettbewerbs beibehalten werden, er kann aber auch in einer modifikation angewendet werden im sinne einer deutlicheren aussage, als einheit der drei schwerpunkte

1 stadt
2 hafen, werften, industrie
3 riviera

das zeichen erscheint an den fahr-zeugen, auf drucksachen und als symbol der stationseingänge. auch als zweidimensionales zeichen ist es in einem sichtbereich von nahezug 360° erkennbar.

Red is the predominant colour in the Metro. Red is also the predominant colour in the city of Bilbao (red and white), and likewise in the flag of the Basque Country (red, green and white). It seems important that the Metro colours should be rooted in heraldic tradition, thereby ensuring the region's identity in the future.

For the emblem of the Metro, the competition design can be maintained or reworked with some useful modification to underscore or clarify the three focal points:

1 City
2 Port, shipyards, industry
3 Riverside

The symbol appears on vehicles, on printed materials and as a sign at the station entrances. The symbol, in two dimensions, is also recognisable from every angle in a 360° field of vision.

die dominierende farbe der metro ist rot.
rot ist die dominierende farbe in den stadtfarben von bilbao (rot und weiß) sowie die dominierende farbe in der flagge des baskenlandes (rot, grün und weiß). es erscheint wichtig, daß die farben der metro sich auf die heraldische tradition beziehen und damit die identität der region auch für die zukunft sichern.

als emblem der metro kann entweder der entwurf des wettbewerbs beibehalten werden, er kann aber auch in einer modifikation angewendet werden im sinne einer deutlicheren aussage als einheit von den drei schwerpunkten

1 stadt
2 hafen, werften, industrie
3 riviera

das zeichen erscheint an den fahrzeugen, auf drucksachen und als symbol der stationseingänge. auch als zweidimensionales zeichen ist es in einem sichtbereich von nahezu 360° erkennbar.

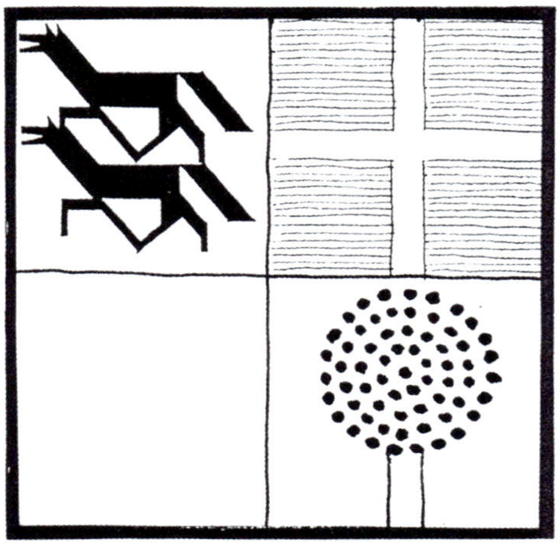

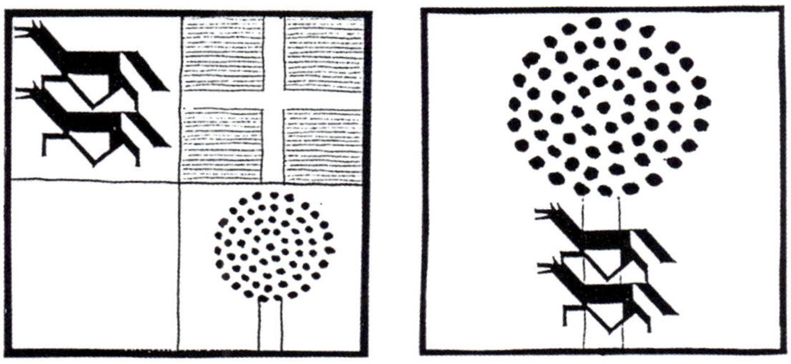

1

2

3

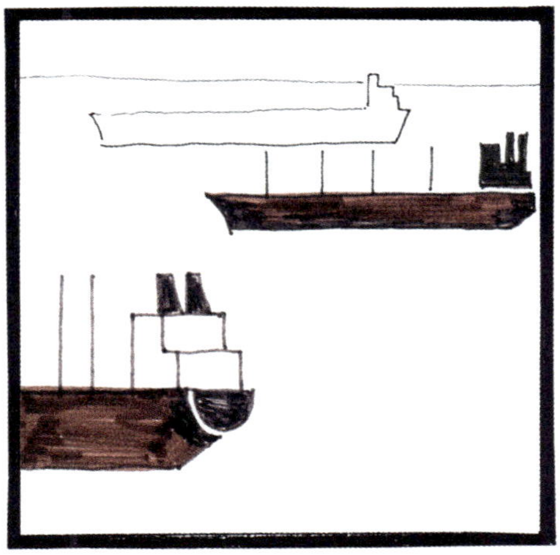

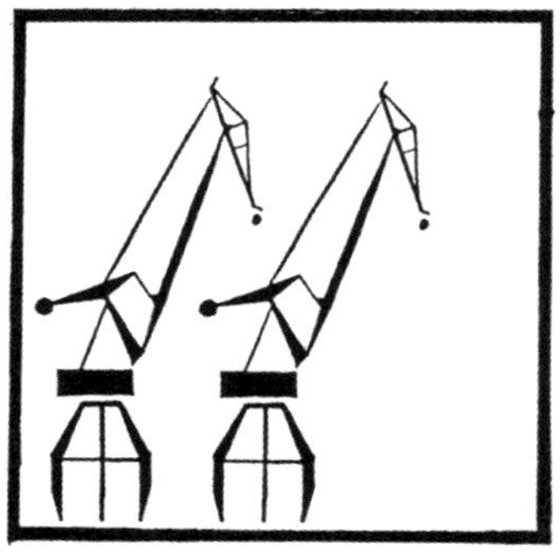

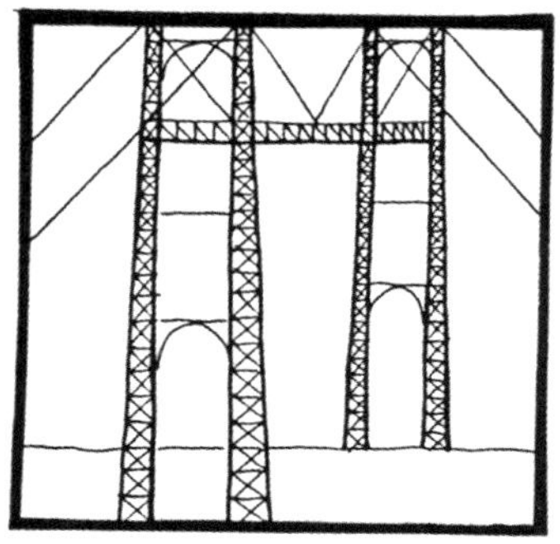

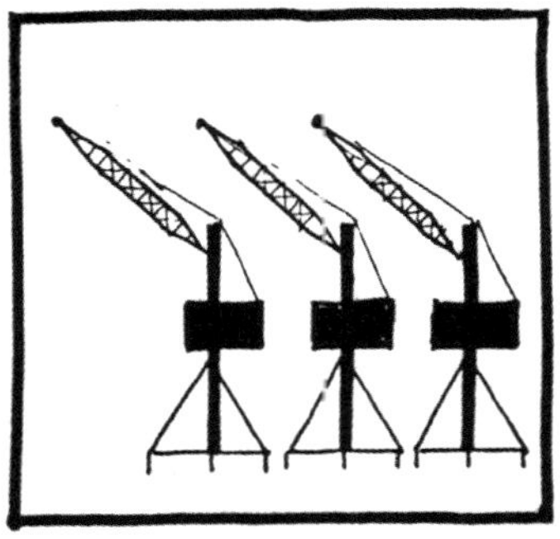

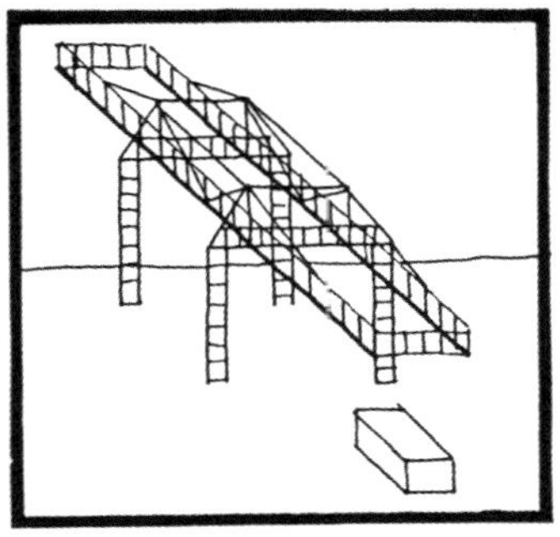

2.

the region

R2 65

Titulo
Headline
Überschrift

Metro Bilbao

Metro Bilbao

Metro Bilbao

Metro Bilbao

Metro Bilbao

Metro Bilbao

Metro Bilbao

Metro Bilbao

Metro Bilbao

Metro Bilbao

was ist bilbao?

strukturwandel von einer stadt an einem
fluß zu einer großregion am meer

What is Bilbao?

The transformation of a city by a river
in a greater region by the sea

was ist bilbao?

strukturwandel von einer stadt am
fluß
zu einer großregion am meer

die hafenregion erweitert sich von der
stadt bis zur flußmündung

The port area extends from the city to the river mouth.

die hafenregion erstreckt sich
von der stadt bis zur flußmündung

ursprüngliche siedlungen
algorta
portugalete
barakaldo
bilbao

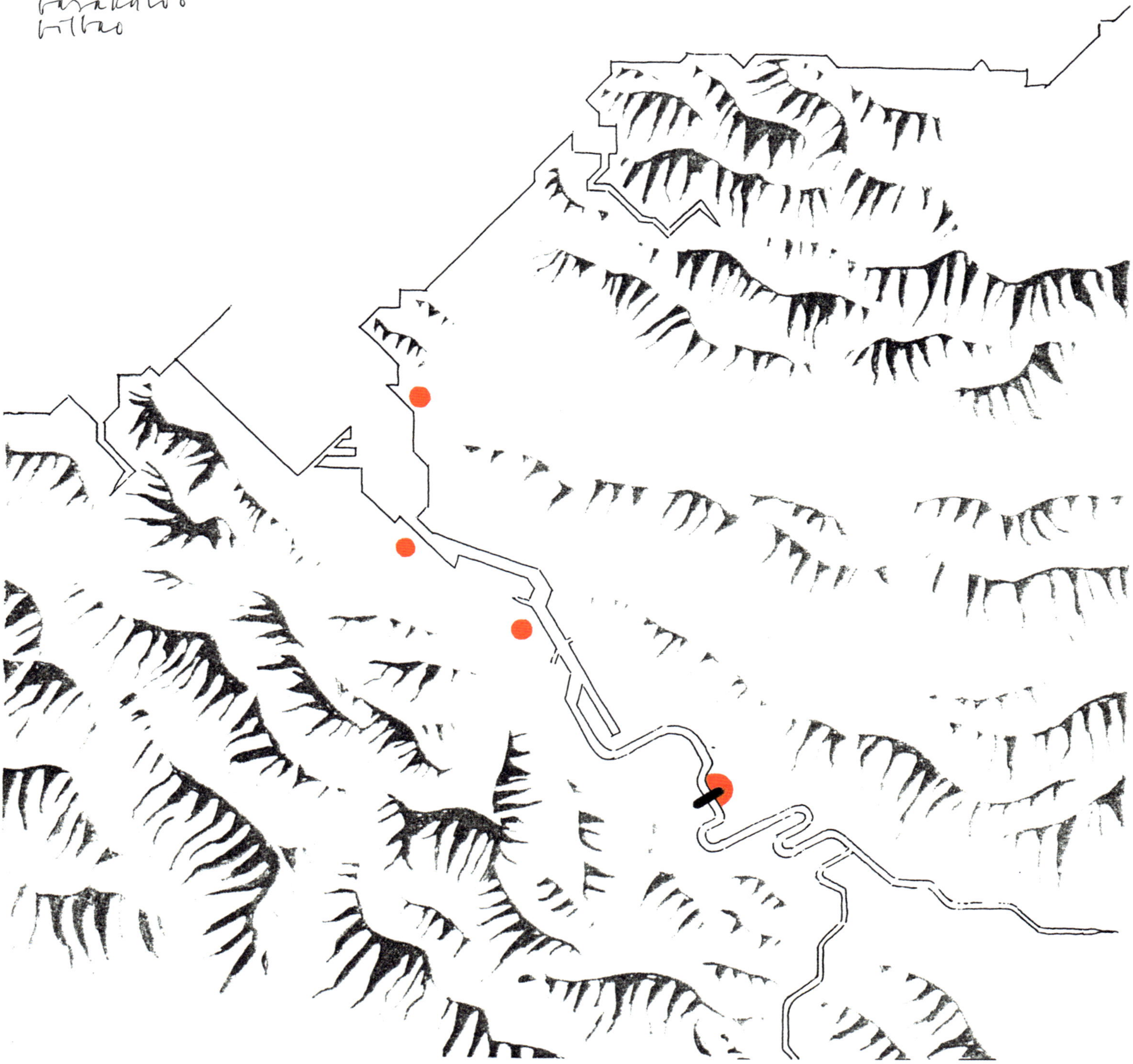

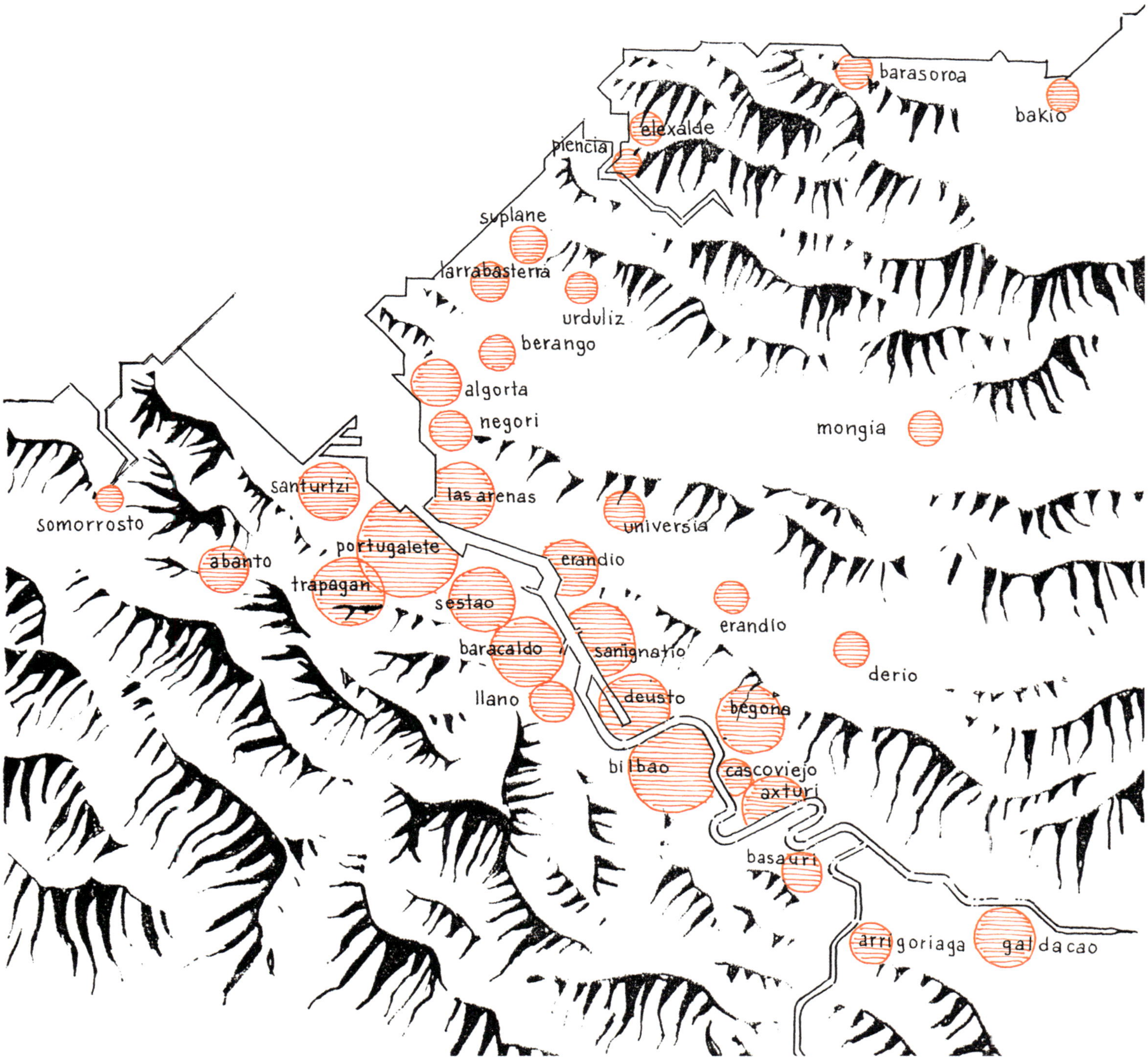
barasoroa
bakio
elexalde
plencia
suplane
larrabasterra
urduliz
berango
algorta
negori
mongia
santurtzi
las arenas
somorrosto
universia
portugalete
abanto
erandio
trapagan
sestao
erandio
baracaldo
sanignatio
derio
llano
deusto
begoña
bilbao
cascoviejo
axturi
basauri
arrigoriaga
galdacao

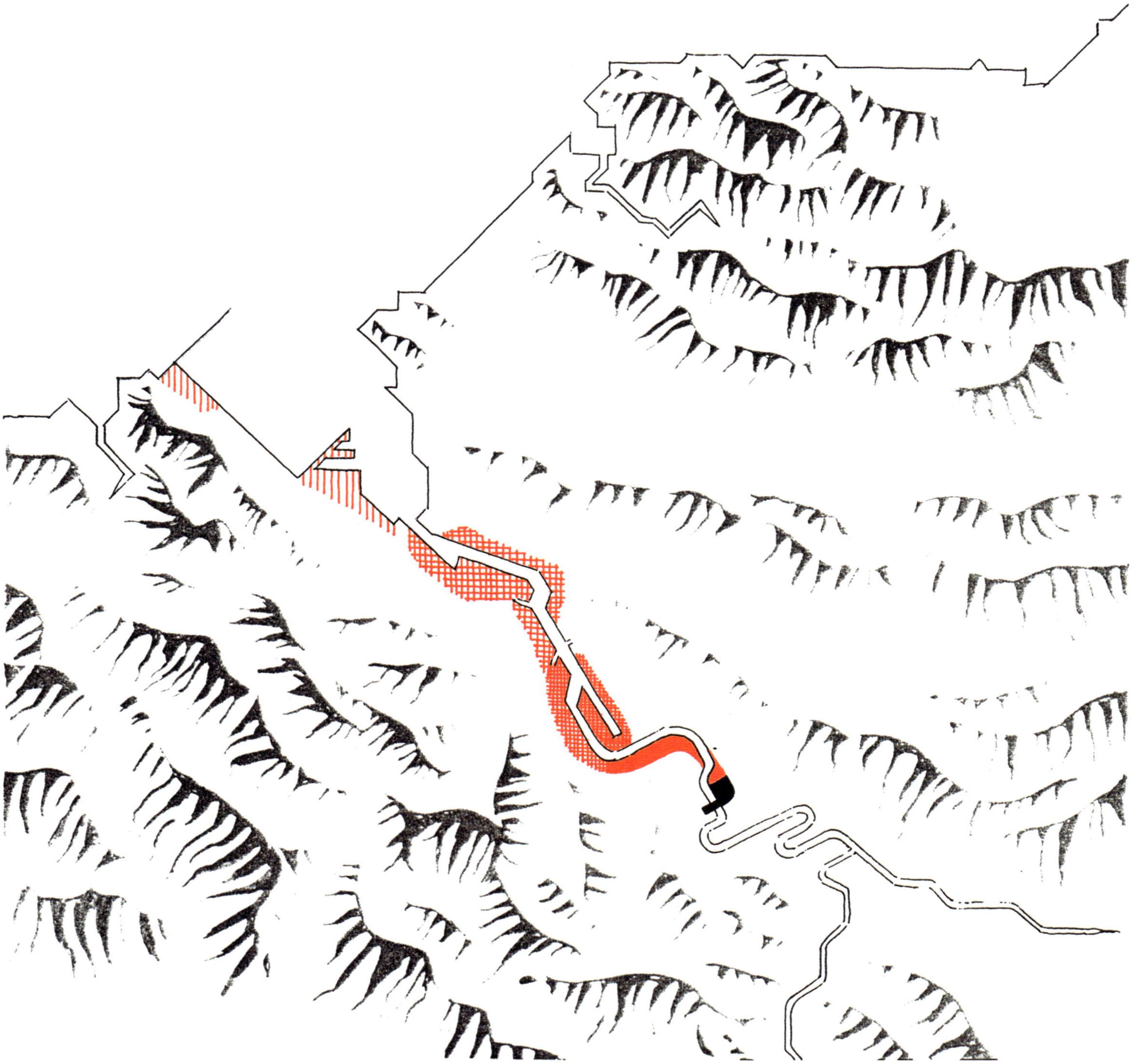

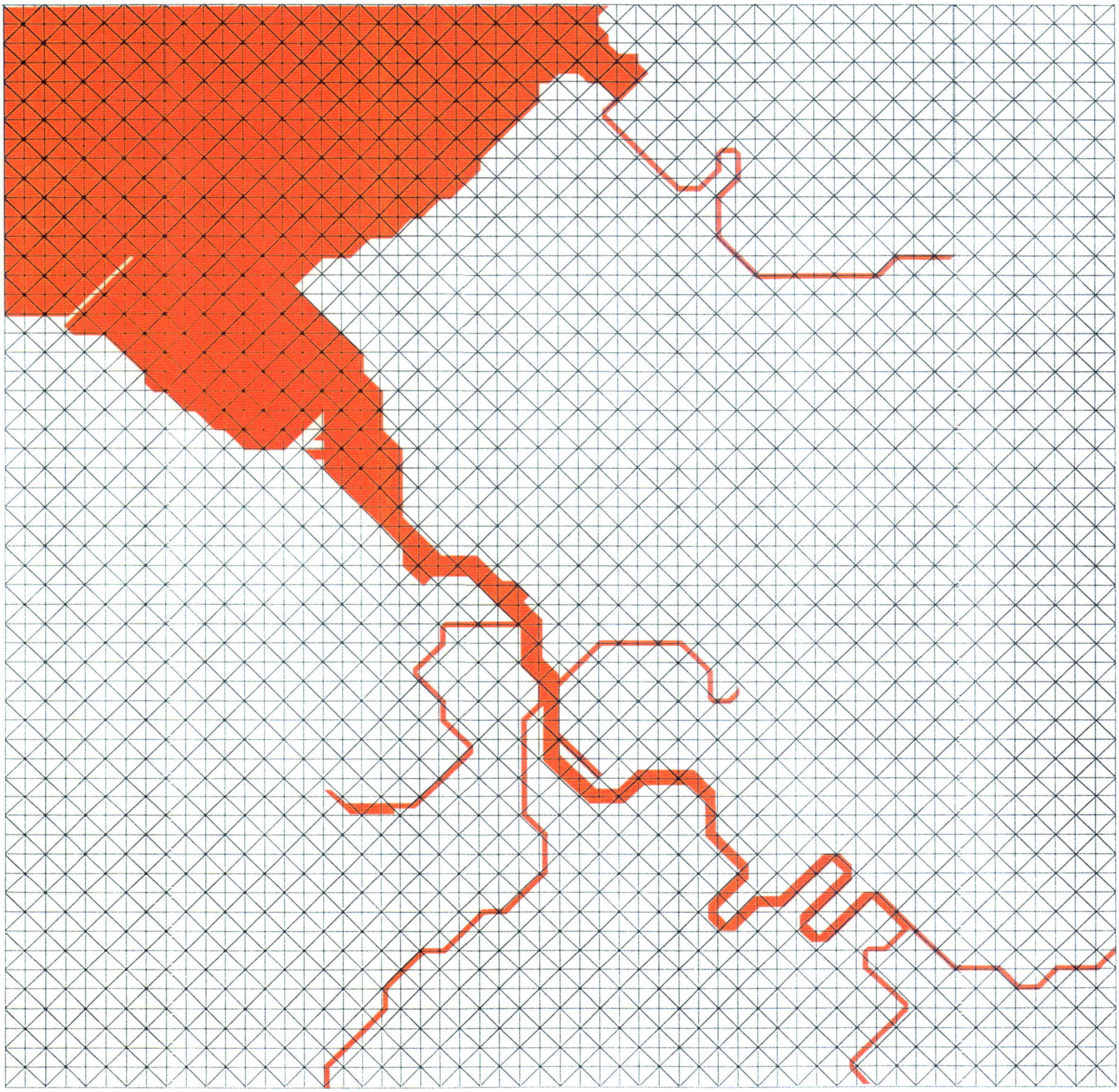

die region ist als eine komplexe einheit zu verstehen
mit unterschiedlichen inhalten. sie umfaßt

1
ein stadgebeit mit historischem kern, geschäfts, verwaltungs und verkehrszentrum

2
eine hafen- und industrieregion mit werften und schwerindustrie

3
eine landschaftsregion mit frei-zeittinhalten (riviera).

The region should be seen as a complex whole with different parts. These include:

1
A metropolitan area with a historic quarter and business, administrative and transport centres.

2
A port and industrial zone with shipyards and heavy industry.

3
A countryside with recreational areas (riverside).

die region ist als eine komplexe einheit zu verstehen mit unterschiedlichen inhalten. sie umfaßt

1
ein stadtgebiet mit historischem kern, geschäft- verwaltungs- kultur- und verkehrszentrum

2
eine hafen und industrie region mit werften und schwerindustrie

3
eine landschaftsregion mit freizeit inhalten (riviera).

FBB

Ferrocarril
Bahia
Bilbao

FBB

Ferrocarril
Bahia
Bilbao

FBB

Ferrocarril
Bahia
Bilbao

FBB

Ferrocarril
Bahia
Bilbao

FBB

Ferrocarril
Bahia
Bilbao

MBB

Metro
Bahia
Bilbao

MBB

Metro
Bahia
Bilbao

MBB

Metro
Bahia
Bilbao

MBB

Metro
Bahia
Bilbao

MBB

Metro
Bahia
Bilbao

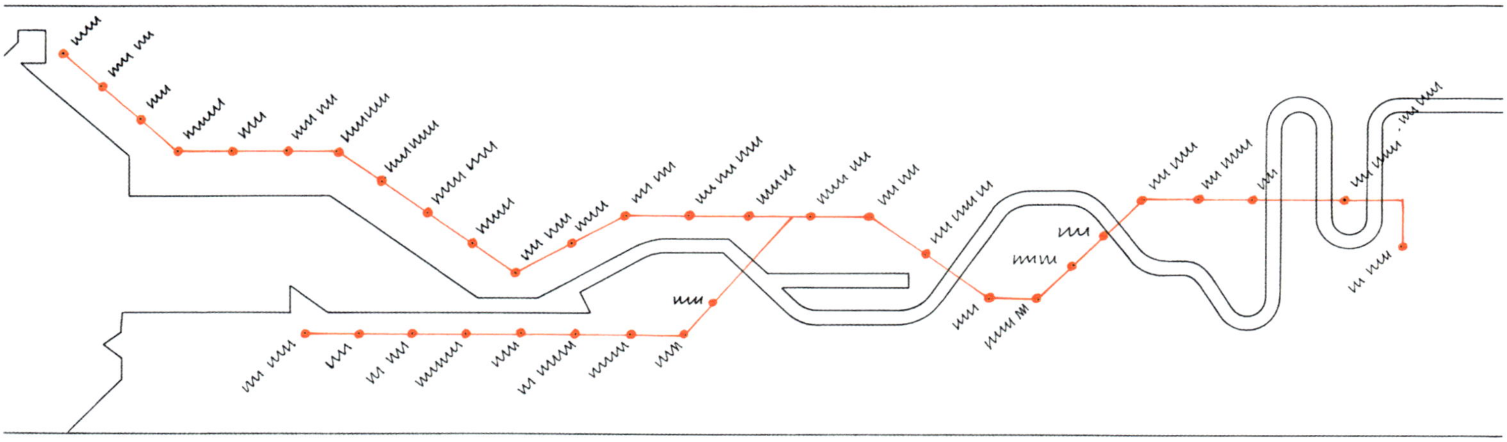

Getxo
Algorta
Aiboa
Neguri
Lamiaco
Ondiz
Axpe
Erandio
Lutxana
1
Llano
Cruces
2
Santurtzi
Peñota
Portugalete
Abatxolo
Sesfao
Urbinaga
Baracaldo I
Baracaldo II

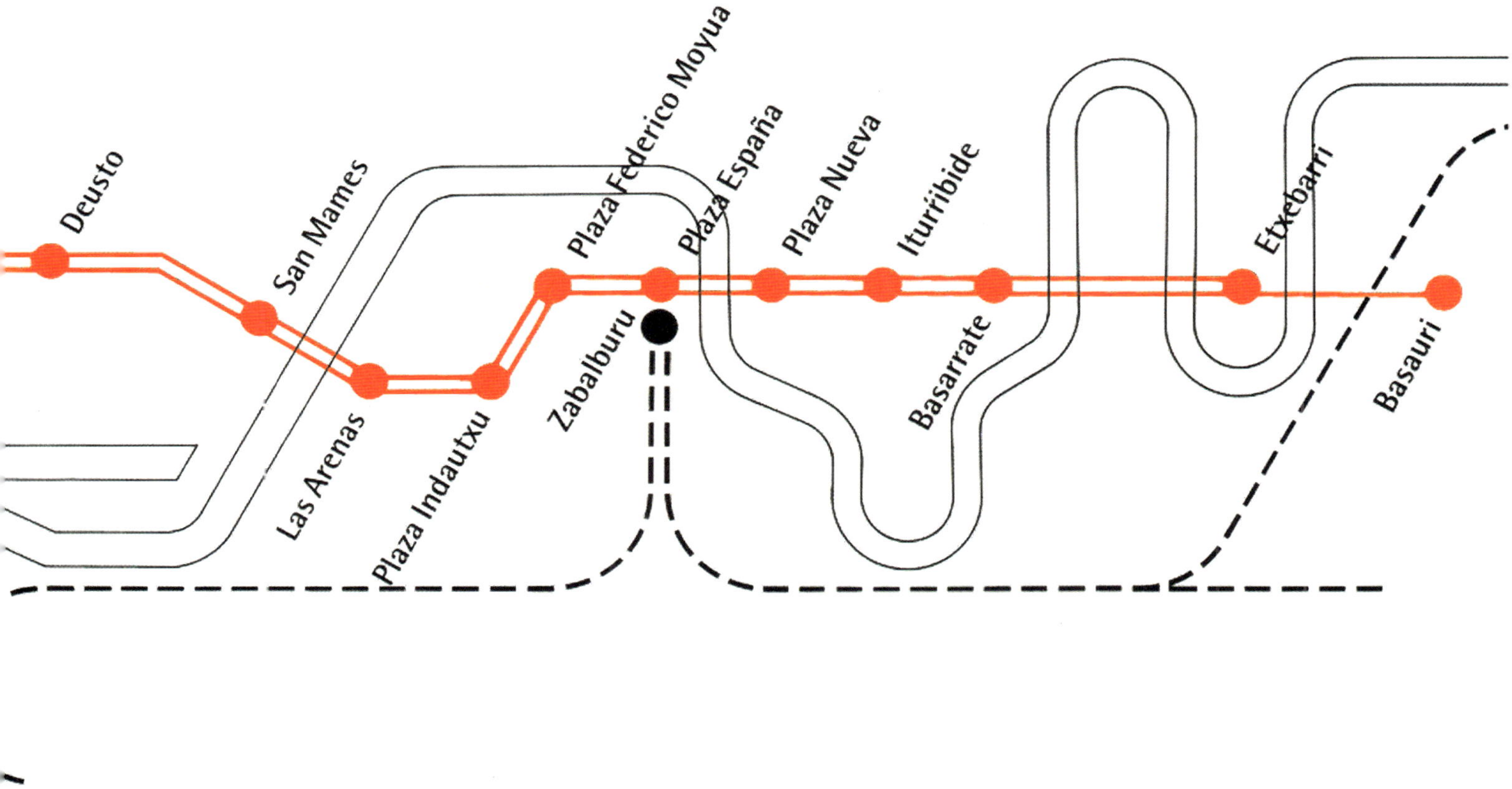
Deusto
San Mames
Las Arenas
Plaza Indautxu
Plaza Federico Moyua
Zabalburu
Plaza España
Plaza Nueva
Iturribide
Basarrate
Etxebarri
Basauri

3.

bird's-eye and ground-level views of the metro

plaucia

die region dokumentiert auf ein-dringliche weise das ende einer industriellen zivilisation, die auf die mechanische technik aufgebaut war. die zukunft gehört einer elektronischen und einer physikalis chchemisch orientierten technologie. diese setzt einen höheren bildungsstandard voraus und gibt der erziehung und der kultur einen neuen stellenwert.

zur kultur dieser region sollte gehören, daß man die industrielle revolution des 19. und 20. Jahrhunderts archäologisch und historisch aufarbeitet und in technik-museen zusammenfaßt und darstellt.

mögliche schwerpunkte könnten sein ein technik-museum, ein park mit werft-kränen, die einen hohen suggestiven Charakter haben und ein schiffsmuseum

ebenfalls von besonderer bedeutung ist der ausbau der erziehungseinrichtungen sowie die errichtung von zentren neuer technologie.

alle diese einrichtungen lassen sich als stationen an die metro anbinden. sie erhält damit eine höhere attraktivität.

The region clearly documents the end of an industrial civilisation built with mechanical technology. The future belongs to a technology more focused on electronics, physics and chemistry, which implies a higher level of studies and increases the value and relevance of education and culture.

The culture of this region has a duty to analyse, archaeologically and historically, the industrial revolution of the 19th and 20th centuries, and to summarise and exhibit it in museums of technology.

The focal points could be a technology museum, a park with the highly suggestive shipyard cranes, and a naval museum.

It is just as important to build educational institutions and create centres of new technology.

All these facilities could be connected by Metro stations, thus increasing their attractiveness.

die region dokumentiert auf eindringliche weise das ende einer industriellen zivilisation, die auf die mechanische technik aufgebaut war. die zukunft gehört einer elektronischen und einer physikalisch-chemisch orientierten technologie. diese setzt einen höheren bildungsstandard voraus und gibt der erziehung und der kultur einen neuen stellenwert.

zur kultur dieser region sollte gehören, daß man die industrielle revolution des 19. und 20. jahrhunderts archeologisch und historisch aufarbeitet und in technik-museen zusammenfaßt und darstellt.

mögliche schwerpunkte könnten sein ein technik-museum, ein park mit werft-kränen, die einen hohen suggestiven charakter haben und ein schiffsmuseum

ebenfalls von besonderer bedeutung ist der ausbau der erziehungseinrichtungen, sowie die errichtung von zentren neuer technologie.

alle diese einrichtungen lassen sich als stationen an die metro anbinden. sie erhält damit eine höhere attraktivität.

basauri

san mames

sestao

portugalete

negurí

getxo

semantik einer fahrt

die metro der region erschließt
unterschiedliche erlebnisbereiche und macht ihre inhalte erfahrbar. sie verknüpft die unterschiedlichen erfahrungswerte zu einem regionalen gesamtprogramm.

insofern reicht ihre funktion weit über ein verkehrstechnisches problem hinaus. diese inhalte sind im einzelnen zu definieren und in die kommunikation der region, sei sie verbaler oder visueller art, einzubringen.

Semantics of a journey

The region's Metro explores different areas of experience and offers various contents to enjoy. It connects diverse sensations in one comprehensive regional programme.

That is why its function extends beyond the technological problem of transport. Each of those contents must be defined separately and integrated in the region's communication plan, whether that communication is verbal or visual.

semantik einer fahrt

die metro der region erschließt unterschiedliche erlebnisbereiche und macht ihre inhalte erfahrbar. sie verknüpft die unterschiedlichen erfahrungswerte zu einem regionalen gesamtprogramm.

insofern reicht ihre funktion weit über ein verkehrstechnisches problem hinaus. diese inhalte sind im einzelnen zu definieren und in die kommunikation der region, sei sie verbaler oder visueller art, einzubringen.

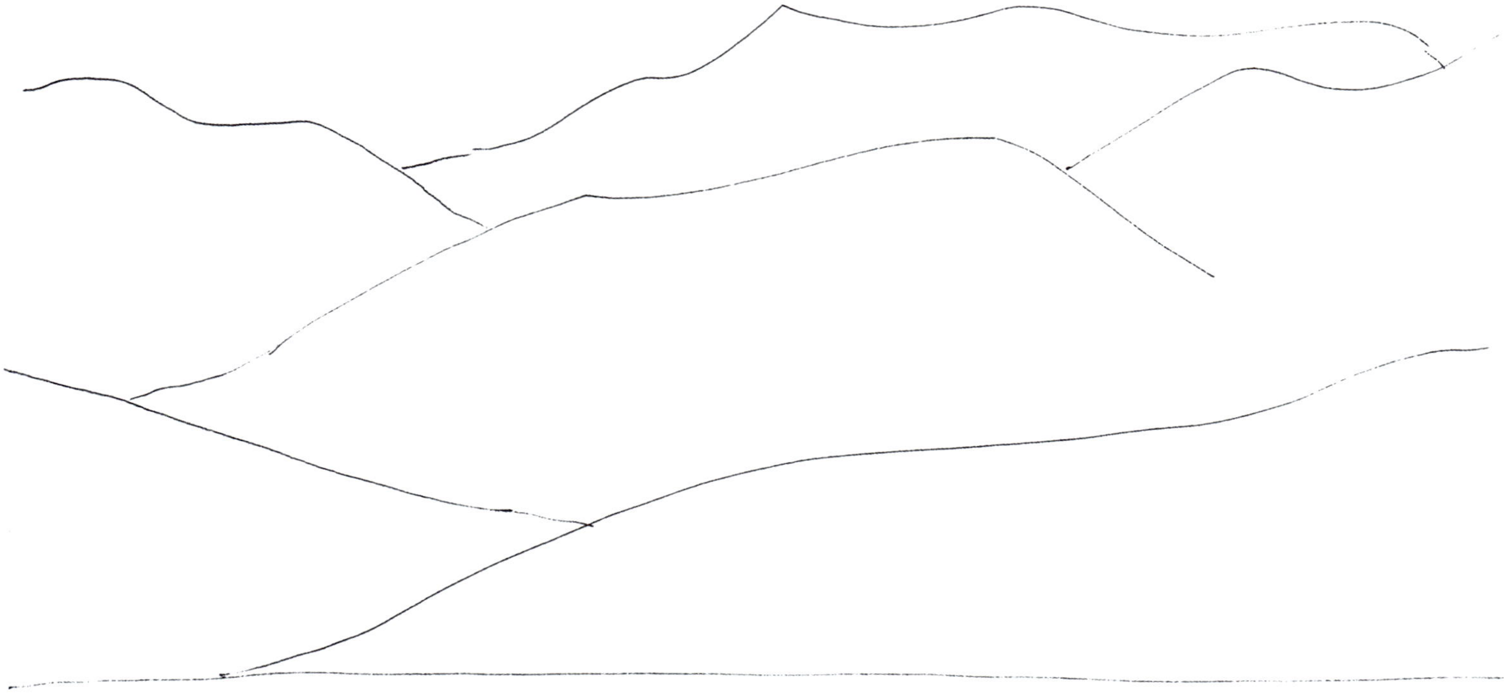

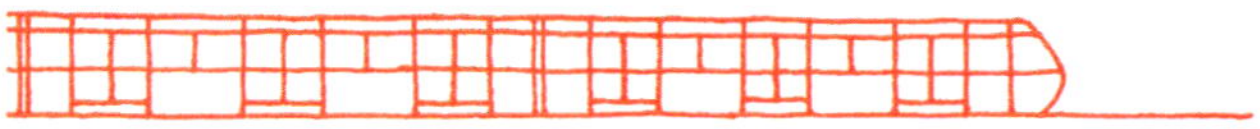

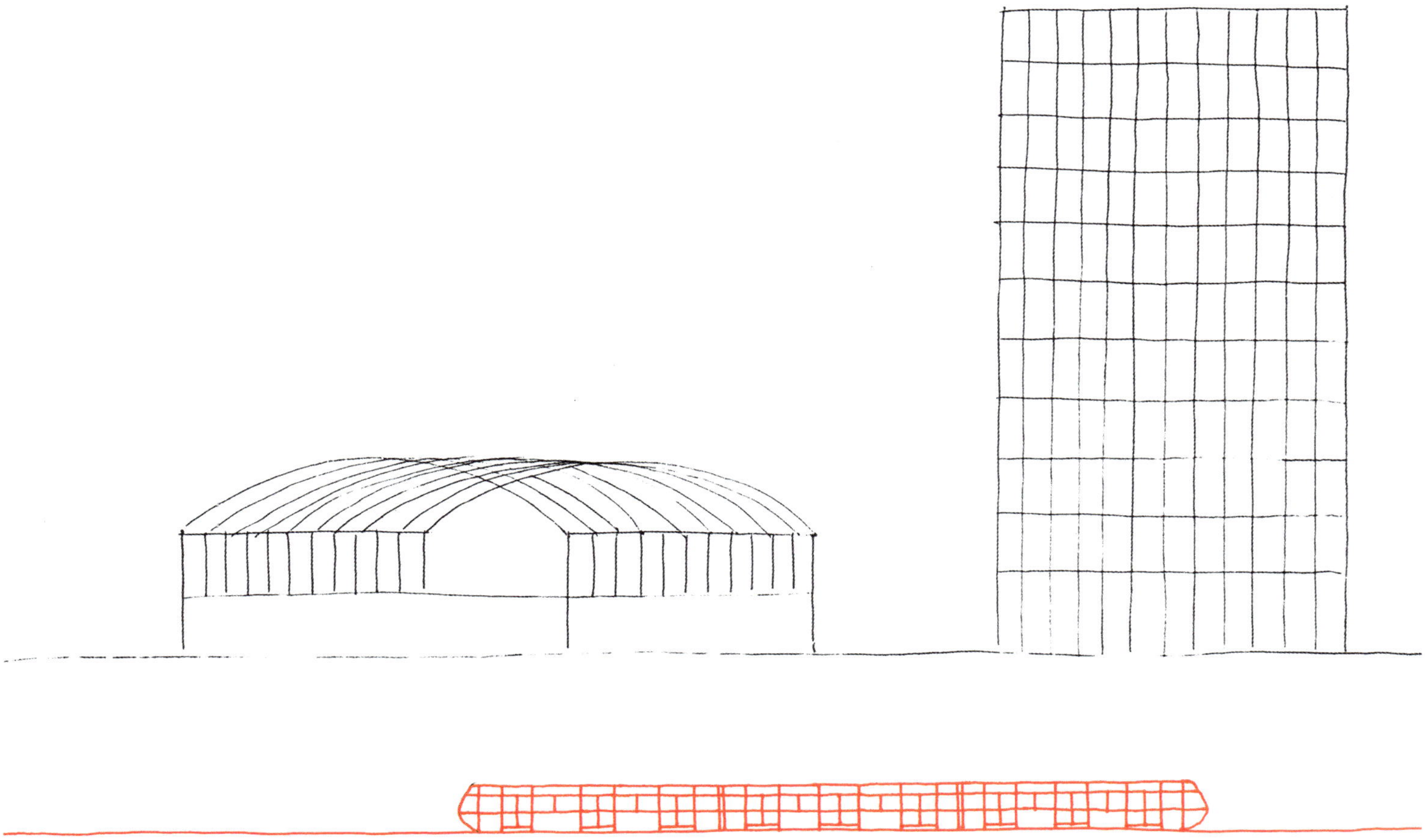

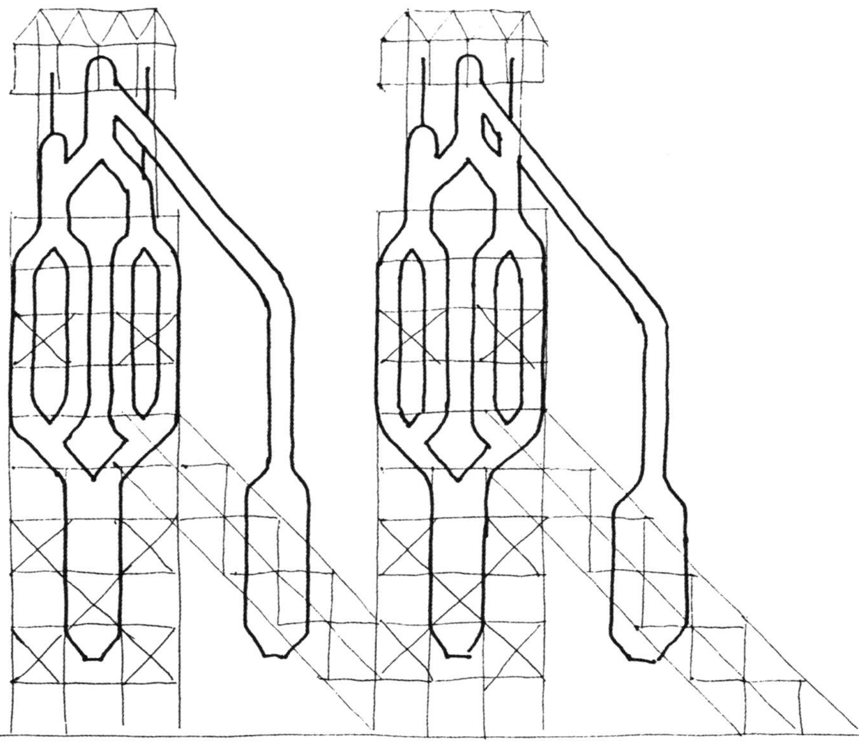

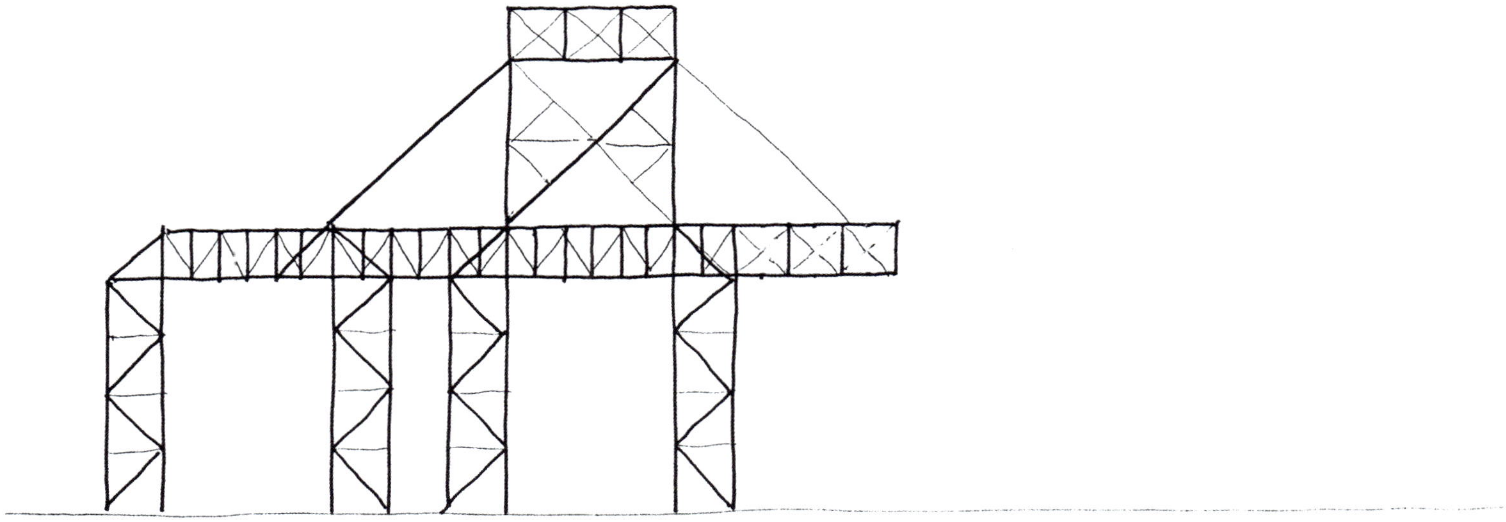

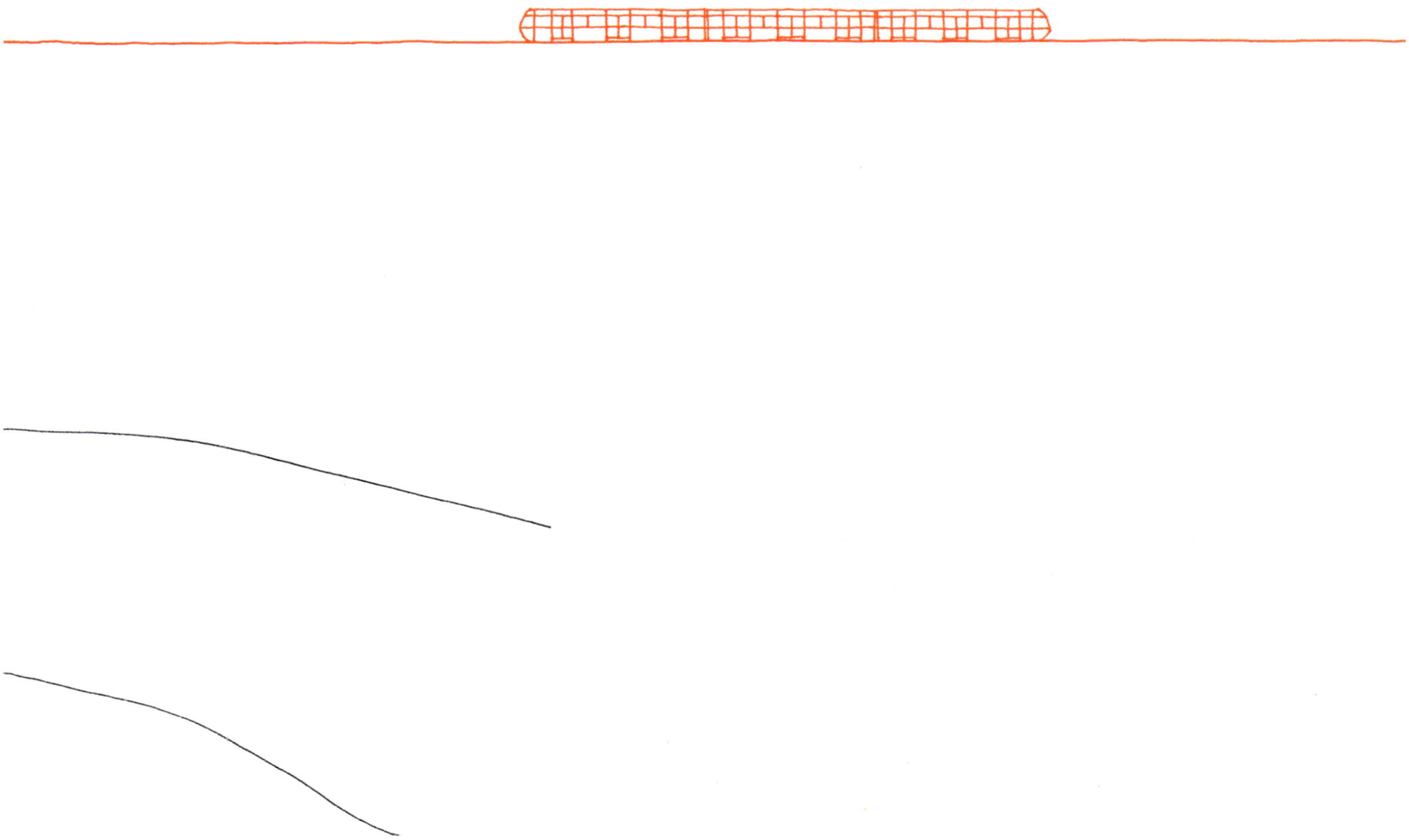

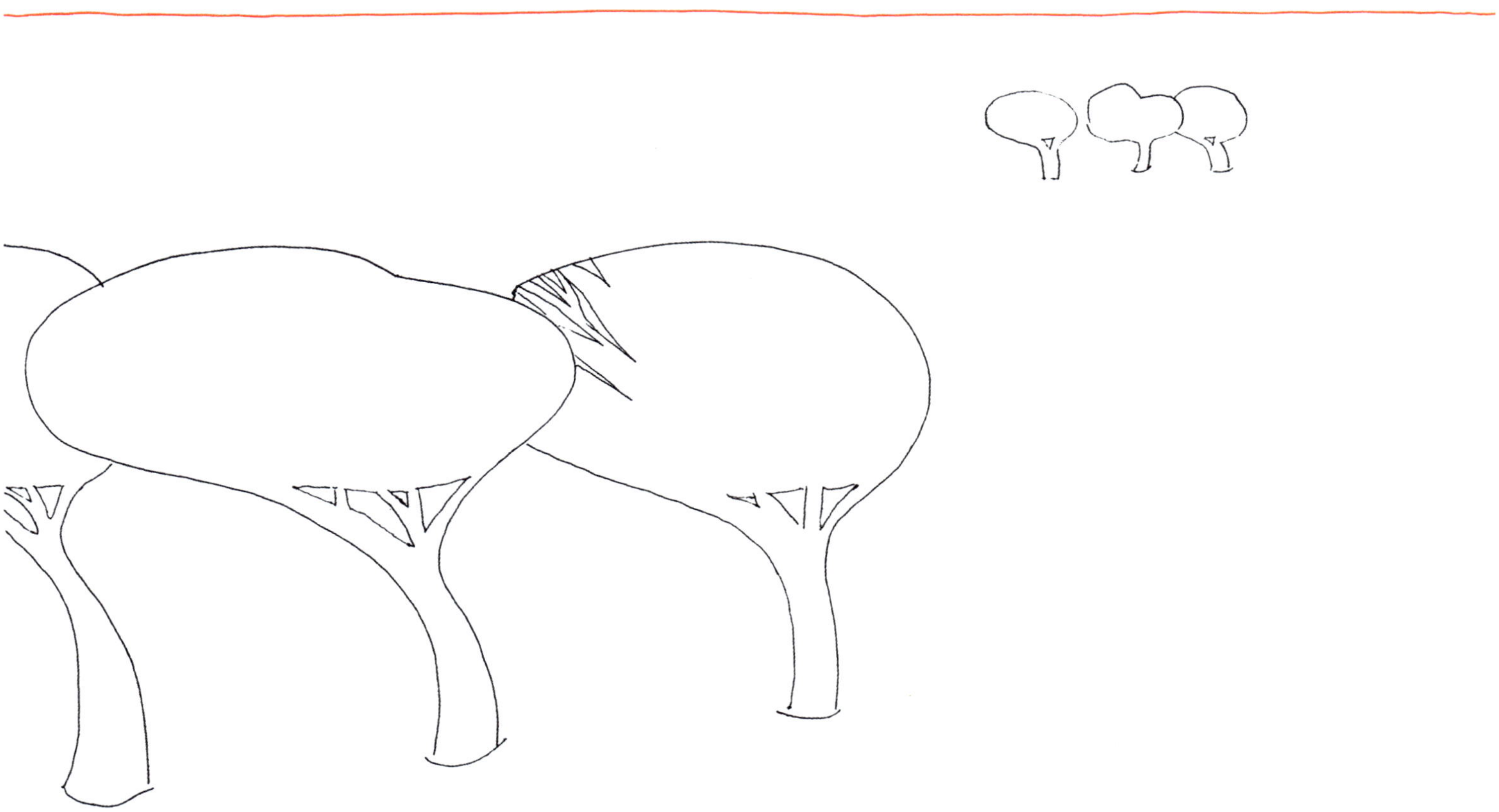

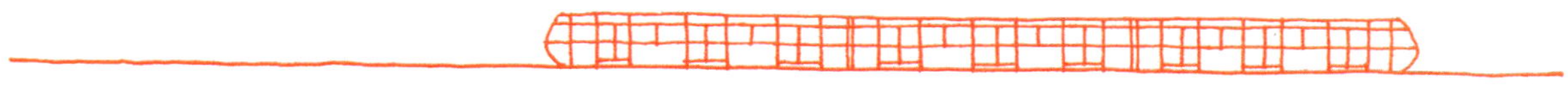

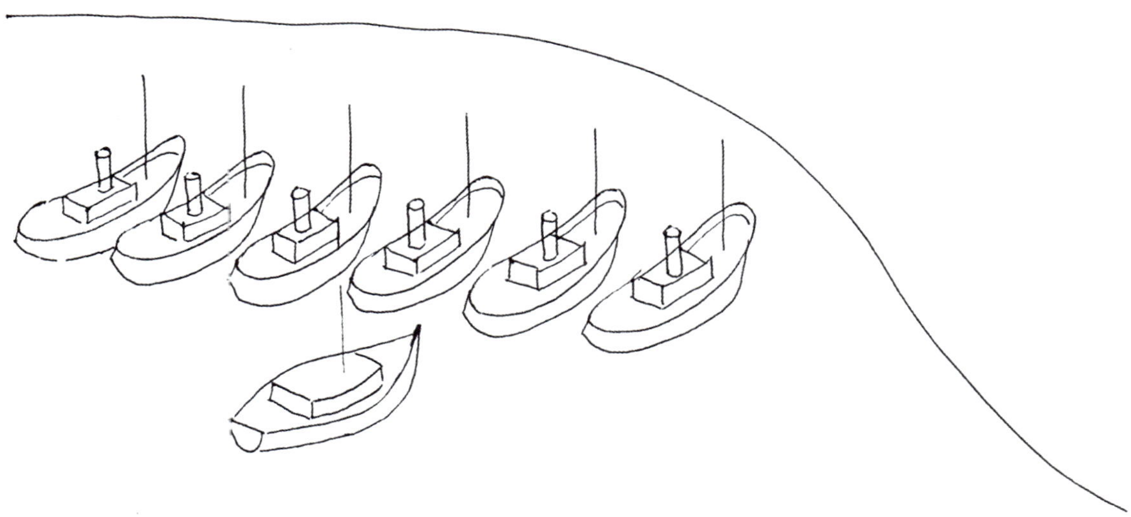

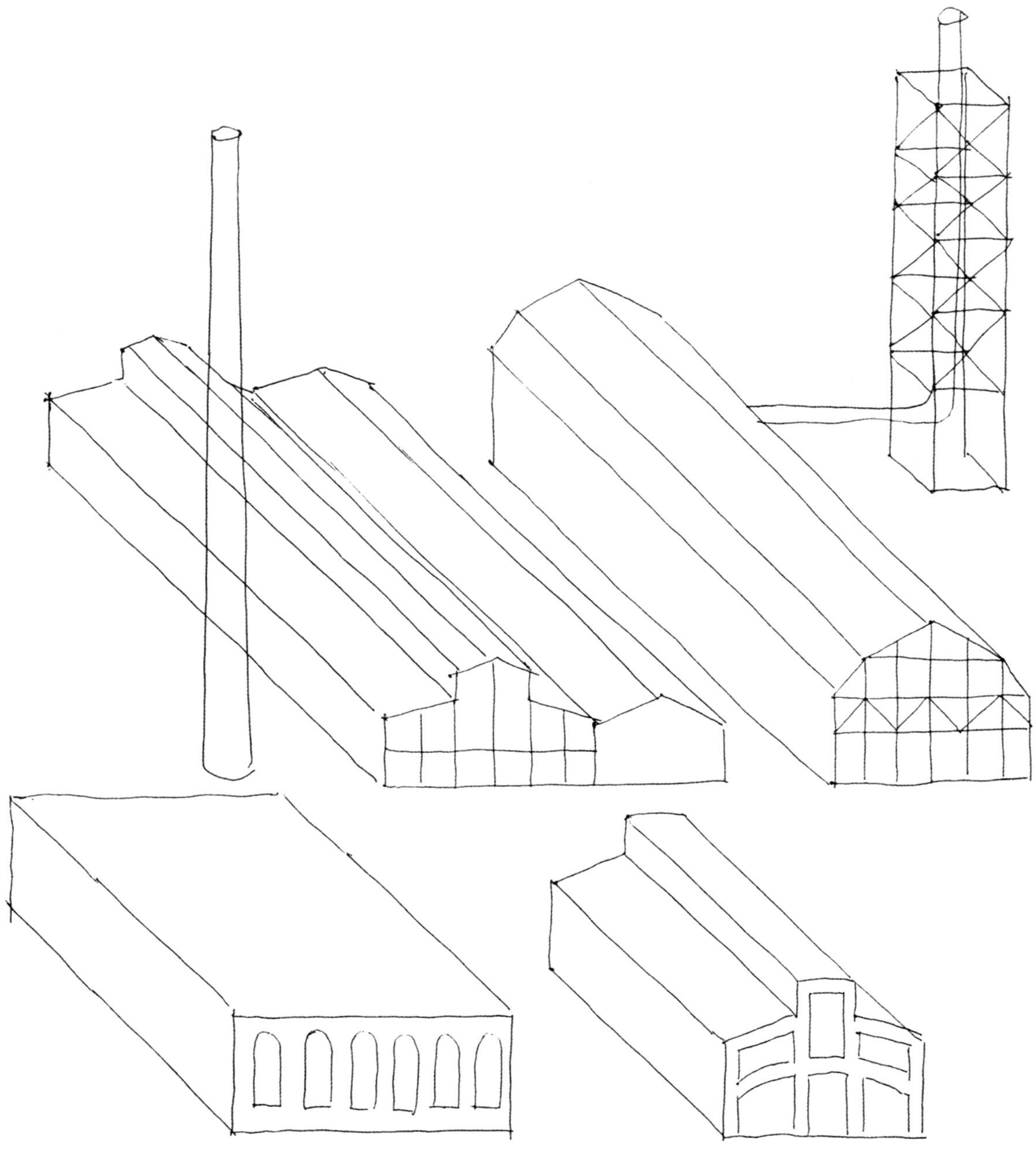

Plaza España
Plaza España
MBB

Plaza España
Plaza Españ
MBB

4.

conclusion

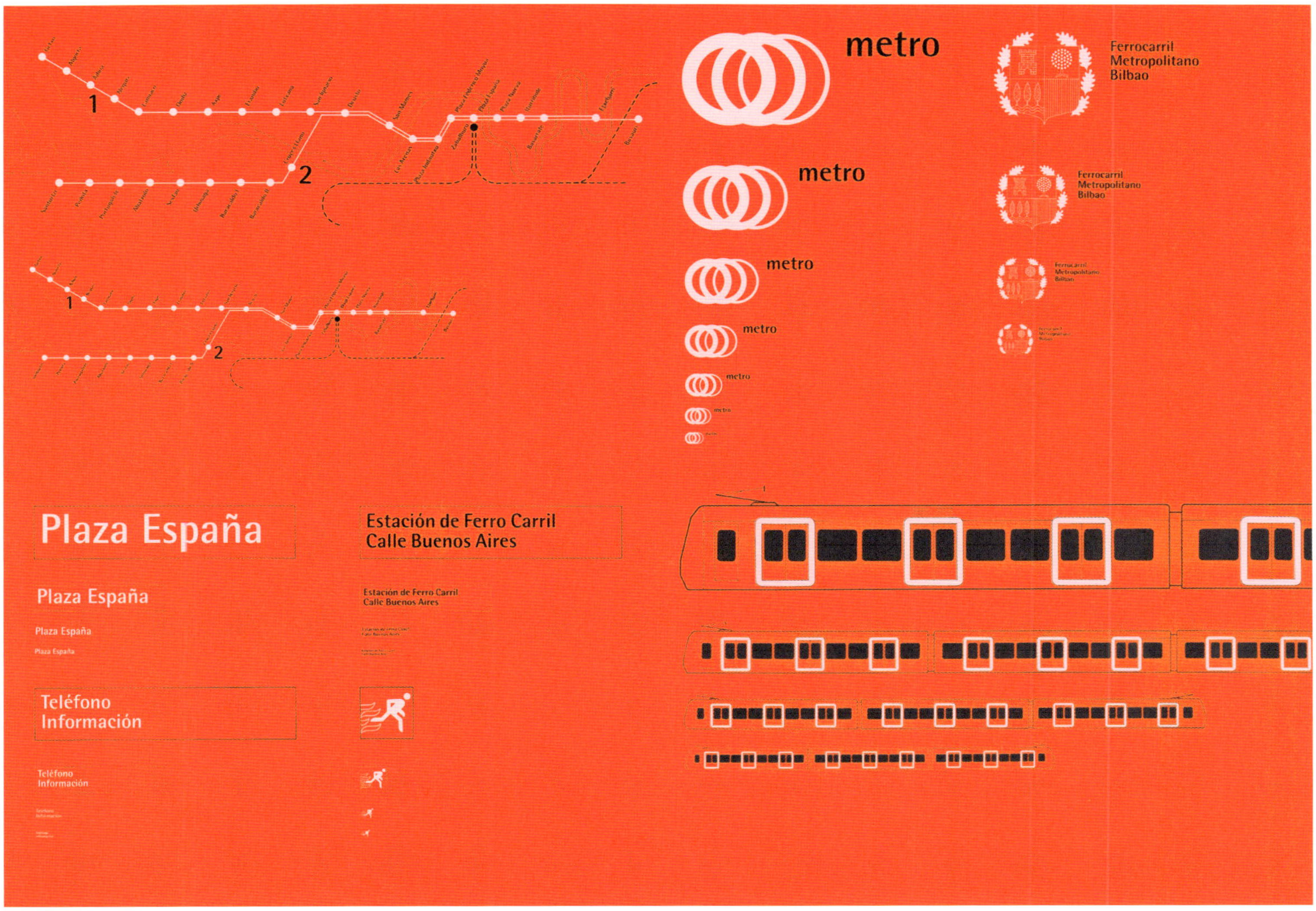
metro
Ferrocarril
Metropolitano
Bilbao
Plaza España
Estación de Ferro Carril
Calle Buenos Aires
Teléfono
Información

karten und pläne sind einmal ein technisches hilfsmittel zur orientierung der verkehrsteilnehmer. darüber hinaus helfen sie, die ganze region im bewußtsein ihrer bürger und besucher verstehbar und überschaubar. als beispiel dienen die metro-pläne in paris. so sind die pläne nicht nur informationsbereich der metrostationen sinnvoll, sondern darüber hinaus im weiteren öffentlichen bereich.

Maps and plans are technical wayfinding resources for travellers. And they also help to make the region comprehensible and manageable in the minds of its residents and visitors. The Paris Metro plans are a good example. Therefore, it makes sense to have plans not only at information points in the Metro stations, but also in public places.

karten und pläne sind einmal ein technisches hilfsmittel zur orientierung der verkehrsteilnehmer. darüber hinaus helfen sie die ganze region im bewusstsein ihrer bürger und besucher verstehbar zu machen. als beispiel dienen die metro-pläne in paris.
so sind die pläne nicht nur im informationsbereich der metro-stationen sinnvoll, sondern darüber hinaus im weiteren öffentlichen bereich.

die metro braucht eine eindeutige und deutliche sprache in ihren bauten sowohl unter der erde im innenstadtbereich wie auch über der erde. diese sprache muß durchgängig sein und alle teilbereiche zu einer einheit zusammenfassen.

The Metro needs clear, unambiguous language at its facilities, not just underground in the city centre, but also on the surface. That language must be universal and form a whole that is the sum of its parts.

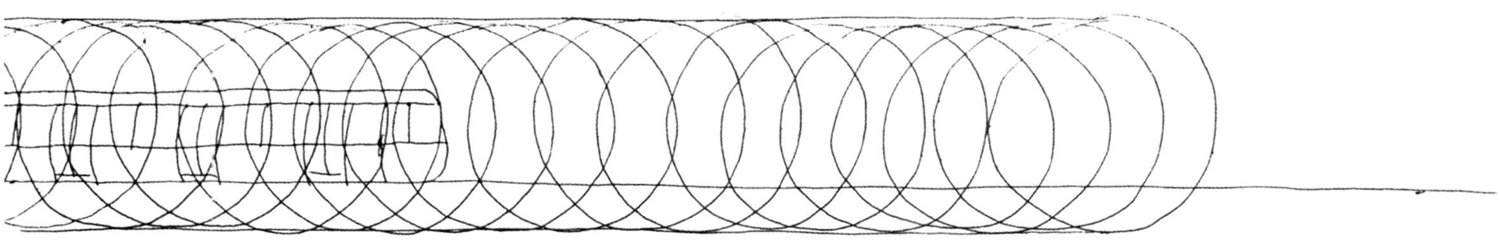

die metro braucht eine eindeutige und deutliche sprache in ihren bauten sowohl unter der erde im innenstadtbereich wie auch über der erde. diese sprache muß durchgängig sein und alle teilbereiche zu einer einheit zusammenfassen.

metro

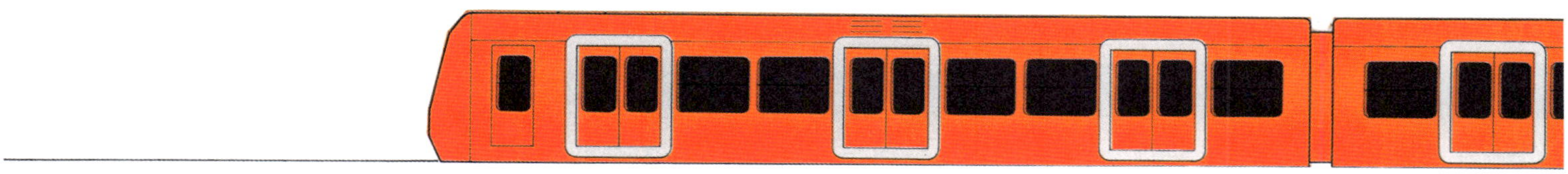

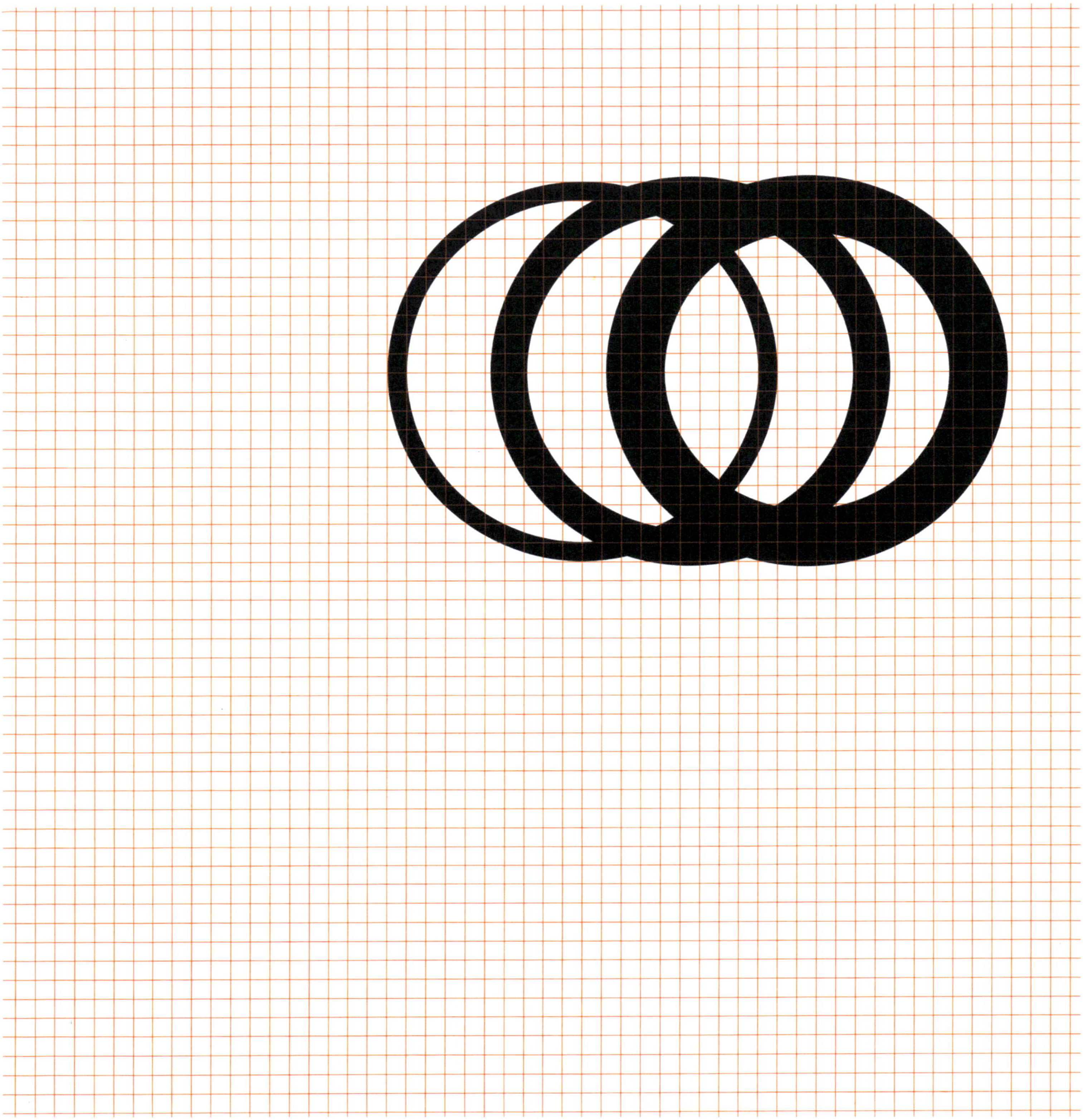

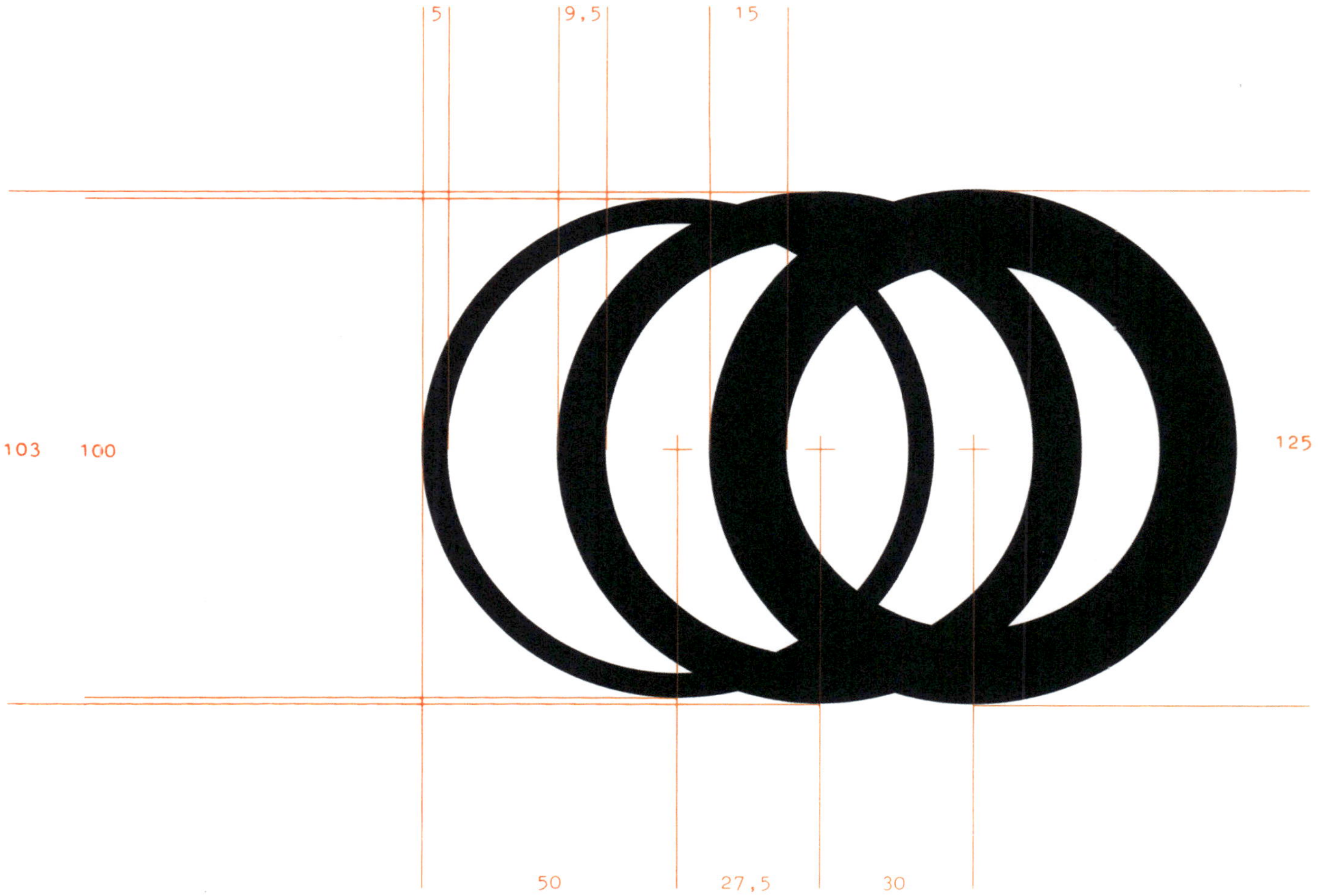
5
9,5
15
103
100
125
50
27,5
30

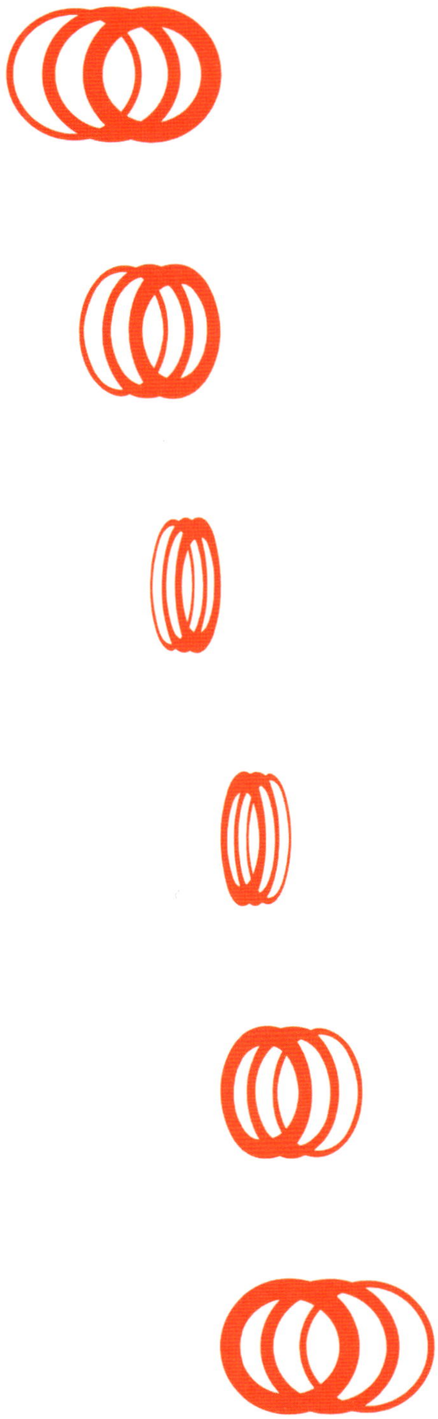

Metro Bilbao

Metro Bilbao

Otl Aicher with a Metro Bilbao team in Rotis. c.1990. Photograph: Hanjörg Brucklacher

Hansjörg Brucklacher in London, c.1990

Norman Foster and Otl Aicher in London, c.1990. Photograph: Hansjörg Brucklacher

Works by Otl Aicher and a Metro Bilbao team in building 17 in Rotis, c.1990. Photograph: Hansjörg Brucklacher

Works by Otl Aicher and a Metro Bilbao team in building 17 in Rotis, c.1990. Photographs: Hansjörg Brucklacher

exhibited works

Otl Aicher and Norman Foster
Metro sign, 1988–1995
98.5 x 64.8 x 12 cm
Truncated cone post 8m
(Ø 20-9.6 cm)
Bilbao Fine Arts Museum

Otl Aicher at the HfG Ulm, c.1955
Photographic print
Museum Ulm / HfG-Archiv
ref. 58_0411

Inge Scholl at the Ulmer
Volkshochschule, c.1950
Photographic print
Museum Ulm / HfG-Archiv
ref. 743

Otl Aicher
Bust of Sophie Scholl, 1991
Bronze. 38 x 22 x 28 cm
Cast by the Anton Gugg foundry
Museum Ulm

Otl Aicher
Bust of Hans Scholl, 1991
Bronze. 38 x 22 x 28 cm
Cast by the Anton Gugg foundry
Museum Ulm

The Ulmer Volkshochschule team:
Inge Scholl, Herbert Wiegandt,
Sven Anker Lindström, Hans
Werner Richter, Otl Aicher, Irm
Lindström, Hans Rupp and Peter
Wackernagel, c. November 1949.
Photograph: Hannes Rosenberg
Photographic print
Museum Ulm / HfG-Archiv
ref. 753_003

Otl Aicher analysing a scale
model of Ulm at the
Volkshochschule, c.1950
Photographic print
Museum Ulm / HfG-Archiv
ref. 754_011

Fashion design class at the
Ulmer Volkshochschule, c.1950
Photographic print
Museum Ulm / HfG-Archiv
ref. 749_017

Hans Neudecker
Otl Aicher modelling the
busts of Sophie and Hans Scholl,
26 August 1991
Photographic print
Museum Ulm / HfG-Archiv
ref. Ai.F.006

Otl Aicher
Poster for the Ulmer
Volkshochschule
'Die Landschaft in der Kunst'
[The Landscape in Art]
Course taught by Dr. Hackelsberger,
Tuesday, 3 November 1953
Offset print. 42 x 42 cm
Museum Ulm / HfG-Archiv

Otl Aicher
Poster for the Ulmer
Volkshochschule
'Die Entwicklungsländer zwischen
Ost und West' [Developing
Countries between East and West]
Course taught by Helmet Jelden,
June 1959
Offset print. 42 x 42 cm
Museum Ulm / HfG-Archiv

Otl Aicher
Poster for the Ulmer
Volkshochschule
'Das Recht auf Widerstand'
[The Right to Resist]
Course taught by Dr. Peter
Schneider, Wednesday,
7 October 1953
Offset print. 42 x 42 cm
Museum Ulm / HfG-Archiv

Otl Aicher
Poster for the Ulmer
Volkshochschule
'Werden und Wachsen alter
Städte' [Development and
Growth of Old Cities]
Friday, 13 January 1956
Offset print. 42 x 42 cm
Museum Ulm / HfG-Archiv

Hans G. Conrad and
Otl Aicher in class, c.1955
Photographic print
Museum Ulm / HfG-Archiv
ref. 1_58_0381

Otl Aicher teaching
at the HfG Ulm, c.1955
Photograph: Hans G. Conrad
Photographic print
Museum Ulm / HfG-Archiv
ref. 2_5_006

Tomás Maldonado and Max Bill
at the HfG Ulm, c.1955
Photographic print
Museum Ulm / HfG-Archiv
ref. 3_dp019_003b

Folded paper studies
Josef Albers's class
at the HfG, 1954–1955
Photographic print
Museum Ulm / HfG-Archiv
ref. 4_pp117_005

Otl Aicher and Tomás Maldonado
at the HfG Ulm, c.1954
Photographic print
Museum Ulm / HfG-Archiv
ref. eh_svs0055_4

Students in the "sawtooth"
hallway at the HfG carrying
their stools, c.1954
Photographic print
Museum Ulm / HfG-Archiv
ref. 5_in_svs0416_4

Josef Albers teaching
at the HfG Ulm, 1954–1955
Photographic print
Museum Ulm / HfG-Archiv
ref. 6_5_0068

Exhibition of the Volkshochschule
on the HfG Ulm campus, c.1955
Photographic print
Museum Ulm / HfG-Archiv
ref. 7_dp090_010_9

Meeting of co-rectors of the HfG
Ulm. Max Bill at the head,
Otl Aicher and Inge Aicher-School
to the right, 1955
Photograph: Hans Conrad
Photographic print
Museum Ulm / HfG-Archiv
ref. 8_55_0022

The HfG building. Design
by Max Bill, 1951–1955
Photographic print
Museum Ulm / HfG-Archiv
ref. schw008_006

Scale model of the HfG Ulm, c.1985
scale 1:750
Wood. 120 x 70 cm
Museum Ulm / HfG-Archiv

Otl Aicher
Site map of Rotis, c.1976
Print and collage. 21 x 29.7 cm
Museum Ulm / HfG-Archiv
ref. 462.1

Otl Aicher
Plan of roofs at Rotis,
17 October 1976
Ink on paper. 21 x 29.7 cm
Museum Ulm / HfG-Archiv
ref. 463.14

Otl Aicher
Bird's-eye view drawing
of Rotis, 1976
Ink on paper. 21 x 29.7 cm
Museum Ulm / HfG-Archiv
ref. 463.38

Otl Aicher
Buildings around the orchard,
17 October 1976
Ink on paper. 21 x 29.7 cm
Museum Ulm / HfG-Archiv
ref. 463.13

Otl Aicher
Bird's-eye view drawing of
Buildings Y, 16 and 18, around
the orchard, 1976
Ink on paper. 21 x 29.7 cm
Museum Ulm / HfG-Archiv
ref. 463.15

Otl Aicher
Axonometric grid projection for a
studio at Rotis, 28 January 1978
Ink on paper. 21 x 29.7 cm
Museum Ulm / HfG-Archiv
ref. 463.2

Otl Aicher
Grid for a studio at Rotis, 1978
Ink on paper. 21 x 29.7 cm
Museum Ulm / HfG-Archiv
ref. 463.36

Otl Aicher
Axonometric projection for a studio at Rotis, 1978
Ink on paper. 21 x 29.7 cm
Museum Ulm / HfG-Archiv
ref. 463.11

Otl Aicher
Scale model for a workshop at Rotis, 1978
Black card. 28 x 12 x 12 cm
Museum Ulm / HfG-Archiv

Otl Aicher
Axonometric projection and side elevation of the carriage house, 17 October 1976
Ink on paper. 21 x 29.7 cm
Museum Ulm / HfG-Archiv
ref. 463.17

Otl Aicher
Perspective view of the entrance pergola, 10 October 1976
Ink on paper. 21 x 29.7 cm
Museum Ulm / HfG-Archiv
ref. 463.45

Büro Otl Aicher. Buildings at Rotis, 1988
Offset print. 59.4 x 84.1 cm
Bilbao Fine Arts Museum

Redrawn buildings at Rotis (1970–1985), 2020
Digital print. 59.4 x 84.1 cm
Bilbao Fine Arts Museum

Redrawn buildings at Rotis (1970–1985), 2020
Digital print. 59.4 x 84.1 cm
Bilbao Fine Arts Museum

Structure and skylights of the power station pavilion, c.1984
Photographic print, colour
Museum Ulm / HfG-Archiv
ref. ai.d.14882

Otl Aicher's office. Building 12, c.1984
Photographic print, colour
Museum Ulm / HfG-Archiv
ref. ai.d.14890

Porch of the photography workshop. Building 18, c.1984
Colour photographic print
Museum Ulm / HfG-Archiv
ref. ai.d.14894; 14995

Rotis compound. Buildings 16, 18 and 05, c.1984
Photographic print, colour
Museum Ulm / HfG-Archiv
ref. ai.d.15015

Otl Aicher's studio and power station, c.1984
Photographic print, colour
Museum Ulm / HfG-Archiv
ref. ai.d.15020

Otl Aicher working in his studio. Studio 12, c.1984
Photographic print, colour
Museum Ulm / HfG-Archiv
ref. ai.d.15057

Workers at Building 18, c.1984
Photographic print, colour
Museum Ulm / HfG-Archiv
ref. ai.d.15064

Power station stairs, c.1984
Photographic print, colour
Museum Ulm / HfG-Archiv
ref. ai.d.15088

Benches and tables designed by Otl Aicher outside the canteen, c.1984
Photographic print, colour
Museum Ulm / HfG-Archiv
ref. ai.d.15120

Otl Aicher
Rotis, c.1984
Offset print. 59.4 x 84.1 cm
Bilbao Fine Arts Museum

Scale model of Rotis (1970–1985), 2020
scale 1: 250
Polyurethane and wood. 100 x 160 cm
Bilbao Fine Arts Museum

Otl Aicher
Promotional campaign for the town of Isny im Allgäu
1. Summer at Isny and Argerbühl; 2. Kitchen; 3. I am the cat; 4. Landscape; 5. The best summer holiday; 6. Synopsis; 7. Farm; 8. Logs; 9. Pine forest; 10. Fox, 1979–1980
Offset print. 59.4 x 84.1 cm
Museum Ulm / HfG-Archiv

Otto Neurath, Marie Reidemeister and Gerd Arntz
Isotype, 1929–1933
Symbols. Workers, unemployed persons. Forest. Arable land. Meadows. Industry. Vehicles. Machines
Linocut and typographic print. 42 x 63 cm
Otto and Marie Neurath Isotype Collection, University of Reading
IC 7.2_15 a; IC 7.2_15 b

Otl Aicher
Rotis der Ort (Rotis the Place), 1988
Offset print on paper. 59.4 x 84.1 cm
Bilbao Fine Arts Museum

Büro Otl Aicher
Development of the Rotis typeface, 20 February 1988
Mixed media on paper. 28 x 29.7 cm
Museum Ulm / HfG-Archiv
ref. ai.p. 326.1; 326.2; 326.8; 326.19; 326.21

Otl Aicher. Volume 2, 1971–1978. Norman Foster
The Buildings and the Projects, 1988
Offset cover proof. 28 x 29.7 cm
Museum Ulm / HfG-Archiv
ref. ai.p. 326.66

Otl Aicher
Metro Bilbao. Complementary study 1. Colours. Heraldry. History, 1988
Mixed media on paper. 28 x 29.7 cm
Museum Ulm / HfG-Archiv
ref. ai.p.108.20; 106.3; fbb-1; 110.1; 108.19; 108.21; fbb-2; 106.29; fbb-3; 106.63; fbb-4; 106.64; 106.65; 108.26

Otl Aicher
Metro Bilbao. Complementary study 2. The region, 1988
Mixed media on paper. 28 x 29.7 cm
Museum Ulm / HfG-Archiv
ref. ai.p. 106.18; 106.75; 106.76 fbb-5; 106.19; 106.20; 106.82 106.92; 500.1

Otl Aicher
Metro Bilbao. Complementary study 3. Bird's-eye and ground-level views of the metro, 1988
Mixed media on paper. 28 x 29.7 cm
Museum Ulm / HfG-Archiv
ref. ai.p. 107.3; 107.14; 107.22; 107.23; 107.27; 107.31; 107.35; 106.79; 106.80; 106.33; 106.35; 106.38; 106.39; 106.42; 106.45; 106.46; 106.47; 106.48; 106.50; 106.54; 106.55; 106.77; 106.78

Otl Aicher
Metro Bilbao. Complementary study 4. Conclusion, 1988
Mixed media on paper. 28 x 29.7 cm
Museum Ulm / HfG-Archiv
ref. ai.p. 106.81; 106.67; 108.36; 106.10; 106.15; 108.16; 106.12; 108.13; 108.14; 108.35; 108.33; 108.32

Otl Aicher
Corporate identity for Metro Bilbao, 1988
Mixed media on paper. 84.1 x 59.4 cm
Museum Ulm / HfG-Archiv

Harry C. Beck
London Map, 1933
Ink on paper. 16 x 22.7 cm
Design Museum of Barcelona
GAGB 124/12

Otl Aicher
Caricature of Norman Foster, 1985
Pen on paper. 29 x 21 cm
Private collection

Norman Foster, Otl Aicher and Ian Lambot
Photographic print
Photograph: Andrew Ward

Norman Foster and Otl Aicher, 1989
Photographs: Rudi Meisel
Photographic print
Norman Foster Foundation
NFF_BT2-03_057Prw; NFF_BT2-03_054Prw

Otl Aicher
Munich Olympics. Olympic Village; Metro; Gymnastics; Weightlifting; Sailing; Boxing; Rowing; Volleyball; Judo; Athletics; Archery, 1972
Screenprint. 84.1 x 119 cm
Museum Ulm / HfG-Archiv

Otl Aicher
Template grid, 1988
Ink on paper. 28 x 29.7 cm
Museum Ulm / HfG-Archiv

Otto Neurath, Marie Reidemeister and Gerd Arntz
Isotype, 1930–1940
Symbols. Work. Sport
Pages from the Isotype Dictionary. 29.9 x 22.4 cm
Linocut
Otto and Marie Neurath Isotype Collection, University of Reading
IC 4.2; IC 4.3

Norman Foster
Type of tunnel section, n.d. (1988–1995)
Digital print. 35 x 27 cm
Norman Foster Foundation
0445_FP205059

Norman Foster
Metro entrance canopy, n.d. (1988–1995)
Digital print. 35 x 27 cm
Norman Foster Foundation
0445_FP374243

Norman Foster
Bilbao, n.d. (1988–1995)
Pencil on paper. 35 x 27 cm
Norman Foster Foundation
I-013

Norman Foster
Platforms, n.d. (1988–1995)
Pencil on paper. 29.7 x 21 cm
Norman Foster Foundation
TNFF_SB00413_017

Norman Foster
Sign of tube ... wheel running, n.d. (1988–1995)
Pencil on paper. 29.7 x 21 cm
Norman Foster Foundation
TNFF_SB00413_018

Norman Foster
Colour in the station, 1 July 1988
Pencil and ink on paper. 29.7 x 42 cm
Norman Foster Foundation
TNFF_SB00432_016v-017r

Norman Foster
Station, sections and axonometric projection, n.d. (1988–1995)
Pencil on paper. 29.7 x 42 cm
Norman Foster Foundation
TNFF_SB00452_009v-010r

Norman Foster
Entrance canopy and information panel, n.d. (1988–1995)
Pencil on paper. 29.7 x 42 cm
Norman Foster Foundation
TNFF_SB00480_028v-029r

Norman Foster
Tunnel sections, n.d. (1988–1995)
Pencil on paper. 29.7 x 42 cm
Norman Foster Foundation
TNFF_SB00495_004v-005r

Otl Aicher
Plaza Elíptica, 1988
Photocollage. 42 x 29.7 cm
Museum Ulm / HfG-Archiv
ref. ai.p.109.22

Otl Aicher
Plaza Elíptica, 1988
Photocollage. 42 x 29.7 cm
Museum Ulm / HfG-Archiv
ai.p.109.23

Otl Aicher
Plaza Elíptica, 1988
Photocollage. 42 x 29.7 cm
Museum Ulm / HfG-Archiv
ai.p.109.24

Otl Aicher
Old Quarter, 1988
Photocollage. 42 x 29.7 cm
Museum Ulm / HfG-Archiv
ai.p.109.28

Norman Foster
Development of access tunnel, n.d. (1988–1995)
Pencil on paper. 29.7 x 42 cm
Norman Foster Foundation
TNFF_SB00522_012v-013r

Norman Foster
Platform, n.d. (1988–1995)
Pencil on paper. 29.7 x 42 cm
Norman Foster Foundation
TNFF_SB00601-019r

Otl Aicher
Bulthaup project. Drawings for the book *Die Küche zum Kochen* (The Kitchen for Cooking), 1982
Ink and collage on paper.
28 x 29.7 cm
Museum Ulm / HfG-Archiv
ref. ai.p. 455.31; 479.8; 455.32; 455.22; 479.15; 455.6; .455.26; 482.1; 480.10; 455.20; 455.9a; 480.34; 455.12; 455.13; 455.22a; 455.46; 455.10a; 455.10b; 455.9b; 455.1

Hans G. Conrad
Düsseldorf system. Designed by Otl Aicher and Hans Gugelot
Adjustable exhibition system for the Max Braun firm, July 1955
Black diazotype on paper.
45 x 62 cm
René Spitz Collection
inv. no. P- 61819

Hans G. Conrad
TV Exhibition, Stuttgart / Braun. Designed by Otl Aicher and Hans Gugelot
Adjustable exhibition system for the Max Braun firm, 10 July 1956
Positive photostat print on paper.
42.6 x 61.6 cm
René Spitz Collection
inv. no. P- 61825

Hans G. Conrad
Structural drawing of the Braun pavilion. Designed by Otl Aicher and Hans Gugelot
Exhibition system for the Max Braun firm, c.1955–1956
Ink on paper. 44.9 x 62.3 cm
René Spitz Collection
inv. no. P- 61929

Hans G. Conrad
TV Exhibition, Stuttgart / Braun. Designed by Otl Aicher and Hans Gugelot, 10 July 1956
Blue diazotype on paper.
44 x 60.5 cm
René Spitz Collection
inv. no. P- 61987

Otl Aicher
Braun. Industrial construction system, August 1960
Ink on paper and typewritten paper
Museum Ulm / HfG-Archiv
ref. ai.p. 512.17; 5; 12.18; 512.19; 512.20; 512.21; 512.22; 512.24; 512.25; 512.26; 512.29; 512.30; 512.78; 512.79; 512.81

Braun pavilion. Düsseldorf system, 1955
Photograph
Museum Ulm / HfG-Archiv
ref. ai.p. 510.3; 510.7; 510-8; 510.13; 510.12; 509.6; 509.8

Braun pavilion.Frankfurt system, 1959
Photograph: Hans G. Conrad
Museum Ulm / HfG-Archiv
ref. ai.p. 510.24; 510.30; 510.33; 511.2; 511.3; 511.4

Otl Aicher
ERCO logo, 1974–1976
Offset print. 42 x 39.6 cm
Museum Ulm / HfG-Archiv
ai.p.80.3; 80.15

Otl Aicher
ERCO information system design. Black, grey and white; Transport; Airport; Communication; Recreation; Religion and Theatre; Hospital; Science; Sport; Winter sport, 1974–1976
Offset print and collage.
42 x 39.6 cm
Museum Ulm / HfG-Archiv
ai.p.80.10; 82.4; 82.5; 82.11; 82.6; 82.2; 82.3; 82.12; 82.13; 82.14

Otl Aicher and Hans Gugelot
Exhibitor's pavilion for Max Braun AG. Düsseldorf system, 1955
Steel, glass, wood and sisal fibre.
600 x 300 x 300 cm
Braun P&G / Braun Archive Kronberg

Otl Aicher and Hans Gugelot
Window display stand for Braun, 1958
Wood and photographic print.
110 x 90 x 2.5 cm
Braun P&G / Braun Archive Kronberg

Hans Gugelot
PKG 1-85. Combination radio and record player, 1960
Wood, lacquered metal and plastic.
120 x 60 cm
Braun P&G / Braun Archive Kronberg

Herbert Hirsch
HF1. Television monitor, 1958
Lacquered metal and plastic.
50 x 50 x 75 cm
Braun P&G / Braun Archive Kronberg

Gerd Alfred Muller
KM3. Food processor, 1957
Metal and blue and white plastic.
100 x 50 cm
Braun P&G / Braun Archive Kronberg

Otl Aicher
Gehen in der Wüste [Walking in the Desert]
S. Fischer, Frankfurt am Main, 1986
Book. 21 x 29.7 cm
Bilbao Fine Arts Museum

Otl Aicher
Photographs for *Gehen in der Wüste* [Walking in the Desert], 1986
Photographic prints, colour
Museum Ulm / HfG-Archiv
ref. ai.d. 17677; 17681; 17687; 17684; 17693.1; 17740; 17768; 17798.1

Otl Aicher
Posters for the *Wilhelm von Ockham* exhibition
Battle of Mühldorf (1322); Rome, heart of the Christian West; Crusade port of Aigues-Mortes (Ockham's flight); the Emperor Louis receives the principal Friars Minor at Pisa; The plague in Europe; Greyfriars in London, Ockham's home monastery; Ockham tried as a heretic in the papal palace of Avignon; The Franciscan Order, 1986
Collage with coloured paper.
84.1 x 118.9 cm
Museum Ulm / HfG-Archiv
ref. ai.t. 360; 361; 364; 376; 378; 377; 379; 386

Otl Aicher
Kuhberg concentration camp: 40 years, 1985
Collage with coloured and offset paper. 84.1 x 118.9 cm
Museum Ulm / HfG-Archiv

Otl Aicher
90. Jahre 1. Mai [90 Years 1 May], SPD, 1980
Collage with coloured and offset paper. 84.1 x 118.9 cm
Museum Ulm / HfG-Archiv

Otl Aicher
Vaterland ist nicht gleich Vaterland [Fatherland Is Not the Same Fatherland], SPD, c.1980
Collage with coloured and offset paper. 84.1 x 118.9 cm
Museum Ulm / HfG-Archiv

Otl Aicher
James Callaghan. Mehr Nachbarschaft, weniger Konflikte [More Neighbourhood, Less Conflict], SPD, c.1980
Collage with coloured paper.
84.1 x 118.9 cm
Museum Ulm / HfG-Archiv

Otl Aicher
Atomkrieg. Wenige vereiten ihn vor, viele fürchten ihn, alle kommen darin um
[Nuclear War: Few Prepare It, Many Fear It, All Perish in It], c.1983
Offset print. 84.1 x 118.9 cm
Museum Ulm / HfG-Archiv

Otl Aicher
Herbst'83. In der Schönste Wiesengrunde ... [Autumn'83. In the Loveliest Meadowland ...], 1983
Offset print. 84.1 x 118.9 cm
Museum Ulm / HfG-Archiv

Otl Aicher
Herbst'83. MenschenKette [Autumn'83. Human Chain], 1983
Offset print. 84.1 x 118.9 cm
Museum Ulm / HfG-Archiv

Otl Aicher
Lufthansa. Im flug über Europa [Flying over Europe]. Germany; Spain, Italy, France, 1974
Photographic print, colour
Museum Ulm / HfG-Archiv
ref. ai.d.8087; 9845; 9440; 10583

Otl Aicher
Lufthansa magazine, 1974
Offset print, colour. 21 x 29.7 cm
Museum Ulm / HfG-Archiv
ref. ai.ki. 55.11; 55.15; 55.17; 55.19; 55.21

Otl Aicher
Lufthansa. Menu covers, 1974
Offset print, colour. 10.5 x 29.7 cm
Museum Ulm / HfG-Archiv
ref. ai.ki. 55.1; 55.2; 55.5; 55.6; 55.7; 55.8; 55.10

This book has been published for
the exhibition *Otl Aicher. Metro Bilbao. Architecture and Landscape*,
held at Bilbao Fine Arts Museum on
the occasion of the 25th anniversary
of Metro Bilbao.

05.11.2020 – 28 .02.2021